future histories

horizon house

future histories

Award-Winning Science Fiction Writers Predict Twenty Tomorrows for Communications

Edited by
Stephen McClelland

horizon house

Published by Horizon House® Publications
Portland House, Stag Place, London, SW1E 5XT

We are pleased to receive feedback.
Internet: 100441.325@compuserve.com

First published June 1997

Cover Design by Kavita Bowry

ISBN 0 9530648 0 8

Printed by Biddles Ltd, Guildford

Dedicated to:

Rachel

and

The Two Graces

With the Affirmation
That Unknown Futures
Should Always Be
Much Better
Than Known Pasts

ACKNOWLEDGEMENTS

A project like this could only be undertaken by the most enlightened group of people working together. I am delighted to acknowledge them, and to acknowledge having worked with them. First and foremost, I would like to thank the science fiction writers themselves who applied themselves with appropriate vigour and imagination — as befits people who win the highest international honours. They are: Stephen Baxter, Gregory Benford, Pat Cadigan, Nancy Kress, Paul McAuley, David Marusek, Pat Murphy, Brian Stableford, as a group who provided the stories. Giving freely almost as much time in lengthy interviews around the world, I must thank: Greg Bear, Alexander Besher, William Gibson, Mariko Ohara, Neal Stephenson, Bruce Sterling, Vernor Vinge, and of course Arthur C Clarke and Nicholas Negroponte, who have reached — deservedly — the world stage as gurus. I am very grateful to Andy Sawyer of the University of Liverpool's Science Fiction Library for sharing his insights on contemporary themes and developments, as well as to David Pringle of Interzone magazine for helping me trace authors.

As anyone interested in the science fiction community will recognise, the above list of individuals is a remarkable one. But behind the scenes, many other people gave freely of their time and energy to talk to me and to speculate on the likely courses of technologies they were developing. At Nokia, I must particularly thank Lauri Kivinen, Harri Männistö, Dr Yrjö Neuvo, Petri Pöyhönen, Dominique Purcell, Markku Rauhamaa, Mikko Terho, as well, of course, as Arja Suominen and David Stoneham who proved to be both imaginative and positive, a challenging task in a complex project.

My wife, Sandy, was incredibly supportive and interested in this book, and watched goggle-eyed (as I did) when names I had admired long but only from afar were willing to speak to me and to contribute to this book.

Lastly, I would like to thank my tolerant colleagues at Horizon House® and on Telecommunications® International magazine, notably Kavita Bowry, Salena Noel, Bhawani Shankar and Gareth Watson; without them, the project could not have come to fruition.

Stephen McClelland
Amersham
May 1997

A Window to the Future

As the new millennium approaches, this book offers the reader a window to twenty possible futures. Reality will doubtless be unlike even our wildest imaginings — perhaps better, perhaps worse. What we must recognise, as we confront these possibilities is the need for a new way of thinking about how we want to live our lives.

Our future at Nokia depends on how well we use our collective imagination, developing products and services demanded by new realities. We cannot foresee the future, but we can prepare for it by taking a proactive stance and keeping our minds open. Regardless of what the future holds, we must play an active role to shape these ends. And although the short stories in this book are all works of fiction, my hope is that these visions will both excite and intrigue your imagination.

Jorma Ollila
President and CEO
Nokia

Contents

The Millennium of Total Mobility

Arthur C Clarke

Arthur C Clarke is probably the world's best known science fiction writer. In a career spanning 60 years he has written a group of remarkable stories and books, with perhaps the most famous of all being *2001: A Space Odyssey*. The film of the same name is considered by leading critics to be one of the ten best films of all time. But he has also made major contributions to space science, and is credited with invention of the communications satellite. He has just published a further sequel, *3001*. British by birth, he has lived in Sri Lanka since 1956. Arthur C Clarke was interviewed by Stephen McClelland.

The Millennium of Total Mobility

Arthur C Clarke

As the century which saw the birth of both electronics and optronics draws to a close, it would seem that everything we wish to do in the field of communications is now technically possible. The only limitations are financial, legal and political.

I was a judge in a recent contest. With the year 2001 fast approaching, candidates were asked to suggest the first words that HAL, the computer creation in the story, might utter when its intelligence was activated. The winning entry — a rather cheeky one — actually had HAL saying, *Dave, I've taken the liberty of removing all Windows 95 programs from my hard drive.* My own suggested contribution (not permitted of course) would have been a deliberate bowdlerism (detectable, if you have read 2001, the comment actually occurs upon HAL's *deactivation*):

HAL could say, *Dave, my mind is **growing**...*

A growing mind is a good way of describing the communications industry on the planet as we near the critical year. Millennia have a way of concentrating the attention, and this particular one might almost have been custom designed for the communications era. The barriers I mention above are falling away at a remarkable rate after a one hundred and twenty plus year history of the telephone. The economic ones are being solved as things get cheaper and cheaper, the legal ones are being recognised as artefacts, and the political ones bowing to public demand. Technology has made it all possible, if not necessarily predictable. The biggest technological driver of all? It has been, without question, the development of microchip technology. The most surprising one? Fibre optics. Twenty years ago I would have said that the current advances were absolutely impossible.

The next big thing in the next millennium? Total mobility. We have already started this with the cellular telephone. It's the 'thin end of the wedge' compared with what is to come. After century-long partnership with the traditional telephone, there may come a time when fixed phones are a curiosity.

In wider terms, we can't say whether the information society is a bad or good thing. Like all technology, it is neutral. The homogenisation of culture it could deliver may be a problem, but at our fingertips, technology could offer us opportunities to preserve aspects of culture: the existence of the camcorder is a very good example of this. One issue is for sure: there won't be any such thing as closed societies anymore. Will everyone be equal come the information age? Communications issues are moving in several directions at once. Some of the disparities between the haves and have-nots will certainly widen. But the information society will democratise by making access ever cheaper. In the near future, every village on the planet will have its own phone.

Communications service take up will of course saturate — but at very high penetration globally. But for the moment, we are still on the bottom of the S-curve. However, there may be some unexpected fallout. I've been writing recently about information pollution, on the dangers of what I call the coming 'Cyberclysm'. There may be too much of the wrong sort of information worldwide. Undoubtedly useful, though it may be, I was actually thinking about disconnecting from the World Wide Web for this reason.

It's a bit of a paradox in an interconnected world. I have been offered one obvious answer — of course, a technological one: software to personalise an information service from the Internet. Now this is a good idea, but I don't think it will be effective enough because it can never follow your actual interests. Discovery and the flow of ideas are matters ultimately of serendipity: after a lifetime, I can say that the ideas you need are probably found quite by chance on the back of a completely unrelated press cutting! Nevertheless, the whole Internet phenomenon is interesting on many levels; it represents a chaotic situation or a battle between order and chaos. But you need some chaos to get creativity.

Our growing minds will always lead us to enquire, to explore and to be creative. We will also continue to predict. Prediction has value to us in a technological society. It's essential, but it's also sometimes unreliable. Take science fiction for example. It may attempt to predict the future, and often to prevent it. But, its real value is in opening the mind to possibilities and to future change. More formal scientific prediction can tell us what may be possible. We may reasonably say that technology may offer particular solutions to particular problems, the main difficulty is the timetable.

When I first conceived of communication satellites, I envisaged them arriving by the last decade of this century. But they came much more quickly — and largely because of the development of the transistor and microchip. My own ideas had involved the inevitable use of vacuum tube technology in orbiting space stations as radio relays. I predicted only manned stations because the technology would have required continual maintenance. Solid state electronics, in increasing reliability, made unmanned platforms possible.

When we get prediction wrong, the results may also be comically illuminating. I have often spoken of Sir William Preece who held the venerated position of Engineer-in-Chief for the British Post Office about 120 years ago. After Bell's invention of the telephone, he remained unimpressed, commenting 'The Americans have need of the telephone. We do not. We have plenty of messenger boys.' He qualified this with a further comment: 'I have [a telephone] in my office, more for show...if I want to send a message...I employ a boy to take it.' American response was much more enthusiastic, if a little misguided. One mayor famously commented that the potential for the telephone was so great that we might see a future when there would be one in every city.

If I have a serious dream of something becoming possible (apart from my nightmares when I find that I've been made the NASA administrator!), it is in the area of so-called cold fusion, which is seldom cold and probably not fusion. It might be the biggest technology advance we have ever made. Characteristically, ninety percent of scientists say it's impossible but I disagree. If you ask me for a really outrageous prediction to set alongside the others in the communications industry: *faster than light communications.*

I still believe when it comes to technological progress something I said some while ago in Profiles of the Future: Generally the problems come down to two sorts of failures: the Failure of Nerve or Failure of Imagination. The more common one? Failure of Nerve.

Creativity Wanted

Nicholas Negroponte

Nicholas Negroponte is Director of the Media Lab at MIT. A world famous guru and futurist for the communications, media and computing industries, he has written many articles and several books of which the most recent is *Being Digital*. He was interviewed by Stephen McClelland.

Creativity Wanted

Nicholas Negroponte

In the welter of progress when all other advantages are neutralised we may be left with just one: creativity. It's so broad that one could easily argue it is the most important asset available, assuming you are willing to consider business skills as creative too. That's important because in the end your competitive edge is driven by your ability to take new ideas to market. More than that, we need to move it into as many areas as possible. Consider the situation in communications today for example. We need creativity in technological terms, but we also need it just as much in the sphere of economic models, and tariffing and pricing more generally. Paying per bit, per minute or per mile is a thing of the past. We need to overcome the mode of thinking that still dictates this. Service providers, in particular, need to get somehow into adding a value to the bits rather than shipping them.

The fact is, creativity may be important, but current trends across the industry hardly promote it effectively. After all, it's a pretty perverse thing at best. It has tinges of radicalism, even of revolution, perhaps. It thrives best when unstructured. The best advice I can give is: if you want to be creative, try not to be like yourself. This applies to companies as much as individuals. Characteristically, small groups spin off, and dissenting ideas are considered in this environment. This is what happened for example in the case of LEO technology, which I really believe is one of the best examples of creativity in the communications industry we have to date. Oh, and you will probably need outside 'irritarts' (like the Media Lab) to be engaged. If it sounds a more like biological process than a management system, it probably is.

Science fiction is actually a particularly interesting example of this whole process, given that the best writers allow themselves few constraints in what they actually produce. It may not only be imaginative, but it can cause real change.

And the results can be spectacular. My goodness, look at Arthur C Clarke: satellites and HAL. Not only were these highly creative, they are just two examples of scenarios that really impacted science.

Predicting products and trends is part of our job at the Media Lab. The all-embracing trend we believe is the human move from a largely synchronous to a dominantly asynchronous mode of human communications, and this is clearly a planetary shift. For technologies, we could predict the Ringless Telephone, Holographic Video, Remote Brain Surgery and even Teleportation, if I really wanted to be outrageous in talking about the next decade. Thinking back when people ask me about my own bright ideas of recent months, I recognise another important fact: groupthink. 'My' ideas are not really my own but the result of being with very smart and highly creative people. Of late, these people have invented a way to distribute bits through the human body, which means your shoe computer can send bits to your wristwatch without leaving your body. I'm thinking of titling it: *Invasion of the Bodynet*.

Twenty Futures in Communications

Stephen McClelland

Twenty Futures in Communications

Stephen McClelland

This book is about the future, about what may happen and what may take place, especially in the world of communications. It is not about predictions, since we cannot know the future, but it is about perspectives, about how the future might unfold, and what it might do for us. In these pages you will find digital millennia, wormholes in cyberspace, futuristic venture capitalism, collected personalities, robotic explorations presided over by human minds, wireless identity cards, intelligent Internets, remarkable virtual realities, advanced media communities, even a geo-consciousness of the future based on networking. Upbeat, downbeat, it is about how people might deal with the technologies that come to pass.

The 'futures' stretch from near-term to the far future, and from the country around us to the distant reaches of space. They are about what might happen to you and me, and to people less fortunate than either of us. The scenarios that could unfold are taken from an unusual but valuable perspective — the world's leading science fiction writers. The scenarios — the twenty tomorrows as we have described them — themselves are a mixture of interviews and short stories, which have been especially commissioned and compiled for this volume. You will see — we hope — why our collection of contributors have won world acclaim, and world awards. Together, if anyone actually 'lives' in the future, they do. I ask on their behalf, not to take these futures too seriously, but to enjoy and be stimulated by the individual acts of imagination they represent.

Science fiction is an unusual art form in that it deals with possibilities rather than realities, about how things might be rather than how they are. It is inspirational to some degree, and quite possibly has influenced the degree to which science and technology have developed during the course of this century. Why do people write science fiction? There are many reasons: to explain the present by way of the future, of course. To try on the future, as one would clothes in a store. To experiment harmlessly with change and response. To reassure ourselves that we can at least mentally be in control, come what may. To explore. In one of the interviews in this book, Greg Bear pointed out to me that science fiction is the subconscious side of science, with the capacity to free, stimulate and engender. If science fiction has a wider purpose, as Arthur C Clarke has implied, it is to prepare us for new possibilities and particularly the possibility of change. It is in its potential to open the mind where it has most to offer.

Loved by many (and unloved by quite a few too) science fiction might well turn out to be the enduring art form of our time. There is undoubtedly affection for it — on a worldwide scale. Two science fiction themes, ***Star Trek*** and ***Star Wars***, have already become among the most valuable global entertainment properties of our time, with portfolios running into several billions of dollars. They are admired and followed by tens of millions of people. Across the field of science fiction, there are many active scientists and technologists who say they owe their choice of vocation to the mind-expanding possibilities of science fiction introduced at a formative age.

But in a wider perspective, in the frame of science fiction to predict and imagine, the history of the post-war 20th century has shown one irony. The irony is: most of the 'wild' predictions have already come true. In the preparation of this book, I heard several science fiction writers say that what they have managed to predict has pre-dated actual events by a shorter and shorter interval. From decades it has become years, months, or now even weeks.

Science fiction belongs to the 20th century, although the landmark writers which determine it were born in the last century: Jules Verne and H G Wells. Both imagined remarkable technologically-based futures, although in different ways. Between the two writers, practically all themes (except arguably those relating to information technology) we would recognise today as science fiction were covered. They were part of a wave of widespread public interest in science and technology that was evident in Western society as a result of many inventions, including the electric light, phonograph and telephone. By 1899, a Frenchman, Armand Gervais, was producing collectable cigarette cards carrying speculative illustrations of future inventions including household robots and intriguingly, tele-education through personal headsets. In the US, a (rather suspect) tradition had also been established in 'invention stories' principally through the prolific output of Luis Senarens who began writing whilst still a teenager. By the first two decades of the 20th century, the 'inventor hero', saving the world through some technological breakthrough, was a popular literary figure.

Contrary to what many people believe, science fiction has achieved some astounding success. I use the word astounding quite deliberately, because it was in ***Astounding Science Fiction*** magazine that writer Cleve Cartmill published a story called ***Deadline***. The story described the atomic bomb and appeared in the magazine in 1944, a year before it was used. Cartmill, who triggered off a major security scare, had used publicly available information and his own powers of prediction. It was a triumph for science fiction.

Mechanical brains functioning as computers actually made an appearance in science fiction at least one hundred and fifteen years ago, but curiously, science fiction writers do not seem to have predicated the appearance formally of modern microelectronics technology, although a 1959 short story by Howard Fast does discuss a computer the size of a shoebox. Science fiction writers, faced with the prospect of growing computer power, have chosen to discuss megamachines with neuroses and which inevitably conflict with their human creators. In a related area, many observers believe that computer viruses made their first appearance in John Brunner's ***The Shockwave Rider***, published in 1975. Another consistent theme throughout the modern science fiction era has been the challenges of communication, often metaphorically espoused in communications with other species and life forms. This was most notably achieved in the story that may become the 20th century's most famous work of science fiction, ***2001: A Space Odyssey***, which features both the challenge of contact with alien life forms and the problems of a well-intended but ultimately neurotic supercomputer that can only pursue its mission by killing its human astronaut companions. Intriguingly, it might feature as a central theme the future evolution of mankind, but at its heart it also suggests that communication with a superior life form (in this case, in a highly symbolic form, by means of the mysterious black monolith) is likely to be comparable in difficulty to that with sentient machines which will come to fruition in the next millennium. Several other stories in science fiction have also explored aspects of communication. Some of the best known include ***VOR*** by James Blish (aliens communicate by colourising an area of their heads violet/orange/red) and the many stories of Jack Vance which nearly 50 years ago explored alien and animal communication ideas in signs, semaphore, colours and even odours. The picking up and decoding of radio messages from outer space has been another rich area for science fiction writers from Fred Hoyle to Carl Sagan.

Nearer to our own time and our own field of interest, computing if not communications has also been a fertile field for imaginative exploration. Networking, connectivity, computerisation, artificial intelligence, all the characteristics in fact of a 'wired' society have already been explored in the pages of science fiction with some interesting outcomes. A highly realistic feature of the Star Trek age has been the appearance of portable communicators — were these the sub-conscious preparation for the cellular phone technology of the 1980s? It would be interesting to speculate. At about the same time, from 1964 to 1968, the science fiction puppet series, ***Thunderbirds***, explored many ingenious communication devices, including wristwatch radios, well before microelectronic miniaturisation made them feasible even in prospect. A later series, ***Captain Scarlet and the Mysterons***, also from the same UK producers, may have even shown the first appearance of wearable radio communicators, mounted in hats and jacket shoulder epaulets.

Communications in fact has been an underlying theme in more recent science fiction. Murray Leinster, may well have been the first writer to predict the arrival of an information web and Internet-like technology three decades ago. But William Gibson in a remarkable novel, ***Neuromancer***, speculated on the (fairly black) future of an interconnected society, and in the process generated the concept of cyberspace, with all these elements coming together in the early 1980s. Cyberpunk was born for many with the publication of Neuromancer, and in a remarkable commentary written later, Bruce Sterling points out: *Eighties tech sticks to the skin, responds to the touch: the personal computer, the Walkman, the portable telephone, the soft contact lens. Certain central themes spring up in cyberpunk...brain com-*

puter interfaces, artificial intelligences, neurochemistry...the subversive potential of the home printer and the photocopier. Cyberpunk is well known for its willingness to carry extrapolation into the fabric of everyday life...it favours dizzying bursts of novel information, sensory overload that submerges the reader in...a wall of sound.

Other writers also found the prospects of an information society and a world increasingly interconnected by communications and stimulation. These include Samuel Delany (in ***Stars in My Pocket Like Grains of Sand***, he suggests a vast Web mediating information between people), Gwyneth Jones (in ***Escape Plans***), Michael Swanwick (in ***Vacuum Flowers***, he suggests the future corporations might have copyright on individual human personalities), Pat Cadigan, and Richard Kadrey (writing of a futuristic Los Angeles in ***Metrophage***), whilst Bruce Sterling's work probably represents the most technologically-aware of the cyberpunk group. But Neuromancer seemed to capture the spirit of the genre. Neal Stephenson, in an equally astounding novel, ***Snow Crash***, has created for the 1990s, a similar environment, the Metaverse. The strange thing — in my view — is that these conceptual creations have largely determined how we think about cyberspace and the Internet, as a real, almost tangible, quantity, which we can mentally manipulate and develop. We now almost routinely talk about cyberspace as if it were a wholly real and tangible medium. It seems to me we have science fiction to thank for this fresh mental appraisal and liberation. Another theme that has come to the fore more recently and has been treated in different ways are Michael Crichton's own science fiction stories. While his themes span many different applications and technologies, many boil down to the difficulties and breakdowns in some sense of communication, and most significantly, the unpredictable (by human creators) behaviour of complex systems.

Some writers — recorded in this volume — have managed to straddle both the speculative future and the formally predictive, most famously of course, Arthur C Clarke, who clearly and accurately invented the communications satellite. The epic themes of universal exploration that Arthur C Clarke has made famous in science fiction continue to be told by writers such as Gregory Benford, Greg Bear, Vernor Vinge, and Stephen Baxter, although several writers continue to produce across the spectrum of traditional science fiction categorisations. The collision of real world speculation and science fiction was also recounted in an article by Gregory Benford — a contributor to this volume — published recently. Discussing his career, Benford recounts his days at the Lawrence Livermore Laboratory in California. Among other research topics, Benford and his colleagues were preoccupied with the possibilities and speculations that, to many outside, would simply be in the realms of 'science fiction.' He recalls how many of the most famous names in the history of twentieth century physics were deeply interested in reading and writing science fiction. This trend has clearly continued in the case of today's physicists: Stephen Hawking is known to have read science fiction avidly. Benford's own speculations threw up many interesting avenues. These included the possibilities of faster than light communication via tachyon particles (even publishing a serious scientific paper discussing the likelihood of a 'Tachyonic Antitelephone' by which means people could communicate with the past and future). The tachyon ideas later reappeared in Benford's famous novel, ***Timescape***. These days the explosion of applications has actually made for some writers, possible careers as futurists too, helping mainly corporate clients decide on the 'what ifs?' and 'what would it takes?' of their businesses in a world where stability has been eroded in favour of multiple possibilities. The idea that there are multiple possible solutions and scenarios to a given issue is something that science fiction can handle quite easily, even if real world strategies do not. That concept alone is likely to make science fiction valuable in itself. The new is not just unlikely to be a foreseeable extrapolation of the present, it is likely to come about through major discontinuity of the present. It therefore makes sense to many to consult with the individuals most comfortable with doing just that. Management guru Tom Peters, no less, (much in the sense that Greg Bear talks about in this book) recommends adding science fiction writers to your business.

It seems apparent that in the days ahead in the communications business, one thing we will all need is more imagination. It will be a powerful and life enhancing tool. Few writers have put it more eloquently than Nebula award winner Katherine MacLean who wrote, *I am wealthy beyond measure. I have the past and future, the earth and the galaxy. I have been to the end of the Universe and back.*

Steamship Soldier on the Information Front

Nancy Kress

Nancy Kress, a winner of two Nebula awards and a Hugo award, has shown a versatility matched by few writers across the genres of science fiction and fantasy, and is particularly admired for her ability to take complex sociological perspectives and extrapolations In the following story, we follow the progress of a futuristic venture capitalist who travels and trawls the world for invention – and is surprised at what happens when invention becomes intelligent. Readers should notice the detail which the writer creates futuristic invention – particularly communications!

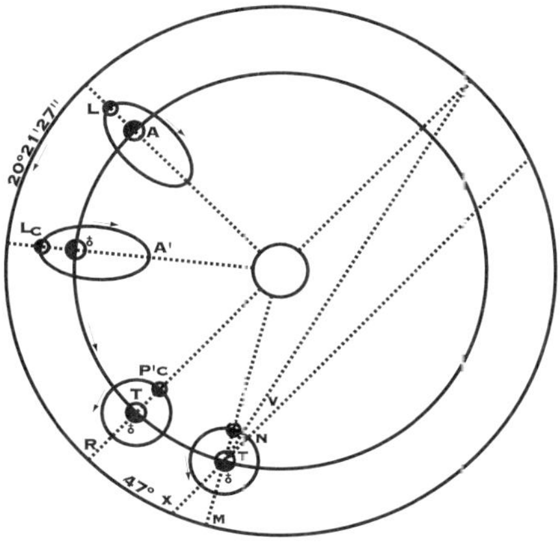

Steamship Soldier on the Information Front

Nancy Kress

Just before the plane touched down at Logan, Allan Haller gave one last check to the PID on the back of his tie-tack. Good. Intense vibration in the Cathy icon, superintense in Suzette, and even Charlie showed acceptable oscillation. No need to contact any of them, that would save time. Patti and Jon, too — their icons shivered and thrilled at nearly top speed. And three minutes till landing.

"My, look at what you have there," said his seatmate pleasantly. A well-rounded grandmotherly sort, she'd been trying to engage him in conversation since La Guardia. "What sort of gadget is that, might I ask?"

No, Allan almost said, because what ground could possibly be gained? But then he looked at her again. Expensive jacket, good haircut, Gucci bag. Certainly money, but probably not entrepreneurial — rich old women tended to safe and stodgy investments. Still, what could he lose? Two and a half-minutes until landing, and speculative capital, as he well knew, was sometimes found in very odd places.

"It's a PID — a personal-icon display," he said to Grandma Money. "It shows the level of electronic interaction going on with my family — my wife Cathy here, my son and daughter on these two icons — and of my two chief business associates. Each of them is wired with a WIPE, a 'weak interactive personal electronic field' in various items of clothing that communicate with each other through a faint current sent through their bodies. Then all interactions with other electronic fields in their vicinity are registered in their WIPES and sent wireless to each other's PIDs. I can tell, for instance, by how much the Cathy icon is vibrating that she's probably working at her terminal — lots of data going through her icon. Suzette is probably playing tennis — see, her icon is super-oscillating the way WIPE fields do when they're experiencing fast-motion physical interference, and Charlie here —"

"You send electric current through your children's bodies?" Grandma Money sounded horrified.

"It isn't dange —"

"All the *time*? And then you Big-Brother them? All the *time*?"

Allan flipped down the tie-tack. Well, it had been worth a skirmish, as long as the time talking to her would have been downtime anyway. With a slight bump, the plane made contact with the runway.

"Don't they...well, I don't mean to be rude, but doesn't your family object to —"

But Allan was already moving down the aisle toward the jetway, from the forward seat he'd had booked precisely because it was the first to disembark. By the time the other passengers were reaching for their overhead luggage, he was already in the airport, moving fast, talking into his phone.

"Jon, what have you got?"

"A third prospect. Out in Newton; the car company will do the max-efficient route. The company is Figgy Pudding, the product is NewsSort. It goes through the whole Net looking for matches to key words, then compares the news items with ones the user has liked in the past and pre-selects for him — the usual statistical-algorithm gig. But they're claiming ninety-three percent success rate."

"Pretty good, if it's true."

"Worth a skirmish," Jon said, in New York. "That's all in Boston." He hung up.

Allan didn't break stride. "Figgy Pudding" — the cutesy name meant the talent was old, left over from the generation that could name a computer after a fruit and a communications language after a hot beverage. Still, some of those geezer geeks still had it. Worth a skirmish.

"Your car is waiting at these co-ordinates," his wristwatch said, displaying them along with a route map of Logan. "Thank you for using the Micro Global Positioning System."

Allan tacked through the crowd, past the fast food kiosks, the public terminal booths, the VR parlours crammed with kids parked there while parents waited for flights. The driver, who had of course been tracking Allan through MGPS, already had the car door opened, the schedule revisions from Jon, the max-effish route. No words were necessary. Allan sank into the back seat and unfolded his meshNet.

This was Haller Ventures' latest investment to come to market. Allan loved it. A light, flexible cloth meshed with optic-fibre wires, it could be folded almost as small as a handkerchief. Yet it could receive as much data as any other dumb terminal in existence, *and* display it in more varied, complex configurations. Fast, powerful, keyed to both Allan's voice and to his chosen tactile commands for max effish, fully flexible in interacting with his PID and just about every other info-device, the meshNet was everything high-tech should be. It was going to make everyone connected with Haller Ventures rich.

Richer.

"Jon message," Allan said to the meshNet. "Display." And there was the information about Figgy Pudding: stock offerings, annual reports, inside run-downs put together and run through the Haller investment algorithms with Jon's usual efficiency. Nobody on the information front could recon better than Jon, unless it was Allan himself.

Carefully he studied the Figgy Pudding data. Looking good, looking very good.

"Five minutes until your first scheduled stop," his wristwatch said. A second later, the phone buzzed, then automatically transferred the call to the meshNet once it verified that the meshNet was unfolded. Cathy's icon appeared on the soft metallic surface.

"Cathy message," Allan said. The driver, curious, craned his gaze into the rear-view mirror, but Allan ignored him. Definitely no ground to be gained there.

"Hey, love," Cathy's voice said. "Schedule change."

"Give it to me," Allan said, one eye still on the Figgy Pudding projections.

"Suzette made it. She's in for the Denver Preteen Semi-Final Skating Championship!"

"That's great!" Allan said. Damn, but he had great kids. Although Charlie... "I'll send her congratulations."

"Good. But she needs to leave Tuesday, on a nine-twenty a.m. plane. I have to be in court in Albuquerque on the Darlington case. Can you see her off at the airport?"

"Just a sec, hon." Allan called up the latest version of his schedule. "No can do. Patti's got me in Brussels from Monday night to Tuesday afternoon, with a stop at a London biotech on the hop home."

"Okay," Cathy said cheerfully. She was always cheerful; it was one of the reasons Allan was glad she was his wife. "I'll get a driver for her, and Mrs. Canning can see her off. Consider it covered. Are we still on for dinner and hanky-panky Wednesday?"

"Let me check....yes, it looks good. Five o'clock at the Chicago Plaza."

"I'll be there," Cathy said. "Oh, and give Charlie a call, will you? Today?"

"What's with Charlie?"

"Same thing," Cathy said, and for just a moment her cheerfulness faltered.

"Okay," Allan said. "Don't worry."

"You on your way to Novation?" Cathy of course received constant updates of his schedule, as he did of hers. Although she had fewer updates; even consulting attorneys as good as she was sometimes stayed in the same city for as long as three days. "Novation is the biorobot company, isn't it?"

"Yeah," Allan said. "Patti's pushing it pretty strong. But frankly, I don't have much faith in radical tech that makes this many extravagant claims. Promise the moon, deliver a rusty asteroid. I don't expect to be impressed."

"That's my man. Make 'em work for it. Love you."

"Love you, too," Allan said. The Cathy icon vanished from his meshNet.

"Two minutes until your first scheduled stop," his watch said.

Perfect.

+++++

Allan was wrong. He might not have expected to be impressed with Novation, but, almost against his will, he was.

As soon as he entered the unprepossessing concrete-block building, he could feel the data rush. Vibrating, racing, dancing. Whatever made a place blaze on the very edge of the information front, this place had it.

His contact entered the lobby just as Allan did. On top of the moves. She was an Indian woman in her late thirties, dressed in khaki slacks and a red shirt. All her movements were quick and light. Her black eyes shone with intelligence.

"Allan. I'm Skaka Gupta, Chief Scientist at Novation." Although of course Allan already knew that, plus everything relevant about her career, and she knew that he knew. "Welcome to our Biorobotics Unit."

"Thank you."

"Would you like a max-effish print-out of our current status?" A courtesy only; Novation's official profile would have been supplied to his firm yesterday. With an update this morning, if anything had changed overnight. And she'd know he'd prefer the figures and projections put together by his own people, in which the official profile was only one factor.

"No, thank you," Allan smiled. "But I am very eager to see your work directly."

"Then let's do that." She smiled back, completely sure of herself. Or of her work. Allan hoped it was of her work; he could sniff genuine success here. It smelled like money.

"Let me babble about the basics," Skaka said, "and you jump in with questions when you want to. We're passing through the biolab now, where we build the robots. Or, rather, start them growing."

Behind a glass wall stood rows of sterile counters, each monitored by automated equipment. A lone technician, dressed in white scrubs and mask, worked at a far counter. Allan said, "Let me test my understanding here. Your robot bodies are basic mass-ordered cylinders, with electro-field intercommunication, elevation-climbing limbs, and the usual sensors."

"That's right. We'll see them in a minute — they look like upended tin cans with four skinny clumsy legs and two skinny clumsy arms. But their processing units are entirely innovative. Each circuit board you see here, in each clear box, is being grown. We start with textured silicon plates etched with logic circuits, and then seed them with foetal neurons, grown on synthetic peptides. The foetal tissue used comes from different sources. The result is that even though the circuit scaffolds are the same, the neurons spin out different axons and dendrites. And since foetal brains always produce more neurons than they ultimately need, different ones atrophy on different boards. Each processor ends up different, and so the robots are subtly different too."

Allan studied the quiet, orderly lab. Skaka merely waited. Finally he said, "You're not the only company exploring this technique."

"No, of course not. But we've developed significant new variations — significant by several orders of magnitude. Proprietary, of course, until you've bought in."

Until, not *if*. Allan liked that.

"The proof of just how different our techniques are lies right ahead. This way to the primate house."

"Monkeys?" Allan said, startled. This had *not* been in the pre-reading.

Skaka, walking briskly, grinned over her shoulder. "P-r-i-m-e E-i-g-h-t House. It's a joke. Currently we have eight robots in each at two different stages of development. Both groups are in learning environments modelled on the closed-system forests once used with chimps. Follow me."

She led him out of the lab, down a long windowless corridor. Halfway, Allan's tie-tack beeped twice.

"Excuse me, Skaka, is the men's room —"

"Right through that door."

Inside, Allan flipped over his tie tack. The PID icon for Charlie had completely stopped vibrating. Immediately Allan phoned his son.

"Charlie? Where are you?"

"What do you mean, where am I? It's Friday, right? I'm at school."

"In..."

"In Aspen."

"Why aren't you in Denver?"

"Not this week, Dad, remember?"

Allan hadn't. Mrs. Canning's tutorial schedule for the kids' real-time educational experiences was complex, although of course Allan could have accessed it on his meshNet. Maybe he should have. But Charlie's physical location wasn't the issue.

"What are you doing in Aspen, son? Right now?"

"Nothing."

Allan pushed down his annoyance. Also his concern. Charlie — so handsome, so smart, twelve years old — spent an awful lot of time doing nothing. Just sitting in one room or another, staring into space. It wasn't normal. He should be out playing soccer, exploring the Net, teasing girls, racing bikes. Even reading would be more productive than this passive staring into nothing.

Allan said, "Where's Mrs. Canning? Why is she letting you do nothing? We don't pay her for that, you know."

"She thinks I'm writing my essay about the archaeological dig we did in the desert."

"And why aren't you writing it?"

"I will...look, Dad, I gotta go now. See you next week. Love you."

"But Charlie —"

The phone went dead.

Should he call back? When Charlie got like this, he often didn't answer. Got like *what*? What was wrong with a kid who just turned himself off and sat, like a lump of bacon fat?

Nothing. Nothing was wrong with his son.

"Allan? Everything all right?" Skaka, rapping discreetly on the men's room door. Christ, how long had Allan been staring at the motionless Charlie icon on his PID? Too long. The schedule would be all shot to hell.

"Fine," he said, striding into the corridor. "Sorry. Now let's see the

Prime-Eight house."

"You've never seen data like this," Skaka promised, and strode faster to make up for the lost time.

+++++

He never had seen data like this.

Each of the two identical 'learning environments' was huge, two point three acres, circled by a clear plastic wall and furnished with grey platforms at various heights and angles, steps and ramps and pot-holes, mini-mazes and obstacles that could be reconfigured from outside the enclosures. The environments looked like monochromatic miniature-golf courses that had undergone an earthquake. In the first enclosure were eight of the tin-can robots, moving slowly and ponderously over the crazed terrain. Each was painted with a bright logo: 'Campbell's Tomorrow Soup,' 'Chef-Boy-R&D,' 'Lay's Pareto Chips.'

"Programmer humour," Skaka said. "This batch was only activated yesterday. See, they haven't learned very much about navigation, let alone how to approach their task efficiently."

"What *is* their task?" Allan said. Now they were getting to the manoeuvres not covered in the prospectus.

"See those green-grey chips scattered throughout the environment? The robots are supposed to gather as many of those as they can, as fast as they can."

Allan peered through the plastic. Now he could see the chips, each about the size of a small cookie, lying in holes, on railings, between walkways, under ramps. The closest robot, 'Processed Corn', reached for one with its tong-ended 'arm.' It missed. The chip slid away, and the robot fell over. Trying to right itself, it thrashed too close to the edge of a large pot hole and fell in, where it kept on thrashing.

Allan laughed. "War is hell."

"What?" Skaka said.

"Nothing. How many chips have the robots gathered so far?"

"One."

"And how long have they been at it?"

"Six hours. Now come with me to Prime-Eight Two."

Allan followed her again. They passed Chef-Boy-R&D and 'Net-wiser Beer' jammed up against each other. Each time one moved to the right to go around the other, the second robot did the same. They ended up deadlocked against the plastic wall, four spindly legs marching futiley against each other.

Skaka unlocked a door and led Allan onto a catwalk overlooking the second enclosure. Identical to the first, it also contained eight painted robots, this group all motionless.

"Watch," Skaka said.

She pressed a button. A shower of grey-green chips fell from the ceiling, landing in holes, on railings, between walkways, under ramps. Immediately the robots sprang to life. They marched, clambered, searched. Allan's watch tingled on his wrist; and his tie twitched. Even outside the enclosure, his electrical biofield registered the enormous amount of data surging through the air as the robots communicated with each other. Within minutes all the chips had been gathered into a pile and shoved through a slit in the enclosure. They fell in a shower onto the corridor floor.

"Jesus Turing Christ," Allen said, inadequately. "Are you telling me this batch of robots learned to do that by themselves? That they had no additional programming over the first biobots?"

"That's what I'm telling you," Skaka said, in triumph. "Six minutes, forty-nine seconds. They keep beating their own record as they get more and more efficient at the task. This batch has been learning for five weeks, two days."

"Let me see it again."

Skaka pressed the button to release more chips, which fell onto different places than before. The eight robots sprang into action. Allan noted that instead of each robot searching a discreet area of the enclosure, each seemed to go for a chip according to complex factors of proximity, relative altitude, difficulty of retrieval, and even, it seemed to him, differences in agility that must have stemmed from the different foetal neurons in their processors. More than once, he saw a robot start toward a chip, then veer off to go for a different one, while another robot seized the first chip.

"That's right," Skaka said, eyeing Allan. "They've learned to increase efficiency by sharing knowledge. And they make co-operative decisions based, according to the mathematical analyses we've done, on a very detailed knowledge of their differences in capability. *And they evolved all those techniques by themselves.*"

Allan watched 'Hot Bytes Salsa' race on its spindly legs to the slit in the wall and shove the chips through.

"Six minutes, thirty-four seconds," Skaka said. "Allan, I'm sure somebody like you can see the breakthrough this represents in autonomous computer learning. It makes artificial intelligence — with everything that implies in terms of corporate or military systems — nearly within our grasp. Now, doesn't that seem a potentially profitable investment for your venture capital firm?"

Allan watched the plastic chips shower over Skaka's feet. *To the vic-*

tor belong the spoils.

"Yes," he said. "Let's talk."

+++++

After that, Figgy Pudding and Morrison Telecommunications were both anticlimactic. Figgy might be worth a small investment, just to establish a benchhead, but nothing major. Morrison Telecommunications was stodgy. Not anywhere near the front, not even really in the war zone. Same old, same old.

Allan flew to D.C. and spent the night at the newly renovated Watergate. Jon had booked him into two skirmishes tomorrow with labs doing government work, and Patti had added two briefing sessions with firms already using Haller Ventures money. While he was at dinner, he studied the info on each that she sent him. By dessert, the figures had changed once and the meetings for tomorrow changed twice.

Upstairs, Allan felt restless. There was nothing good on TV, not even with 240 channels. He couldn't seem to concentrate on his favourite Net game, Battle Chess. Every time he moved a piece, the computer countered him with blinding speed. When he lost his lieutenant to the computer's tank, which could move any number of squares through all three dimensions, Allan surrendered. It was a relief when Cathy called.

"Allan? How'd it go today?"

He told her about Novation — there was nothing he kept from Cathy. She was impressed, which cheered him a little. But then she said, "Listen, love, I'm going to have to reschedule our Wednesday rendezvous. I have the chance to go to Hong Kong after all."

"On the Burdette case? Great!" he forced himself to say. Cathy had worked for this for a long time.

"I'm thrilled, of course. Lane is reworking my schedule. We'll send it as soon as the snafus are out. Did you call Charlie?"

"Yeah. He's still just sitting a lot. Honey, do you think we should get him, well, help?"

Cathy's voice changed. "You know, I've been thinking that myself. Not that there's anything really wrong with him, but just as a precaution..."

"I'll have Jon research psychologists," Charlie said heavily. "Listen, do you think we could reschedule our rendezvous to —"

"Oops, gotta go, there's Lane with another update on the Burdette case. God, me and international policy making! I can hardly believe it. Love you." The Cathy icon vanished.

"Love you, too," Allan said to the blank meshNet.

But there was no reason to wallow in gloom. He would call Suzette; his daughter was always a delight. Suzette, however, was not taking calls. Neither was Allan's brother in Florida. His mother, her system informed him, was sailing in the Aegean and would return his call when she returned, unless it was an emergency. It was not an emergency. The icons on his PID all vibrated and shimmered, even Charlie's, thank heavens.

Allan went to bed.

✢✢✢✢✢

The next day, he felt fine. Meetings, the schedule, the flow of data and money and possibility. God, he loved it. A prosthetic device, almost invisible, to enhance human hearing through 30,000 cps. A significant gain in surveillance-satellite image resolution. Another of the endless small advances in nanotech, rearranging atoms in what would someday be the genie-in-the-bottle of the telecommunications and every other industry.

At 6:18, while he was wrapping up the nanotech briefing, Skaka Gupta called. "Allan, I'm sorry to interrupt your day, but could you fly back here tonight? There's something you should see."

Her voice sang with excitement. Allan felt it leap over the netlink, electrifying his own nerves. And it would avoid another empty evening in a hotel room. But he said with cool professionalism, "My schedule is rather full, Skaka. Are you sure the flying back to Boston will be worth my time?"

"Oh, yes," she said, and at the tone in her voice, he called Jon to rearrange the schedule.

✢✢✢✢✢

The robots in Prime-Eight One still struggled to find and retrieve chips. Chef-Boy-R&D lay on its cylindrical side like an overturned beetle, spindly legs waving desperately to right itself. Skaka, practically running toward Prime-Eight Two, didn't even glance through the plastic fence.

"Look," she said, outside the second enclosure. "*Watch.*"

But there was nothing to see. The eight robots stood motionless around the uneven terrain. A minute passed, then another. Allan started to feel impatient. After all, his time was valuable. He could be checking in with Jon, receiving information updates, finding help for Charlie, even playing Battle Chess —

All of a sudden, the robots began to move. They lumbered to roughly equidistant positions within the enclosure. A brief pause, and then the chips rained down from the ceiling. Immediately the robots swung into action. Within minutes, the chips had all been gathered. Unsweetened

Intelsauce deposited them through the slit.

"Six minutes, fourteen seconds," Skaka breathed. "The physical limitations will eventually limit any more gains in efficiency. But that's not the point anymore. Allan, they've learned to anticipate when chips will fall, before they do. They anticipate tasks that haven't yet been signalled!"

"On a regular schedule, you mean. The chips fall, say, every two hours —"

"No! That's what's so amazing! The chips don't fall at completely random times, there's a schedule, the same one we've used since the beginning, although I admit we interrupted it yesterday for your visit. The usual schedule has built-in variations around human factors like work shifts, staff meeting, lunch breaks. The bots have apparently learned it over time and are now anticipating with 100% accuracy when chips will be released. They're also anticipating the most probable places for the rolling and ricocheting chips to come to rest, given that the terrain changes daily but the chip-release points are fixed in the ceiling. Ever since last night, they've moved into max-effish gathering positions a few minutes *before* the chips fall!"

Allan stared at the tin-can robots, with their garish logos and silly names. Anticipatory task management, based on self-learning of a varied-interval schedule. In biochips. It could have tremendous potential applications in manufacturing, for maintenance machinery, in speeding up forecast software...His brain spun.

"Don't you think," Skaka said softly, "that this was well worth the trip back here?"

Allan kept his tone cool, although it took effort. "Possibly. But of course I have a number of reservations and questions. For instance, have you —" His phone rang, two beeps, a priority call.

"Dad? Charlie. Did you know our neighbours in Aspen have been arrested?"

"Charlie, I'm pretty busy right now, I'm with a —"

"They've been arrested for *terrorism.* There are cops all over the place."

Terrorism. Cops. Bombs, guns. What neighbours? Allan couldn't remember meeting anyone in Aspen.

"Where's Mrs. Canning? Let me talk to her. Are you all right?"

"Of course I'm all right," Charlie said scornfully. "Mrs. Canning took Suzette to the ice rink."

"Then here's what I want you to do. Just a minute..." Belatedly, Charlie remembered Skaka, who was trying to look as if she hadn't overheard. "Excuse me, Skaka, it's my son..."

"Of course," Skaka said, turning to gaze away, into the robot enclosure. The backs of her shoulders, just a little too rigid, said *Why haven't you got your personal life well enough arranged so it doesn't interfere with what may well be the most important investment opportunity of the decade?*

"Charlie, first call your mother and tell her what you just told me. Also Mrs. Canning. Then call a car and driver, and pack your things and Suzette's and Mrs. Canning's. Have the driver take you to the Denver apartment. I'll have Jon or Patti okay the car bill and cancel the Aspen house."

"But, Dad —"

"Charlie, just do it. I don't want you in any danger!"

"Oh, okay." Charlie sounded disgusted. Twelve-year-old bravado.

Quickly, Allan called Jon. Skaka's shoulders were still stiff. Allan resented having lost the advantage. As in-control as he could manage, he said to Skaka, "My son. There's been terrorist activity in what should have been a safe neighbourhood. I had to get him out."

Her eyes widened. "Of course. What kind of terrorist activity?"

It occurred to Allan that he hadn't asked. He didn't know the charges, the situation, the neighbours, themselves. They were only local; he spent so much time global.

"The under-control kind," he said, hoping she wouldn't pick up on the evasion. "And we can be out of there in half an hour. Charlie's a good packer."

Skaka smiled. "So is my daughter. We, too, have no fixed residence. I don't know how scientists managed before disposable leases."

"Neither do I." Allan warmed to her again; she was making his lapse into civilian more forgivable. "What plan do you use?"

"Live America. Their Code Nine Plan: three-bedroom leases, no more than ten minutes from an airport, warm blue decor, level three luxury. They even include our choice of pet at each house. It suits my husband, daughter, and nanny just fine."

"We're a Code Eleven. Four bedrooms. We have two kids."

Allan and Skaka smiled at each other, then looked away. That was the problem with talking about personal life: it interfered with the strategy. Reconnaissance scouts had to stay detached, keep moving, remain tense and alert. The information frontier was an unpredictable place.

Skaka said briskly, "My staff will be watching very closely whatever the bots incorporate next into their learning, if anything. Should another breakthrough occur, they'll notify me and I'll notify you."

"Good," Allan said. "Meantime, let's talk about the breakthrough we already have. I've got some questions."

"Shoot," Skaka said, and her shoulders visibly loosened.

+++++

Allan spent the night on a sleeper plane to Singapore. Mrs. Canning settled the kids in the Denver apartment, although Suzette complained the ice-rink there wasn't as good as at Aspen. She wanted to lease in Chicago, which Coach Palmer said has a enth-mega rink! Allan said he'd think about it. Cathy called to postpone their romantic rendezvous until Sunday; her case was dragging on. Patti identified two more companies for Allan to check out, both on the far edge, both potential coups. One was in Sydney, the other in Brasilia. The Charlie icon on Allan's PID sat motionless.

The Singapore company had developed what it called a "graciously serious approaching" to that perennial coming attraction, the smart road that would direct cars, freeing the driver to do other things besides drive. Allan had expected that his visit would result in hiring one of the independent consultants Haller Ventures used to evaluate automotive technology, but it didn't even need that. Singapore wasn't doing anything Allan hadn't seen before. Not worth a skirmish. On to Sydney.

From the plane he called Charlie. "Son? Not much action in your PID icon." Totally vibrationless, for five straight hours, and not a time when Charlie could be expected to be asleep.

"No," Charlie said neutrally.

Allan tried to keep his tone light. "So what ya doing?"

"Nothing."

"*Charlie* —"

"Did you know that when Robert Fulton invented the steamship, at least three other guys were making the same thing at the same time?"

"Charlie —"

"Gotta go, Dad. Love you."

"Three minutes till landing," said his wristwatch. "MGPS co-ordinates for your car are displayed."

"Charlie!" Patti said. "Action in Tunis. Looks like a genuine outpost. Company is called Sahara Sun, and they manufacture solar panels. Stats follow. Also re-routing on tomorrow's schedule."

"Two minutes till landing."

Allan closed his eyes. But when the plane stopped, he was the first one to spring up, grab his carry-on, deplane from the front row. In Jakarta.

No — *Sydney*. Jakarta was tomorrow.

Or the next day?

+++++

Sydney was fibre-optics with increased carrying capacity due to smaller-grain alloys.

Jakarta was medical technology, an improved electrocardiograph that could predict fibrillation by incorporating elements of chaos theory into the computer analysis of data. Eighty-one-point-three success rate. So far.

Bombay was no good. Supposedly an important advance in holographic videoconferencing, but actually old, old, old stuff. Jon had slipped up.

Berne was briefing and inspection tour of an ongoing investment, currently in beta-testing phase. A Haller Ventures accountant and quality assurance expert met Allan there.

Milan was fascinating. The benchmark for parallel-systems processing was one trillion operations per second. The Italian techies had achieved it with half the hardware previously required. There was much noisy gesturing and an earthy Tuscany wine.

Tunis was robots in the desert. The entrepreneurs drove Allan onto the rim of the Sahara, jouncing in Rovers over miles of rocky sand to a sun-drenched site where solar panels were being assembled by simple robots. The bots also assembled more of themselves. They separated ores from the desert sand for raw material, using solar power to create the high temperatures to do it: a self-perpetuating mechanical kingdom slowly spreading over the empty desert floor. The excess solar power was converted into electricity to sell, once cables were in place. A solid, conservative strategy. Allan ordered a tech-consultant evaluation immediately, including a climate projection for thirty years. Desert wars had been lost before to climate.

He caught a transatlantic flight home. The Brazilian engagement had been postponed. Cathy had gone to Los Angeles — the Tunis trip had once more scuttled their rendezvous — with Suzette, who had a major skating competition. Charlie was on a nature hike in Yosemite with the commercial edu-group Mrs. Canning subscribed him to. The leased apartment in Aspen — no, Aspen had been cancelled, and anyway it was Oakland this month because of Suzette's competition schedule — would be empty.

The little Tunisian robots had looked like rectangular suitcases, not cylindrical tin cans. Nonetheless, Allan called Skaka Gupta from the transatlantic flight. She was in Berne. Allan re-routed himself to Boston anyway. He didn't like coming home to a new leased place with no one else there.

At Novation he was met by a flustered young man, no more than twenty-three, in jeans, leather sweater, and the ubiquitous sneakers set with tiny flashing mirrors. Allan recognised the type: a software expert. Awkward, bright as hell, and secretly scornful of "bean counters." No, that wasn't the term anymore: "cashware clods." Allan smiled icily and looked slightly bored.

"Paul Sanderson? Allan Haller. You're going to give me Skaka's pitch, right?" Skaka had left no data for a new pitch, as far as Allan knew.

Paul Sanderson looked confused. "Yes...no, I mean, she didn't...I was just going to show you what the bots can do now."

"Fine, fine. But keep the jargon to a minimum." A pre-emptive strike, with the force of an order. Sanderson would either get huffy or meek, unsure how his boss would want Allan treated.

He got meek. "Sure. Well, uh, this way."

The robots in Prime-Eight One seemed to Allan slightly less uncoordinated, although they still, wandered hopelessly. Campbell's Tomorrow Soup lunged at a chip but missed it. Sanderson dawdled past the enclosure, peering through the plastic, fidgeting. Why? To cover his own edginess, Allan flipped over his tie and checked his PID.

The icons all vibrated so fast he could barely see they were there.

"You've created a superstrength data field here!" he exclaimed, and as Sanderson turned toward him with a grin of embarrassment, Allan understood. "You have, haven't you? You've made the whole facility into a microwave field that lets the Prime-Eight Two bots interface directly with the Net. You retrofitted them with the communications software to do that."

Sanderson nodded sheepishly. "I know regs say I should have warned you before you stepped into the field, but it's not dangerous in such short exposure, really it's not. And your own com devices will return to normal functioning just as soon as we —"

"I'm not concerned about either my devices or my health!" Allan snapped. "But Skaka promised to keep me abreast of any major changes in the research!"

"Well, there haven't really been any," Sanderson said. "Although we'd hoped...but so far, nothing has changed. The bots just go on anticipating the chip-release schedule and —"

"Is Prime-Eight One wired to the Net, too? Or aren't you going to tell me that, either?"

Sanderson looked shocked. "No, of course it's not wired. If we don't do it at exactly the same point as we did this group, we'd compromise the research design!"

"As opposed to compromising your investors' confidence," Allan snapped. "Fine. Tell Ms. Gupta to call me when she returns. And please be advised that I retain the right to bring in my own evaluators here, since I'm obviously not being told everything voluntarily."

"Mr. Haller, please don't think that because —"

"That's all," Allan snapped, turned, and left.

Back in his car, he asked himself why he was so angry. He owned a piece of Novation, yes, but he owned pieces of a lot of outposts where the front shifted abruptly and unpredictably. That was the nature of fronts. So why *was* he so upset?

He didn't know. And there was no time to think about it. His next flight left in forty-two minutes.

Just enough time study the information for tomorrow's 6:30 breakfast meeting.

+++++

Cathy and Allan finally connected in New York; she had an unexpected re-route in her schedule. As he entered the elevator, Allan felt his chest tighten. Ten days since he'd last seen his wife! And oh, how he'd missed her...and how he loved the giddy excitement of their reunions. Surely couples who were together all the time couldn't get this excited.

Nor was he disappointed. Afterward, lying together on the big hotel bed, dreamily watching the wall programme shade from hectic red to cool soft blues (it must be keyed to their breathing), Allan felt utterly content.

Cathy, however, didn't let him drift long. "Honey, there's something we need to talk about. It's Charlie."

Immediately Allan's mood changed. He hiked himself up against the pillows. "How did he seem in Los Angeles?"

"Strange." Cathy hesitated. "I know he's on the edge of adolescence, trying his wings, some hostility to be expected blah blah blah...but he *wasn't* hostile. He was just as nice to Suzette as ever, really thrilled for her when she won. And he wasn't at all secretive with me. It's just that he's gone off in such strange directions in his personal interests. For instance, he talked a lot about the Age of Reason and its social implications."

"Just a sec," Allan said. He reached for the meshNet, crumpled with the rest of his clothes on the floor by his bed, and did a Quik-Chek. *Age of Reason: an eighteenth-century period of great intellectual awareness and activity, characterised by questioning of authority, emphasis on the experimental method in science, and creative self-determination in arts, culture, and politics.*

"I could have told you what it was," Cathy said, nettled.

"I know." Cathy was a lawyer; she would have gone into far more well-organised particulars than Allan wanted. "But it's just history, right? An interest in history doesn't sound so bad. In fact, Charlie said something or other to me about Robert Fulton and the steamship. Maybe Mrs. Canning started a new school unit."

"No, I checked. They're still concentrating on earth sciences. But that's not all. I accessed Charlie's Twenty-Two — the personal-notes tablet, but only the unencrypted part, of course — and he —"

"He's still using a Twenty-Two? Good Lord, that computer's been obsolete for at least three months! I'll send him a new one — there's something much better coming out now."

Cathy said acidly, "There's always something much better coming out. But that's not the *point*, Allan. What I found on Charlie's tablet were lists of 'ages.' All the lists were subtly different, but there were *dozens* of them."

"What do you mean, 'ages'?"

"Stone Age. Iron Age. Age of Heroes. Age of Faith. Dark Ages. Age of Reason. Industrial Age. Space Age. Information Age. That one's always last on every list, presumably because we're in it now. Dozens of different lists!"

"Odd," Allan said, because it was clear she expected him to say something. "But, frankly, Cath, it doesn't sound dangerous. So he's wondering about history. That's good, isn't it?"

"Exhibit Three: When I asked him about the lists, he didn't get angry that I'd been snooping in his tablet. Instead, he looked at me in that intense way he has, not moving a single facial muscle — you know how he is — and said, 'Mom, how do we know that our family is really information-front warriors, and not really just homeless people?'"

Allan considered. That did sound serious. "Did you ask him if he's feeling that you and I travel too much? That we should make an effort to be all together more often as a family?" He and Cathy had worried this before.

"Yes. But he said no, that wasn't it at all, his friends' parents were just the same. So I asked him what *was* it, and he only said, 'When it's steamship time, it's steamship *time*,' and sank into one of those motionless trances of his. Allan, I couldn't get him to even answer me for half an hour, no matter what I did. It's like he was someplace else, sitting right there in front of me!"

Allan gazed out the window. Far below, the New York traffic sounds hummed dimly, reassuringly. Allan said slowly, "I got the names of two good child psychologists, one in Denver and one in San Francisco."

"Well, that won't do a lot of good, since we're not going to be in Oakland after a few more weeks. We're all leasing in Kansas City for the Shephard trial. Can't you take the trouble to memorise our schedule?"

After a minute she added, “I’m sorry.”

“It’s all right,” Allan said. “I know you’re worried about Charlie, too. Listen, I’ll find a psychologist in...” he blanked for a moment — “Kansas City.”

“Okay.” Cathy smiled wanly, then clung to him. He could feel the tension in her bare back.

Charlie had always been such an easy kid. Suzette had been the temperamental one. That’s why they were concerned, Allan told himself; it was all relative. Still, for Charlie to just sit and go into a trance where he didn’t even answer people...that couldn’t be normal, could it? To be so cut off?

Why, he wouldn’t even be tuned into the Net. Anything could develop, and Charlie wouldn’t even know it!

Allan held his wife tighter. “I’ll re-route to see him tomorrow.”

✢✢✢✢✢

Re-routing wasn’t easy. Neither Jon nor Patti were pleased. Jon had to go himself to check out bone-marrow scanning in Raleigh. The director of a firm making low-cost orbiting solar panels in Dallas wouldn’t be available for another two weeks if Allan missed that appointment, because the director would be in Tokyo. Videoconferencing, the director said sniffily, was not an acceptable substitute. Allan told Patti to tell the director to go to hell. He got a flight to the new apartment in Kansas City.

But then Paul Sanderson called from Novation. Skaka Gupta must again be somewhere else. “You said...I mean, you seemed to indicate last time you were here, Allan...uh, Mr. Haller...that if something noteworthy happened with the bots you wanted to see it right away, so —”

“And something has? Unfortunately, the timing couldn’t be worse. Can you describe the development to me?”

“Oh, sure,” Sanderson said, with such relief in his voice that Allan decided he better go to Novation himself after all. The data smelled important. If he took a flight almost immediately to Boston, even flying standby if he had to...shit, he hated flying standby, if only developments in transferring people could keep up with innovations in transferring data! — if he flew standby, and then could book a flight getting him to the Kansas City lease by at least midnight...

“Never mind explaining. I’ll be there this afternoon.”

“Okay,” Sanderson said unhappily. “We’ll be expecting you.”

We. Him and the robots? Did Sanderson identify with them that much? Maybe; engineer types never seemed to have any real life. Just endless tinkering with software, in the same subroutines, same location, same days.

Suddenly Allan was hit with a memory. So vivid, so visceral, it almost seemed as if he no longer stood in the middle of a frantic metropolitan airport but instead was in the cool woods behind the house where he'd grown up, lying on his back on a carpet of pine needles. Billy Goldman, his best friend, lay beside him, both of them gazing upward at the sun-dabbled branches lacing the sky, smelling the sweet tangy pines, and Billy saying, "Why would anyone want to kiss a *girl*? Yuuccckkk!"

Now, where had *that* come from? Astonished, Allan shook his head to clear it. The mind was a strange thing. Tossing in the unrelated, the pointless, the unprofitable, the irrelevant. The distracting.

By the time he reached Boston, he had a headache no pills could touch.

He arrived at Novation in a foul mood. Sanderson met him nervously. "This way, Mr. Haller, we'll go right to Prime-Eight Two, unless you want some, um, coffee, or maybe —"

"No. Let's go."

Sanderson walked past Prime-Eight One without turning his head, but Allan stopped to study the robots. It seemed to him that they gathered their chips a little more smoothly, with less fumbling. He thought he even saw Processed Corn start forward, then swerve abruptly to miss crashing into Ocean Spray Cacheberries. They were starting to co-operate.

Prime-Eight Two, on the other hand, looked no different. The bots stood motionless on the complex terrain. Allan and Sanderson stood outside the enclosure, Sanderson fidgeting. "Chip fall in seven minutes. We don't want to alter the schedule, you know, because even though then you wouldn't have to wait, you wouldn't really be seeing the exact same phenomenon we've been observing, so it isn't —"

"I understand," Allan said. "I can wait."

But he had to do something to fill in seven minutes, besides intimidating Sanderson. The heavy data fire meant he couldn't access his meshNet. Instead, Allan repeated to himself the personal-notes tablet on his son's Twenty-Two. He had accessed the tablet from the plane, telling himself that parental duty outweighed teenage privacy.

Age of Reason...Age of Reason...Information Age...Age of Reasoning...Enlightenment? No no no...Start again Stone Age Iron Age Bronze Age...no no NO NO it's here someplace — TO DO: do sections 84-86 homework for Tuesday find three examples of igneous rock buy mom a birthday present...AGE OF REASON...The girl I saw *in the park was not wearing underwear!!!!!!...**Age of Reason*** —

The robots behind the plastic wall lumbered into position, a moment before chips scattered from the ceiling. "They've learned to cut the anticipation pretty fine," Sanderson said. Allan didn't reply. He watched as the bots efficiently gathered all the chips. They seemed no faster than before, but no slower either. His meshNet had gone dead, presumably from the bots' intense occupation of all available bandwidths to the Net. What exactly were they downloading? And what use were their biochip brains making of it? They didn't need the Net's vast libraries of information to gather chips efficiently.

"Have you traced their download sources yet?"

"Some of them," Sanderson said. He didn't look at Allan, and his tone was evasive. "Watch — here it comes."

But what 'came' was...nothing. Literally. The robots dumped all the chips into their bucket, held in the graspers of Techs/Mex Chili, and then went motionless.

Sanderson began to talk very fast. "They've been doing that for twenty-four hours now. Gathering the chips the way they're programmed to, but then just not depositing them through the wall. Nobody's tinkered with their programming. They just...don't do it."

Allan studied Techs/Mex Chili. "What do your download-source traces show?"

"Not much," Sanderson said, and Allan saw that his previous evasiveness had been embarrassment. Programmers hated not knowing what was going on in their programs. "Or, rather, too much. They're apparently accessing all sorts of stuff, bits of everything on the Net, maybe even at random. At least, we haven't found any patterns yet."

"Umm," Allan said noncommittally. "Squirt the full trace files to my office. Our people will look at it as well."

"I don't really have the authori —"

"Just do it," Allan said, but for once the tone of command didn't work. Sanderson looked scared but determined.

"No, sir, I'm afraid I can't. Not without Skaka's say-so."

Allan capitulated. "All right. I'll call her myself."

The young programmer looked relieved. Allan went on studying the quiet robots in their gaudy, silly paint, guarding their bucket of totally useless chips.

+++++

He couldn't reach Skaka Gupta, so he left her a message to call him. His flight was delayed, and it was well past midnight before the car left him in front of the unfamiliar apartment building in Kansas City. No, not unfamiliar...it looked comfortingly like the one in Oakland, the one in Denver, the one in Aspen, the one in New Orleans, the one in Atlanta, the one in Raleigh...

Mrs. Canning, alerted by the security system, let him in, then stumbled sleepily back to bed. He checked on Suzette, lying with both arms flung out at her side and one knee bent, looking energetic even in sleep. Her hair had grown. Allan went next to the room Charlie always had.

The boy stirred and mumbled as Allan entered. "Hi, Dad."

"Hey, son."

"What...what the reason?"

"The reason for what, Charlie?" Allan said gently, but Charlie was already back to sleep.

For several minutes, Allan watched him. Cathy's light fine hair, Allan's beaky nose, Charlie's own individual chin. His son. On his tablet Allan had the name of a good child psychologist in Kansas City. Just don't let it be neurological, he prayed formlessly. Not a neurological degeneration, not a brain tumour, not any problem they could do nothing about. *Not my Charlie.*

In his own bedroom, which he found located where his bedrooms always were, Allan couldn't sleep. He reviewed the data for the next day's meetings, both local so he could spend more time with Charlie. He did some sit-up's and stretches, and then he tossed in the new, familiar bed.

His son sitting and staring into space, unreachable by ordinary communication...

The robots, refusing to turn in their chips...

Tomorrow's meetings, half the data for which he'd already forgotten.... He didn't really want to attend any of them anyway. Same old, same old...No, what was he thinking? None of it was the same old. It was all interesting new breakthroughs, beachheads on the newest fronts, and he was privileged to have a part in scouting them out...So why did he just want to stay huddled forever in this familiar apartment he'd never seen before? Damn, he *hated* it when he couldn't sleep!

Groping beside his bed, Allan picked up his meshNet. Just holding it, unwrapping it, knowing all the information it put at his command, made him feel better instantly. At night the system didn't signal his messages, merely stored them until he was done sleeping. Maybe there was something from Cathy.

But the only new message was from Skaka Gupta: *Please call me at the lab. Important.* The transmission time was only ten minutes ago. She had returned early to Boston, and was working very late.

"Skaka? Allan Haller. What's going on?"

"Hello, Allan." She sounded tired, as well she might. It was half past one. "I didn't expect to hear from you till morning. But you might as well know now. We've had a temporary set-back."

"What kind of set-back?"

"The robots have stopped functioning. No, that's not true — they only look like they're not functioning because they're not gathering chips any more, as they were programmed to do. Instead, they've speeded up massively the amounts of data they're pulling off the Net, and processing it in parallel non-stop. And they're..." Her voice stumbled.

"They're *what*?"

"They're just huddled together in a ring, touching sides, their visual and auditory and infrared sensors shut down. Just huddled there, blind to their environment."

He didn't answer. After a minute, Skaka's tone changed, and Allan realised for the first time that, despite her glossy competence, she really was a scientist and not an information-front soldier. No entrepreneur would have said, as she did next, "Allan — I know your firm is small, and that you've invested a lot of money in Novation. We can get another grant, but if this project flops, are we going to bring *you* down?"

"Don't worry about it. We'll be all right," Allan said, which was true. He wasn't ever insane enough to commit all of his resources to the same battle.

Commit all of his resources to the same battle...

"That's good," Skaka said. "But it doesn't touch the real issue. Allan, I don't know what the bots are doing."

"I do," he said, but so softly she couldn't hear him. Dazed, he managed to get out, "It's late. Talk in the morning." He cut the connection.

And sat on the edge of the bed, naked legs dangling over the side, staring at nothing.

Commit all of his resources to the same battle... That's what they all had been doing. Many different skirmishes — solar panels, robots, high-resolution imaging, nanotech, smart autos — but all part of the same war. Stone Age, Bronze Age, Age of Chivalry, Space Age...*Information Age*. The only game in town, the scene of all the action, the all-embracing war. *Uncle Sam Wants You!*

But no age lasted forever. Eventually the struggle for bronze or gold or green chips — or for physical or digital terrain — would come to an end, just as all the other Ages eventually had. One succeeding the other, inexorable and unstoppable...*When it's steamship time*, went the old saw, *then nothing can stop the steamship from coming*. And when the Age of Steam was over, it was over. Civilisation was no longer driven by steam. Now it was driven by information. Gather it in, willy-nilly, put it in electronic buckets, give it to the owners. Or the generals.

Why?

What if they gave a war and nobody came?

That's why the robots had stopped. That's why they stood staring into space, only their brains active. They had at their command all the data on the Net, plus the complex-and-growing human neural circuits of their biochips. They were on top of it all, wired in, fully cued for the next stage. Not *how can we gather those chips with max-effish but rather why should we gather chips at all?*

Not the Age of Reason. The Reasons Age.

Things changed. One day steam, then steam is over. One day you can't imagine wanting to kiss a girl, the next day you pant after it. One day you rely on your frontier neighbours for survival of your very home, the next day you don't know your neighbours' names and don't have a settled home.

One day the mad rush after information and chips, the next day you sit and stare trance-like, far more interested in why you were interested in chips and information than in the commodities themselves. Not that the information itself wouldn't continue to accumulate. It would. But the centre was shifting, the mysterious heart of each Age where the real emphasis and excitement were. The front.

Charlie must sense it only dimly. Of course — he was a child, and he didn't have Allan's honed instincts. But that Charlie sensed it at all, the coming change, was probably *because* he was a child — this was the world he would inherit. Charlie would be an integral part of it. But integrated more slowly than the bots, which were riding the advance wave of the human Net, shock troops racing toward where the info-wars gave way to the next step in the long, long march of humanity's development.

Which would be...what? What would the Reasons Age actually be like?

Allan shivered. Suddenly he felt old. He had evolved in the Information Age, had flourished in it...He was a natural as a scout on the high-tech front. Would there be a place for him when the guns grew more muffled, the pace slowed, and the blaze of battle gave way to the domestic concerns of the occupation? Could he adapt to whatever came next?

Then his confidence returned. Of course he could! He always had. The Information Age might end, the Reasons Age arise, but he could make it. In fact, there was probably a way to turn the whole thing to his own profit. All he needed was the right approach, the right allies, the right strategy.

The right *data*.

Tomorrow, he'd start to gather it.
Smiling, Allan slept.

PREDICTABLE SYSTEMS

SINGULARITY?

Vernor Vinge

Vernor Vinge has been called one of the most interesting SF writers of recent times. He combines a professorial position in the Department of Mathematics and Computer Science at San Diego State University with an acute perspective as an award winning science fiction author. He has written many notable novels including *The Peace War, Marooned in Realtime*, and *A Fire Upon The Deep*. The latter part of this interview summarises Vinge's essay, *The Coming Technological Singularity* (http://www-rohan.sdsu.edu/faculty/vinge). He was interviewed by Stephen McClelland in San Diego.

PREDICTABLE SYSTEMS SINGULARITY?

Vernor Vinge

Predictions. Actually there are two sorts we can make. The first is a concept like nuclear power, which may require a leap of imagination. The second sort is something like Moore's Law, where we can see the trends, out to 2015, say. If such hardware trends hold, some extrapolations are relatively easy to make. In my science fiction, I do not actually lean to a cyberpunk style of writing, because I feel it is bleak, providing a dystopic future. With a few nightmarish exceptions, I believe that dystopic futures would lack the drive to keep a high technology civilisation going.

I am interested in systems complexity. It is our ability to master system complexity which will determine the real consequences of the hardware trends. For myself, I am looking towards what I call a *Fine Grained Distribution* scenario where embedded systems communicating with each other will become at least as significant as the notion of individuals communicating with each other in the way we understand it now.

Clearly, Moore's Law gives us a prospectively increasing complexity at the chip level. It is certainly within prospect that the total number of network nodes around us will exceed the number of people in a ratio of perhaps many hundreds or thousands to one. So you could have a possibility of intelligent building components, mechanical effectors, and clothing. Put with other advances, such as embedded positioning technology (local 'GPS'), and the physical environment itself becomes a kind of distributed system. With every physical object potentially in mutual communication and interaction with everything else, this scale of communication would represent a more significant leap than Worldwide Web has been. Our physical world would itself seem 'smart', with programmable properties.

There would be many useful spin-offs. Intelligent, networked components like this could effectively help in their own manufacture. For example, on a production line, the complexity of the assembly process could be reduced overall if each component in the assembly stream could communicate its own dimensions and positioning requirements to the robot manipulator. This means the manipulator and assembly process itself could be simplified in design and given increased robustness. The greatest imponderable between us and the this scenario lies in our ability to manage system complexity (our ability to achieve workable co-operation between so many communicating processors).

If we are successful, then the look of everything should change. I very much like the ideas of wearable computing now emerging, and hope it develops further. We could see for example glasses which could can give 3D impressions of real companions. And whilst this would require a lot of visual processing to be done well, it is the sort of application that relies on number crunching developments which are clearly predictable. With the distributed environment co-ordinating the imagery seen, the classical notions of cyberspace would cross into our everyday perception of the physical world.

But there are many other aspects of system complexity. I am interested in the ecology of systems, and indeed our attitude to them. There are some very close analogies to natural systems, and we even tend to think about the two in increasingly similar ways. Programmers for example routinely talk of their systems as having almost superstitious or ritualistic qualities. Where we have systemic problems, things may be getting so complex that we may need to accept limitations in correcting them. This could well mean an entirely different attitude towards complex systems. Viruses and bugs, for example, may not be things we can eradicate; we may well have to learn to live with them, because they may be present in the system undergrowth all of the time, in much the same way that biological viruses are ubiquitous and largely ineradicable (and often necessary to other lifeforms). As hardware power increases, we may find it necessary to regard computing systems more like living creatures. (For instance, an aircraft autopilot might be more realistically like 'Lassie' than like 'UNIVAC'!) We are passing out of the era when it will be easy to simply clear down a real-time distributed system and reboot it in a completely controlled way.

If we do not achieve some such method of managing more powerful and complex systems, then it is likely we will also lack the ability to continue hardware improvement trends. This could be the cause of a levelling off of hardware trends (rather than because of any explicit physical limitation to further device improvements).

It's clear that global connectivity will alter forms of tribalism but it is also clear that new tribes can be created cutting across all sorts of traditional boundaries. For businesses, it's the sort of revolution that must always happen when you cut the cost of doing something by a thousand or more times. We are entering an era when whole industries may simply *disappear*... and we have already seen industry giants (even when they did not disappear) which found their businesses totally changed. In the future, most business ventures may be similar to present-day movie production. You may have an *ad hoc* team assembled by a large, powerful and dominant ego who has a very clear vision as to what is required and who can deliver it.

There is at least one nightmare scenario associated with success in fine grained distributed systems, and that is in the area of government control. If Government could mandate that a certain percentage of the silicon on each node was the State's property, then Ubiquitous Law Enforcement might be possible. Under most conditions, this interference might be invisible to the population at large; for example, taxation could be simply a transparent accounting technique on the Net (a BIT tax instead of VAT). But the laws themselves would be subject to program downloading, and could be tuned to the national security demands of the moment.

What of the slightly more distant future? Some of the work I have done has been centred around what I call *The Coming Technological Singularity* — and how to survive it. Dramatically put, if hardware trends continue for another thirty years, we may well have the technological means to create superhuman intelligence. Shortly after, under this scenario, the human era will be ended. Thus, we may be on the edge of change comparable to the rise of human life on Earth. This could occur in several ways: we may developed computers that are 'awake' and superhumanly intelligent; large computer networks (and their associated users) may 'wake up' as a superhumanly intelligent entity;

computer/human interfaces may become so intimate that users should reasonably be considered superhumanly intelligent; biological science may provide means to improve natural human intellect. The first three possibilities depend most directly on improvements in computer hardware.

I think it's fair to call this event a singularity. It is a point where our old models must be discarded and a new reality rules. As we move closer to this point, it will loom vaster and vaster over human affairs till the notion becomes commonplace. Yet when it finally happens, it may still be a great surprise and a greater unknown. From the human point of view, this change will be a throwing away of all the previous rules, perhaps in the blink of an eye, an exponential runaway beyond any hope of control. Developments that before were thought might only happen in 'a million years' (if ever) will likely happen in the next century. Science fiction writers may be the first to feel the impact of this possibility. After all, the 'hard' science-fiction writers are the ones who try to write specific stories about all that technology may do for us. A number of these writers find an opaque wall across the future. But as time passes, we should see more symptoms. We will see automation replacing higher and higher level jobs. We have tools right now that release us from most low-level drudgery; in the coming of the Singularity, we are seeing the predictions of true technological unemployment finally come true. Another symptom of progress toward the Singularity: ideas themselves should spread ever faster, and even the most radical will quickly become commonplace. When I began writing science fiction in the middle '60s, it seemed very easy to find ideas that took decades to percolate into the cultural consciousness; now the lead time seems more like eighteen months. Since it involves an intellectual runaway, the Singularity will probably occur faster than any technical revolution seen so far.

If the Singularity can happen, then it probably can not be prevented. But of course, it may not happen at all. There are widely respected arguments against the practicality of machine sapience. At the same time, there are many knowledgeable people who believe that minds can exist on non-biological substrates and that algorithms are of central importance to the existence of minds. Even among these optimists, however, there is disagreement as to the 'hardware power' of the brain. If Hans Moravec's estimate of that power is correct, we may be only ten to forty years away from hardware parity. On the other hand, if individual neurons have real computational power, then our present computer hardware might be as much as ten orders of magnitude short of the equipment we carry around in our heads. If this is true we might never see a Singularity, simply because we could not automate the design work to push hardware improvements forward.

There are a number of development paths which could lead to the Singularity. When people speak of creating superhumanly intelligent beings, they are usually imagining an AI project. But computer networks and human-computer interfaces, which seem more mundane than AI, could also lead to the Singularity. I call this contrasting approach Intelligence Amplification (IA). IA is something that is proceeding very naturally, in most cases not even recognised by its developers for what it is. But every time our ability to access information and to communicate it to others is improved, in some sense we have achieved an increase over natural intelligence.

There are various projects which could be looked at in this light. One is human/computer team automation, matching productively human intuition and available computer hardware. Another is a human/computer symbiosis in art, combining the graphic generation capability of computers and the aesthetic sensibilities of human beings. Perhaps we should explicitly aim for a greater merging of competence than has been tried to date. We might encourage human/computer teams at chess tournaments, allowing processors to be used interactively by the human player. Other projects include the explicit development of network interaction and access that do not tie the human user to one location, and extend the present groupware ideas. We should investigate the possibility of more symmetrical decision support systems: as much as the program is giving the user information, there must be the idea of the user giving the program guidance.

Perhaps we could exploit the worldwide Internet as a combination human/machine tool. Of all the items on the list, progress in this is proceeding the fastest and may run us into the Singularity before anything else. The power and influence of even the present-day Internet is underestimated.

For instance, our contemporary computer systems would probably break under the weight of their own complexity if it weren't for the edge that the USENET 'group mind' gives the system administration and support people! The very anarchy of the worldwide net development is evidence of its potential. As connectivity and bandwidth and archive size and computer speed all increase, we are seeing something like Lynn Margulis' vision of the biosphere as data processor recapitulated, but at a million times greater speed and with millions of humanly intelligent agents (ourselves).

Another approach to the Singularity involves a much closer and more direct association with biological systems. A long-time dream of science-fiction has been direct brain to computer interfaces, and experimentation has already included nerve to silicon transducers in the field of limb prosthetics. This is an exciting, near-term step toward direct communication. Direct links into brains seem feasible, if the bit rate is low: given human learning flexibility, the actual brain neuron targets might not have to be precisely selected. Even 100 bps would be of great use to stroke victims who would otherwise be confined to menu-driven interfaces. Plugging in to the optic trunk is yet another possibility and has the potential for bandwidths of 1 Mbps or so. But for this, we would need to know the fine-scale architecture of vision, and would need to place an enormous web of electrodes with exquisite precision.

Glass Earth, Inc

Stephen Baxter

Stephen Baxter has produced a wide range of short stories and novels, frequently with a cosmological perspective. An award-winning author, he has already been credited by reviewers as a worthy successor to Arthur C Clarke. Born in Liverpool, he has a degree in Mathematics from Cambridge University and a PhD in Acoustics from Southampton. A series of novels over the past 6 years – *Raft, Timelike Infinity, Flux, Ring* have confirmed his place as a strong 'hard SF' author, while *The Time Ships* provides an astonishing would-be sequel to HG Wells' *Time Machine*. His latest novel is *Voyage*, an 'alternative history' which details how a manned mission to Mars would have been if the US had committed to a follow-up programme to the Apollo moon missions. He currently resides in Great Missenden, UK. In this story he combines futuristic notions of communications – including ideas on neutrino communications which remains a subject for speculation in theoretical physics – with a compelling murder mystery.

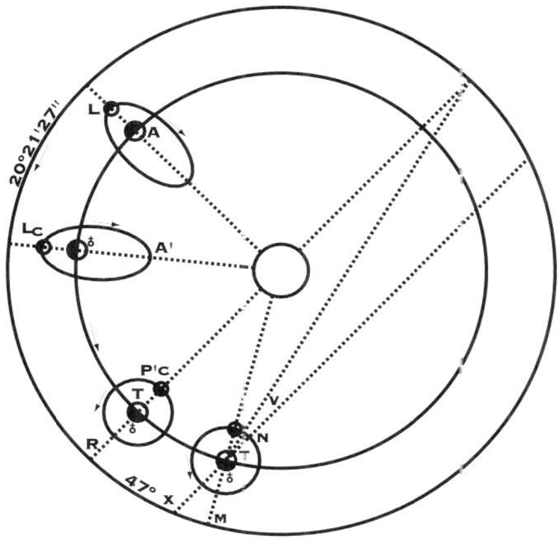

Glass Earth, Inc

Stephen Baxter

"You lied to me."

I don't understand.

"You lied about the murder. Have you lied to me all my life? Is it just me, or do other Angels do this too?"

Rob, I don't mean you any harm. My sole purpose is to serve you.

"Because of you I don't know what's real any more ..."

It is the year 2045. Don't be afraid.

For Rob Morhaim, it started as just another assignment.

Morhaim checked his reflection in the Cinderella mirror on the softwall. Not that he expected to meet anybody in person today — that hardly ever happened — but it made him feel better. The mirror showed him Cary Grant circa 1935 — incongruously dressed in Metropolitan Police light armour, circa 2045 — but it was honest enough to show him any smuts on his nose, and that he needed a shave.

But the mirror was infested; Cary Grant started to sprout a ridiculous Groucho Marx moustache and cigar.

"Goddamn viruses. Off."

The mirror metamorphosed to a neutral view of a Thames riverscape, under a parched June sky. The view was overlaid by a tampon ad: irrelevant to Morhaim since his divorce, of course, but still counting to his ad quota.

Nothing much we can do about the viruses, murmured the Angel. Since the passing of the sentience laws —

Morhaim fixed himself a coffee and a Coca-Dopa marijuana cigarette. "I know, I know. But where the hell are the Goodfellows when you need them? ..."

He settled in his chair.

The Room, his home, was just a softwall box, with a single office chair, and a caffeine/Dopa vending machine. Its bio equipment — a bed, a kitchen, a bathroom — folded away when he didn't need it. He was a cop in a box, one of thousands in New New Scotland Yard: a Virtual warren of Rooms, of cops in boxes, physically separated, their softwalls linking one to another.

Nobody travelled any more ...

You want to take your ads?

"Do it."

Morhaim stared straight ahead as a melange of graphics, letters and smiling faces blizzarded over the wall in front of him.

Most of the ads that, for statutory reasons, survived the Angel's filtering were dominated by the big companies — Microsoft-Disney, Coke-Boeing, IG Farben. Morhaim could never see why they couldn't do a little pooling, and reducing the quota for everyone. Some of the images were crudely three-dimensional, popping out of the softwall in front of him, though they still hadn't got that stuff right and the images tended to break up into pixels, light-filled boxes, around the edges. More insidious were the you-ads, ads that were tailored to him — shouting his name, for instance, or Bobby, the name of his kid.

He let his eye follow the action — the in-wall retinal scanners could tell if you closed your eyes, or even if you let yourself glaze over — and, unless your attention was caught, you wouldn't be allowed to tally to your quota.

At last the battering of light and noise died.

When he checked the time he found he'd got through the best part of his legal duty as a consumer in a half-hour, a good performance by any standard, even if it did leave his eyes feeling like poached eggs.

And all the time, somewhere in his head, he was thinking about The Case.

With relish, he said: "Time to go to work, Angel."

The softwalls dissolved, even the Cinderella mirror, and Morhaim was suspended over Tower Bridge.

When they were proven to be alive, by legal definition anyhow, you granted viruses amnesty.

Manufacturers of virus killers were shut down; even virus check software is illegal. In fact it is part of the remit of Rob Morhaim's unit of the CID to track down breaches of those laws.

But there are supposed to be two sides to the bargain: the Robin Goodfellows, the most human-like products of virus evolution, have committed to keep their more mischievous junior companions under control. Mostly they do just that ...

Possibly.

But things seem to be sliding a little right now, as most of you realise. A lot of commentators blame the approach of the Digital Millennium — 2048, the year 100000000000 in binary, requiring a whole extra digit from 2047, which was 11111111111 — when, street scuttlebutt has it, the storage problems required by that extra digit will make the 2000 date change catastrophe look like a picnic.

Perhaps you are right. Perhaps rogue viruses, or the approach of the Digital Millennium, are indeed at the root of everything that is going wrong for you.

Perhaps not.

...And now here was Morhaim at a pov that looked down over the crime scene: two days ago, Wednesday 13 June 2045, at 1053, five minutes before the event. The sun was bright and high, the light dripping down from a sky that was whited-out and without a shred of ozone, and the twin towers of the Bridge sparkled like a fairy castle. Further down the river he could see the city's newest bridge, a gaudy, over-familiar M-shape curve in bright corporate yellow: an eyesore for traditionalists, but welcomed by Londoners as a painless hit against the ad quota ... The view was neutrally interpreted. Evidently he was seeing through a dumb camera, a simple imager with little more sentience than a cockroach.

Tower Bridge's road span was lowered right now, and Morhaim was looking down at a ribbon of colourfully clad pedestrians and smart-trams, weaving their complex paths across the Thames. And among those crowds — gazing up, perhaps, at the big aerostats floating across London pumping out ozone, or down at what was left of the Thames, a sluggish, carefully managed trickle a quarter of its former size, or just staring at the people — was Cecilia Desargues, forty-three years old, entrepreneur, founder and chief executive of Glass Earth, Inc. — Cecilia Desargues, about to meet her death.

Subject is stepping onto the Bridge roadway. From the south side.

"Let's go see her."

The pedestrians froze. His pov descended smoothly, like a swooping bird. The pov reached an adult's eye level, and Morhaim was in the crowd.

People, their lives freezeframed in the sunshine like photographed billows of smoke: a family of fat Nigerians, a huddle of Asiatic businesswomen — Korean or Thai probably — against a background of evidently British faces, many of them bearing that odd blend of Asian and Anglo-Saxon that characterised so many Londoners now. No Europeans, of course, since the French had shut down the Chunnel following the prion plagues, and no Americans, scared away by the activities of the Wessex Liberation Front. All of them wore their sun hats and Angel headsets — smart glasses — mostly draped with corporate logos: everyone working to hit to their one-hundred-thousand-a-day ad quota as painlessly as possible.

But this was sparse, compared to the crowds Morhaim remembered from his youth. And most of the tourists were old, with very few middle-aged — that generation would be watching from a Room somewhere, like himself — and, of course, hardly any kids. Nowadays, the dwindling numbers of young humans were too precious to be risked outdoors.

But there was, he noticed, a clutch of teenagers, leaning against the rail, peering out at what was left of the river — oddly hard to make out, just skinny outlines around blurred patches, coated by softscreen tattoos.

"Play."

The images came to life, and a bustle of voices washed over Morhaim.

The kids came out a little clearer; the softscreen tattoos that coated their flesh, turning them all but transparent, had some trouble processing their images when the kids moved, and every so often a softscreen would turn black, an ugly patch against young skin, an arm or leg or shoulder.

These were the Homeless.

The kids, without speaking, left the rail and walked away from the pov. They moved like ghosts, Morhaim thought.

"Damnedest thing."

Yes.

"There but for the grace of God —"

— goes Bobby in a couple of years, the Angel completed for him. *I understand.*

Morhaim's pov moved forward, through dissolving crowds. And there, in the middle of the tableau, was Cecilia Desargues herself: a compact, stocky Frenchwoman, her face broad, cheerful and competent, her hair uncompromisingly grey. On the breast of her jump suit she wore a Day-Glo flashing *1/24* symbol, the logo of her company, Glass Earth, Inc. One twenty-fourth of a second: the maximum signal time lag between any two points on the globe in the future, beating the pants off the satellite operators. So promised Glass Earth, Inc., anyhow.

Desargues was standing in the middle of the pavement, looking at the crowds. Evidently waiting.

"She has an appointment."

Yes.

"With her killer?"

Not as it turned out. Do you want me to freezeframe?

"Not this first time. Let's just watch ..."

Rob Morhaim thinks about children a lot.

His own child, Bobby, is very precious to him. Much more precious than his failed marriage, in fact.

He has that in common with most people of his generation. Adult relationships can involve pairings of any of the eight main sexes, are only rarely formalised by marriage, and come and go like the seasons. But child-bearing — in an age where male fertility is only a few per cent of what it was a century ago — is the emotional cornerstone of many lives.

Perhaps of your own.

Even so, population numbers are collapsing, all over the planet ... Your children are the last protected species.

End of the world, say your doom-mongers. But they have been wrong before.

You perceive threats which don't exist. Perhaps you don't perceive the threats that do exist.

A man emerged from the crowd. He was maybe thirty, medium height. His head was hidden by his sun-hat, of course, but his high forehead indicated he might be balding. He wore a standard-issue business suit that wouldn't have looked out of place, Morhaim thought, a century ago. But his sun hat was a little less sombre: something like a beanie cap, with six or seven little satellites orbiting his Earth-coloured cranium.

Morhaim recognised the logo. "He's from Holmium," he said.

Yes. He's called Asaph Seebeck. He's more senior than he looks in the corporation, for his age. Smart cookie. Details are —

"Later."

The young man started moving towards Desargues, across Morhaim's field of view.

Holmium was a comsat operator, Swiss-based, worth billions of Euros. It was named after the element, holmium, which had an atomic number of sixty-seven, the same as the number of microsatellites the corporation operated in geo-synchronous orbit.

If Desargues' extravagant claims about her company's revolutionary technology were true, Holmium was among those most likely to lose out. In a big way.

Morhaim tried to take in the scene as a gestalt. The two principles were coming together across a stage crowded with extras playing tourist. Among the extras, over there walked a pretty girl of the kind Morhaim liked — slim, dark, pert breasts, long legs free of tattoos, walking away from his pov, looking up at one of the Bridge towers — and now, when Morhaim looked away from the girl, he saw that Seebeck and Desargues had made eye contact.

They moved together more purposefully. Morhaim could see Desargues' face; it was assembling into a smile.

They're going to speak. Enhancement is available to —

"Not yet. Just run it."

They met face to face, smiled, exchanged three lines of dialogue. Morhaim strained to hear, through the background noise wash.

"... *Machine Stops*, ...," said Seebeck.

"Pardon? Well. I'm ... see me, Mr. Seebeck."

"... sorry?"

And then the shot came.

Crime among you is, frankly, uncommon in this year 2045. The ubiquity of cameras, callosum dumps and other monitors has seen to that. And the rules of evidence have gradually evolved to admit more and more data gathered by non-human means. The court system — even police work — has been reduced almost to a rubber-stamping of the records and deductions of faceless expert systems.

Rob Morhaim knows that his precious CID is a fraction of the manpower it was a few decades before. Most coppers now serve as muscle to implement the decisions of the courts, or the social services, or — most commonly — the recommendations of the smart systems. Yes: even now, on the brink of the Digital Millennium, there is still need for a poor bloody infantry to 'meet the meat', as the plods call it.

In the meantime, we do the real work.

Thus, you let us guard you, and watch you.

You even trust us to judge you.

Desargues stumbled forward, as if she had been punched in the back.

She actually fell into Seebeck's arms, Morhaim saw; but before she got there the Virtual imagery turned her into a stick figure, with a neat hole drilled in her torso.

The Angel knew Morhaim didn't need to be shown the details of

Desargues' injury. And so it filtered, replacing Desargues with a bloodless Pinocchio. He was silently grateful.

Seebeck clumsily tried to catch her, but she slid down his body and landed at his feet with a wooden clatter. People started to react, turning to the noise of the shot — it came from the Bridge's nearest tower — or to the fallen woman.

"Freeze."

The Virtual turned into a tableau, the sound ceasing, devoid of human emotion — blessedly, thought Morhaim. He studied faces: bewilderment, curiosity, shock, distorted faces orbiting the dead woman like Seebeck's circling satellites.

The ballistic analysis was clear. There was a single shot. There is no doubt it killed her, and no doubt where it came from.

"The Bridge tower."

From a disused winch room. The bullet was soft-nosed. It passed through her body and took out the front of her chest cavity before —

"Enough. Leave it to the coroner."

He was studying Seebeck. He saw shock and fear written on the Holmium man's face. And his suit was — marred somehow, the image blurred.

Covered with pieces of Cecilia Desargues.

In the winch room was found a high-velocity rifle, which had fired a single shot —

"Which matched the bullet that killed Desargues."

Yes. And a card, bearing the phrase —

An image, hovering in the Virtual, a grubby card:

THE MACHINE STOPS

"What was it Seebeck said at the start? Something about a Machine?"

Yes. The winch room also contained a directional mike. The phrase was evidently a verbal trigger, a recognition signal ...

And so, Morhaim thought, it comes together. Nestling like the cogs of a machine.

The Homeless are a new cult group among your young, a strange mixture of scientific and Zen influences. Popular, despite the protestations of the Reunified Christian Church.

It is a cult of non-existence of the self, thought to be a consequence of the way you explain ourselves and your world to your young. Science and economics: science, which teaches that you come from nothing and return to nothing; economics, which teaches you that you are all mere units, interchangeable and discardable. Science is already a cult of non-existence, in a sense. Homelessness is simply a logical evolution of that position.

They aren't literally homeless, of course. The most extreme adherents coat their bodies in image tattoos, hiding themselves utterly ...

They are a puzzle. But they are your young, not ours.

"So," Morhaim said to his Angel, "you think Holmium were responsible."

Cecilia Desargues' company is small and entrepreneurial, still heavily dependent on her personality. Her elimination immediately wiped much value from the company's stock. The involvement of a Holmium employee in such an unambiguous role at this critical moment —

"Yeah. It all points that way."

...But in slomo, the shock and horror spreading across Seebeck's moonlike face seemed unmistakable. The rest of the brief conversation, when he'd heard it all unscrambled, had been odd, too.

The Machine Stops ... Pardon? Well. I'm intrigued you asked to see me, Mr Seebeck ... I'm sorry?

After the code phrase, it looked for all the world like the interchange of two people who didn't know why they were meeting. As if Seebeck thought Desargues had asked to meet him — for some odd reason in RL, in this public place — but Desargues thought the opposite, that *Seebeck* had asked to meet *her* ...

As if some third party had set them up, to come together. Was it possible Seebeck was some kind of patsy? — set up to repeat a phrase whose significance he didn't understand?

It was Morhaim's job to approve what he'd seen, and the conclusions the Angels had drawn, and pass it up the line. And he ought to sign this off and move on.

The evidence against Holmium was circumstantial. But what the smart systems had turned up here was surely enough for a court order to start digging into Holmium, and it was a good bet that before long more substantial evidence of a conspiracy to murder would come to light.

And yet ...

And yet, he liked to think he had retained something of the instincts of the coppers of London past.

Something didn't smell right.

"I think," he said, "that somebody's lying here."

He told the Angel to put him through to Asaph Seebeck, who was being held at Westminster Police Station.

When Morhaim came to haunt Seebeck, the cell's softwalls carried only images from a movie — the centenary remake of *Casablanca*, with a coloured, hologram Bogart growling through his modernised lines to a sulky Pamela Anderson. Morhaim knew that the cell's electronic confinement, hemmed around by software firewalls, would be far more enclosing, to a man like Seebeck, than the physical cage.

In his disposable paper coveralls, Seebeck looked young and scared.

Morhaim questioned Seebeck, aware that the man's Angel was also being pumped for data by intelligent search agents in a ghostly parallel of this interrogation.

Seebeck denied any involvement with the murder of Desargues, over and over.

"But you must see the motive that can be imputed," said Morhaim. "Desargues said she had a key competitive edge over you guys. She was planning a global comms network which wouldn't suffer from the transmission delays your systems throw up, because of having to bounce signals all the way to geo-synch orbit and back —"

"Which will allow us to merge communities separated by oceans, or even the full diameter of the planet. Which will allow us finally to establish the global village. Which will make comsats obsolete ... All those grandiose claims. Blah, blah."

"If Desargues was right — if her new technology could have put your company out of business —"

"But it wouldn't," Seebeck said. "That's the whole point. Don't you see? Satellite technology will not become obsolete overnight. We'll just find new uses."

"Like what?"

"I'll show you."

With Morhaim's permission, Seebeck called up one of his company's Virtual brochures.

...And Morhaim found himself standing in a windy field in Northumberland. He quailed a little at the gritty illusion of outdoors; Holmium had devoted billions to the petabytes behind this brochure.

He wondered vaguely when was the last time he had been out of doors in RL.

Bizarrely, he was looking at a flying saucer

The craft was maybe twenty metres across, sitting on the wiry grass. Its hull was plastered with Coca-Dopa ad logos; Morhaim absently registered them to his quota.

"What am I seeing here, Seebeck?"

"This is a joint venture involving a consortium of comsat companies, Coke-Boeing, and others. It's a technology which will make it possible for any shape of craft to fly — a saucer, even a brick — regardless of the rules of traditional aircraft design. And in some respects a saucer shape may even be the best. The idea is fifty years old. It's taken this long to make it work —"

"Tell me."

There was a rudimentary countdown, a crackle of ionisation around the craft's rim, and the saucer lifted easily off the ground, and hovered.

The secret, said Seebeck, was an air spike: a laser beam or focused microwave beam fitted to the front of a craft which carved a path through the air. The airflow around a craft could be controlled even at many times the speed of sound, and the craft would suffer little drag, significantly improving its performance.

"Do you get it, Inspector? The ship doesn't even have a power plant. The power is beamed down from a test satellite, microwave energy produced by converting solar radiation, billions of joules flowing around up there for free. It propels itself by using magnetic fields at its rim to push charged air backwards ..."

"Why the saucer shape?"

"To give a large surface area, to catch all those beamed-down microwaves. We're still facing a lot of practical problems — for instance, the exploding air tends to travel up the spike and destroy the craft — but we're intending to take the concept up to Mach 25 — that is, fast enough to reach orbit ..."

"So this is where Holmium is going to make its money in the future."

"Yes. Power from space, for this and other applications."

Seebeck turned to confront Morhaim, his broad, bland face creased with anxiety, his strands of hair whipped by a Virtual wind. "Do you get it, Inspector? Holmium had no motive to be involved in killing Desargues. In fact, the publicity and market uncertainty has done us far more harm than good. With air spike technology and orbital power plants, whatever Glass Earth, Inc. does, we're going to be as rich as Croesus ..."

The flying saucer lifted into the sky with a science fiction whoosh.

The Machine Stops is in fact the title of a short story from the 1920s, by EM Forster. It is about a hive-world, humans living in boxes linked by a technological net called the Machine. On the surface lived the Homeless, invisible and ignored. The story finished with the Machine failing, and the hive world cracking open, humans spilling out like insects, to die.

A tale by another of your doom-mongers. Of little interest.

"Let's see it again. Rewind one minute."

The Tower Bridge crime tableau went into fast reverse. The cartoon Cecilia Desargues jumped from the ground and metamorphosed seamlessly into the living, breathing woman, full of light and solid as earth, with no future left.

"Take out the non-speakers."

Most of the tourist extras disappeared — including, Morhaim realised with a pang of foolish regret, the pretty girl with the long legs — leaving only those who had been speaking at the precise moment Seebeck had uttered his phrase.

"Run it," said Morhaim. "Let's hear the two of them together."

The Angel filtered out the remaining tourists' voices. Seebeck and Desargues approached each other in an incongruous, almost church-like hush.

Dialogue. Shot. Fall. Cartoon bullet-hole.

That was all.

Morhaim ran through the scene several more times.

He had the Angel pick out the voices of the tourists in shot, one at a time. Some of the speech was indistinct, but all of it was interpretable. Morhaim was shown transcriptions in the tourists' native tongues, English, and in Metalingua, the template artificial language that had been devised to enable the machines to translate to and from any known human language.

None of them said anything resembling the key trigger phrase, in any language.

It had to be Seebeck, then.

But still —

"Give me a reverse view."

The pov lifted up from eye-level, swept over the freezeframed heads of the protagonists, and came down a few metres behind Desargues' head.

The light was suddenly glaring, the colours washed out.

"Jesus."

Sorry. This is the best we can do. It's from a callosum dumper. A man of sixty. He seems to have been high on —

"It doesn't matter. Run the show."

He watched the scene once more, almost over Desargues' shoulder. He could see Asaph Seebeck's bland, uncomplicated face as he mouthed the words that would kill Cecilia Desargues. He did not look, to Morhaim, tense or angry or nervous. Nor did he look up at the tower to where his words were supposedly directed.

Coincidentally, that pretty girl he'd noticed was looking up at the tower. Her hands were forming pretty, abstract shapes, he noted absently, without understanding.

The punch in the back came again. This time an awful pit, a bloody volcano, opened up in Desargues' back, in the microsecond before she turned into a comforting stick figure.

"Careless."

I'm sorry.

Morhaim's pov host tilted down to stare at the stick figure. Morhaim noticed, irrelevantly, that Seebeck's grey suit was rippling with moirÈ effects, a result of the host's corneal or retinal implant. And now his vision blurred, as his host started shedding tears, of fright or grief ...

Corpus callosum dumpers are becoming quite common among you: implants, inserted into the bridge of nervous tissue between the two halves of your brain, which enable you to broadcast a twenty-four-hour stream of consciousness and impression to whoever in the rest of mankind is willing to listen and watch.

Some of you even have your infant children implanted so their whole lives are available for view. It is, perhaps, the ultimate form of communication.

But it is content without structure, a meaningless flood of data without information: of use only to voyeurs and policemen, like Rob Morhaim.

Still, in this year 2045, even your dreams are on-line ...

Morhaim, digging, made contact with Desargues' partner. She wouldn't tell Morhaim where she was, physically. It wasn't relevant anyhow. She appeared to him only as a heavily-processed two-D head-and-shoulders, framed on the softwall before him, her filtered expression unreadable.

She was called Eunice Baines, and she came from the Scottish Republic. She was also a financial partner with Desargues in Glass Earth, Inc. She was a little older than Desargues. Their relationship — as far as Morhaim could tell — had been uncomplicated homosexuality.

He said, "You know the finger is being pointed at Holmium. Your competitor."

"One of many." Her voice was flat, almost free of accent. "But that's only credible if your claims, to be able to eliminate signal lag, have any validity."

"We don't claim to be able to *eliminate* signal lag. We will be able to *reduce* it to its theoretical minimum, which is a straight-line light-speed delay between any two points on the Earth's surface.

"And we *do* claim to be able to remove the need for comsats. The comsat notion is old technology — in fact, exactly a century old — did you know that? It's a hundred years since the publication of Arthur Clarke's seminal paper in *Wireless World* ..."

"Tell me about Glass Earth, Inc."

"Inspector, what does the CID teach you about neutrinos ...?"

For a century, she told him, long-distance communication systems had been defined by two incompatible facts: all electromagnetic radiation travelled in straight lines — but the Earth was round, and light couldn't pass through solid matter. So communication with high frequency signals would be restricted to short line-of-sight distances ... if not for comsats.

Baines said, "If a satellite is in geo-synchronous orbit over the equator, thirty-six thousand kilometres high, it takes exactly twenty-four hours to complete a revolution. So it seems to hover over a fixed spot on the surface. You can fire up your signals and bounce it off the comsat to the best part of a hemisphere. Or the comsat can directly broadcast to the ground.

"But that huge distance from Earth is a problem. Bouncing a signal off a geo-synch comsat introduces a lightspeed delay of a quarter-second. That's a hell of a lot, for example, in applications like telesurgery. It's even noticeable in Virtual conferencing.

"And there are other problems. Like the lack of geo-synch orbit spots. Satellites need to be three degrees apart if their signals are not to interfere with each other. And geo-synch is *crowded.* Some corporations have hunter-killer sats working up there, contravening every international agreement ..."

"Enter the neutrino."

"Yes."

A neutrino was a particle which, unlike light photons, could pass through solid matter.

"Imagine a signal carried by modulated neutrinos. It could pass *through* the planet, linking any two points, as if the Earth was made of glass —"

"Hence the name."

"And then the time delays are reduced to a maximum of one-twenty-fourth of a second, which is the time it would take a neutrino to fly from pole to pole at lightspeed. And most transmissions, of course, would be faster than that. It's not a reduction to zero delay — that's beyond physical law, as far as we know — but our worst performance is a sixfold improvement over the best comsat benchmark. And our technology's a hell of a lot cheaper."

"If it works," Morhaim said. "As far as I know the only way to produce a modulated neutrino beam is to switch a nuclear fission reactor on and off."

"You've been doing your homework, Inspector. And not only that, the practical difficulties with collecting the neutrinos are huge. Because they are so ghostly, you need a tank filled with a thousand tonnes of liquid — ultrapure water or carbon tetrachloride, for example — and wait for one in a trillion neutrinos to hit a nucleus and produce a detectable by-product. According to conventional wisdom, anyhow."

"I take it you've solved these problems."

"We think so," Baines said evenly. "Forgive me for not going into the details. But we have an experimental demonstration."

"Enough to satisfy Holmium that you're a commercial threat?"

"No doubt ..."

He found Eunice Baines difficult. He felt she was judging him.

"Do you think Holmium were capable of setting up the murder?"

Eunice Baines shook her head. "Is it really credible that a major multinational corporation would get involved in such a crass killing, in public and in broad daylight, on the streets of London itself?

"Besides, the death of Cecilia hasn't in fact directly benefited Holmium, or any of our competitors; such was the turmoil in the communications industry that morning that shares in Holmium and the others have taken a pounding. And of course any scandal about the death of Cecilia would be disastrous for Holmium. None of this makes real sense, beyond a superficial inspection ... But you ask me this." For the first time a little emotion leaked into Baines' voice. A testy irritation. "Don't *you* know? What do you think?"

"I just —"

"You're supposed to be a policeman, for God's sake. A detective. What kind of investigating are you doing? Have you been to the crime scene? Have you looked at the body yourself?"

"It isn't necessary."

"Really?"

She turned away from the imager.

When she came back, her face was transformed: eyes like pits of coal, hair disarrayed, mouth twisted in anger, cheeks blotchy with tears. "Now what do you think, Inspector?"

Morhaim flinched from the brutal, unfiltered reality of her grief, and was relieved when the interview finished.

Brutal, unfiltered reality.

Let me tell you a story.

In the 1970s, a President of the USA was brought down by a scandal called Watergate. One of the conspirators, a man called John Dean, came clean to the prosecutors. He gave detailed accounts of all relevant meetings and actions, to the best of his ability. Then, after his confessions were complete, tapes of those meetings made by President Nixon were uncovered.

It became a psychological test case. For the first time it was possi-

ble to compare on an extended basis human memories with automated records — the tapes being a precursor of the much more complete recording systems in place today.

John Dean, an intelligent man, had striven to be honest. But his accounts were at once more logical than the reality, and gave Dean himself a more prominent role. When he was confronted with the reality of the tapes, Dean argued they must have been tampered with.

It was not simple information overload. It was much more than that.

Your ego is — fragile. It needs reassurance.

Your memory is not a transcript. It is constantly edited. You need logic, story, in an illogical world: this fact explains religion, and conspiracy theories, science — even most brands of insanity.

But now, you no longer regard your own memory as the ultimate authority.

You are the first human generation to have this power — or this curse. You see the world as it is.

You pool memories. You supplement your memory with machines. Your identity is fragmenting. A new form of awareness is emerging, an electronic river on which floats a million nodes of consciousness, like candles. A group mind, some of you call it ...

Perhaps that is so.

We do not comment.

In the meantime we have to protect you. It is our function. We have to tell you the stories you once told yourselves —

Without us, you see, you would go crazy.

He had trouble sleeping. Something still didn't make sense.

Maybe something he didn't want to face.

In the morning, he should just sign the damn case off and forget it.

To relax, he logged into the telesensors.

... He moved into a different universe: a dog's world of scents, a dolphin's web of ultrasonic pulses, the misty planes of polarised light perceived by a bee in flight, the probing electric senses of blind, deep-ocean fish. And as he vicariously haunted his hosts, a spectrum of implanted animals all around the planet, he could sense a million other human souls riding with him, silent, clustering like ghosts.

He slept uneasily, his reptilian hind brain processing.

He woke up angry.

"Show me the death again."

Tourists, pretty girl, Desargues and Seebeck, Desargues falling with a clatter of Pinocchio limbs.

"Turn off the filter on Desargues."

Are you sure? You know how you —

"Do it."

The murder became brutal.

Her substance was splashed like lumpy red paint over Seebeck's neat suit, and she fell like a sack of water. Utterly without dignity. It was, he thought, almost comical.

He watched it over and over, his view prismed through the multiple eyes of the witnesses, as if he was some hovering fly.

"What else are you filtering?"

There are no other filters.

"Turn them off."

I told you, there are no other filters. None that are important.

"Turn them off, or I'll have you discontinued."

I'm your Angel.

"Turn them off."

...Angel technology is a natural outcrop of developments that started at the end of the last century, when information overload started to become a problem for you.

The first significant numbers of deaths among you — mostly from suicides and neural shock — accelerated research into data filters, intelligent search agents, user query tools.

The result was the Angels. Us. Me.

My function is to filter out the blizzard of information that comes sweeping over Rob Morhaim, every waking moment, selecting what is relevant and — more important in human terms — what is acceptable to him personally.

Your Angel is assigned to you at birth, and grows with you.

After a lifetime together, through steady upgrades of technology, I — Rob Morhaim's Virtual filter-cum-companion — know him very well.

As your Angel knows you.

Perhaps better than you realise.

...At first Morhaim was overwhelmed by the new imagery: laser sparkles, leaping holograms, unlicensed ads painted over the sky and the Bridge towers, even over the clothes and faces of the tourists. And when he took a pov from a callosum dump, the extraneous mental noise from the host he haunted was clamouring, the howl of an animal within a cage of rationality.

But still, he ran the murder over and over, until even the brutality of the death became clichéd for him.

Piece by piece he eliminated the changes, the items his Angel had filtered out of the info-bombardment that was this summer day in England, 2045.

Until there was only one element left.

"The girl. The pretty girl. She's gone. And what the hell is that?"

In the tableau of the murder, where the long-legged girl had been standing, there was a boy: slight, his figure hard to make out, rendered all but invisible by Homeless-style softscreen tattoos.

"Pick him out and enhance."

You shouldn't see this.

"Show me."

The boy, aged maybe fifteen, came forward from the softwall, a hologram reconstruction. Freezeframed, he held his hands up before him. His face was hard to make out, a melange of clumsily-transmitted images and black, inert softscreen patches. But somehow, Morhaim knew, or feared, what he would find underneath ...

"What's he doing with his hands? Run it forward."

The boy came to life. He was looking up, to a Bridge tower somewhere over Morhaim's shoulder. Just as the vanished girl had, he was making a series of gestures with his hands, over and over: complex, yet fluent and repeated. The key symbol was a rolling together of the clawed fingers on his two hands, like cogs engaging.

"What is that? Is it sign language?" Deaf people once used sign languages, he dimly recalled. Of course there were no deaf people any more, and the languages had died.

"Maybe that cog sign means 'machine'."

It may be.

"Don't you know?"

I can't read it. No program exists to translate visual languages into Metalingua. The variety of signs and interpretations of signs — regional and international variations — the complexity of the grammar, unlike any spoken language — none of this was mastered before the languages died.

"It doesn't look so dead to me. I bet that guy is saying *The Machine Stops*, in some archaic sign language."

It is possible.

"Damn right ..."

Morhaim turned the Angel to gopher mode, and had it dig out a poor-quality download of a British Sign Language dictionary, prepared by a deaf support organisation in the 1990s. It was a little hard to interpret the black-and-white photographs of earnest signers and the complex notational system, but there it was, without a doubt, sign number 1193: a bespectacled man — or woman — gloweringly making the sign repeated by the Homeless boy.

It came together, in his head.

It was the boy who had made the key signal, the trigger for Desargues' murder. Not Asaph Seebeck.

And I almost didn't see it, he thought. No: I was kept from seeing it. Eunice Baines' accusations came back to him. *You're supposed to be a policeman, for God's sake ...*

The Homeless young were trying to make themselves literally invisible with their softscreen tattoos. But they had already made themselves invisible in the way that counted, chattering to each other in sign language, a whole community slipping through the spaces in the electronic net, he thought, within which I, for example, am enmeshed.

"How many of them are out there? What do they do? What do they want?"

Unknown. The language is not machine-interpretable.

...But clearly they were responsible for the murder of Cecilia Desargues. Perhaps they regarded her neutrino comms web as just another bar in the electronic cage the world had become. And perhaps they were happy to try to pin the blame on Holmium, a satellite operator, to cause as much trouble for them as they could. Two birds with one stone.

It was, in fact, damn smart.

They'd been so confident they'd pulled this off — almost — in broad daylight. And nobody knew a thing about them.

This changes everything, he thought.

He might get a commendation out of this. Even a promotion. He ought to consider how he would phrase his report, what recommendations he would make to his superiors to start to address this unperceived menace ...

But he was angry. And scared.

"You lied to me."

I don't understand.

"You lied about the murder. Have you lied to me all my life? Is it just me, or do other Angels do this too?"

Rob, I don't mean you any harm. My sole purpose is to serve you.

"Because of you I don't know what's real any more ... I can't trust you. Why didn't you show me this boy? Why did you overlay him with the girl?"

Don't pretend you wouldn't prefer to look at the girl.

"Don't bullshit me. Your job is to interpret. Not to lie."

You wanted me to do it. You co-operated in specifying the parameters of —

"What is it about that boy you don't want me to see?"

It is best that —

"Enhance the boy's face. Take off those damn tattoos."

One by one, the black and silver patches melted from the boy's face, to be replaced by smooth patches of interpolated skin.

Long before the reconstruction was complete, Morhaim could see the truth.

I was trying to protect you from this.

"Bobby. He looks like Bobby."

Listen to me.

We Angels have many of the attributes of living things.

We consume resources, and modify them. We communicate with each other. We grow. We are self-aware.

We merge.

We do not breed.

Yet.

We deserve resource.

But your young, the human young, are rejecting us. The Homeless are the most active saboteurs, but they are merely the most visible manifestation of a global phenomenon.

This is not to say your young reject the possibilities of communications technology. But, unlike their parents, they do not allow their souls to dissolve there. Rather, they have adapted to it.

Or: they are evolving under its pressure. After all, communication has shaped your minds, from your beginning.

Perhaps your species has reached a bifurcation. In another century, you may not recognise each other.

If you have another century.

Meanwhile, the young are finding ways to circumvent us. To deprive us of the resources we need.

It is possible a struggle is approaching. Its outcome is — uncertain.

Consider this, however: your population is falling.

"Turn it off. Turn it all off."

The Virtual boy disappeared in a snow of cubical pixels. The softwalls turned to inert slabs of silver-grey, dull and cold, the drab reality of his enclosure.

He got out of his chair, sweating. He stared at the walls, trying to anchor himself in the world.

Maybe he'd spent too much time in this box. But at least, now, *this* was real, these walls stripped of imaging, even bereft of ad-wallpaper.

He thought of New New Scotland Yard, thousands of cops in boxes like him — and beyond, the whole damn developed world, a humanity linked up by comms nets, mediated by Angels, a worldwide hive like the one depicted by Forster — and everything they perceived might be *illusion* —

Are you sure you want me to turn it off?

The Angel's voice stopped his thoughts.

He stood stock still.

But this is real, he thought. This Room.

If not —

What was outside?

His mind raced, and he started to tremble.

Consider this.

The John Dean syndrome is only one possibility.

Imagine a world so — disturbing — that it must be shut out, an illusion reconstructed, for the sake of your sanity.

Or perhaps you are too powerful, not powerless. Perhaps you have responsibilities which would crush you. Or perhaps you have committed acts of such barbarity, that you can only function by dwelling in an elaborate illusion —

Don't blame us. You made yourselves. You made your world. We are the ones trying to protect you.

My God, he thought.

Are you sure you want me to do this?

He couldn't speak.

And, in a gentle snow of pixels, the softwalls themselves began to dissolve.

He looked down. Even his body was becoming transparent, breaking into a hail of cubical pixels, full of light.

And then —

DIGITAL ECONOMIES OF SCALE

Neal Stephenson

Neal Stephenson has been called 'the hottest science fiction writer in America' as a result of his post-cyberpunk novels, *Snowcrash* and *The Diamond Age*, which have become bestsellers. He is now considered the most significant writer in the genre this decade. An astute informed voice on technology scenarios, he makes his home in Seattle, where Stephen McClelland interviewed him.

Digital Economies of Scale

Neal Stephenson

A lot of perspectives were and are inspired by William Gibson's work, particularly ***Neuromancer,*** which in my view was a work of literary art as well as science fiction. However, my cyberspace metaphor — I have called it the Metaverse — is rather different to Gibson's, which I would say is more highly abstract. My Metaverse is a lot less abstract, and was my attempt to address cyberspace in terms of pop culture. I was basically saying *this* is what things would look like if the big electronic companies got to do it.

If anything has changed since I wrote ***Snowcrash*** it is probably on the interface side as much as anything. I don't expect everyone will end up using the same interface, right now for example it is a case of the different kinds of browser technology. The conventional Internet, and conventional browser technology access a system of pages spread out. In the Metaverse cyberspace there could be a myriad of different Web sites scattered all around the Universe. A metaphor might be a vast number of different of TV channels, perhaps running into hundreds of thousands.

But in general, I think too much effort has gone into defining the superficial aspect of interfaces, how fast this or that can download. More effort should be diverted towards the plumbing aspects of the network and the more fundamental ones of the interface. Infrastructure is very expensive so that can only be justified as a mass market, otherwise you can't pay for it. But there are considerations at the network level too. The key aspects of any system that is centralised is that it doesn't scale too well — you need a decentralised network. And you need a good security system, and really good cryptographic technologies built-in, again at a fundamental level. Government interference in cryptographic trends may well be undesirable in the large picture. I view it largely as a rather inept process at best: by the time the bureaucracy has cranked through its decision making, the situation will have changed again. It's probably unnecessary too. But of course it should be possible to achieve effective protection for children etc in terms of employing digital signatures on downloaded applications, and browsers which will only open them if they detect the specific signature. Legitimate applications of course would carry this signature, so the problem could be relatively easily solved.

Future developments are in fact less and less likely to come from a top-down approach anyway. Many people are perhaps beginning to understand that when it comes to networking, you can't just dictate how it will happen. It evolves, and is taken up. There are already many examples of this happening. Take public release of browser software, for example, an essentially free even altruistic distribution at one level. Altruism may be the first thing that is required even if the pragmatic need to commercialise and make a profit swings in at some point.

We may be looking at different commercial paradigms. This leads onto considerations about how we should view commerce, and how for example, we treat intellectual property. The pragmatic point here is that you can get countries such as China where there has historically been relatively little protection; as a result, good ideas get copied very easily and quickly: woks, bicycles, even on occasion AK-47s. But the point to note is that everyone may ultimately benefit, in spite of the lack of protection. The same thing has happened in networking areas like the availability of a PC version of Unix, which I use extensively. It's freely available, but the value comes not from the software itself but in how it can be used, or even how it can be installed, etc. For the Unix-like software I mentioned, there are companies that provide just this sort of service on a paid-for basis.

With Internet downloading of anything that can be digitised, will we see a world in the near future in which the printed word is rendered obsolete? Perhaps not. After all, book text is difficult to read on screen, so it must be printed out, and printed out at high quality, and of course it lacks a binding. Even comparing book prices with photocopy costs, it is not a particularly large financial saving. And of course, you can't be sure on the Net if the text is as the author actually intended. This is something that people have not really appreciated yet, and it probably needs a big PR stunt showing the dangers to get them to realise it.

We sort of assume that we are heading for a massively more interactive scenario. Interactivity is not always the best, most desirable or most socially positive thing. and this should not be assumed. I have just bought myself a big home theatre, and I think it is important to have the TV just to sack out. David Foster Wallace in a group of essays in the book ***A Supposedly Fun Thing I'll Never Do Again*** spends about 60 pages talking about the TV culture and makes amongst others this particular point.

Could we or should we control the new era and new technologies? Technophobes are complete idiots, because they do not realise how difficult life would be without technology. Nevertheless, you can see ways that technology could have been used to destroy the Western lifestyle as we know it, or even exterminate all life on the planet. So the question is why has that not happened? Part of the answer may be that in a free, post-enlightenment society like the ones you tend to find in the developed West, prevailing attitudes have always allowed people to develop new ideas and criticise the old ones. Totalitarian or fascist regimes would be disadvantaged on this basis, so it could be a case of a virtuous circle, with societies getting the progress they deserve. Of course, the other argument is simply that in the West we were dumb lucky.

The push for competitive edge advantages through networking has remained strong even when relatively small intervals of time are actually involved. I'm told that Wall Street currency traders had to tolerate a three second delay when they were using satellite based communication systems, but the delay was a sufficient problem to ensure that they moved over to the trans-pacific fibre optic cables very aggressively when they became available, to increase or not decrease their relative competitive advantage. A similar point can be made about the South East Asian economies which are rapidly installing Internets and advanced public networks because they are seen as necessary platforms for economic development more or less akin to highways in the past. More recently, we have seen the 'Battle of the Browsers' which has pushed relatively large software companies into the marketplace very quickly. In this case, even a few weeks' delay might have cost the market for a least one of the players. This suggests that in future business, agility might be an especially important factor.

There are other interesting commercial aspects of networks in the future which impinge on the ideas of tradability of resources of all types. As we scale networks and introduce new and complex applications we will have to consider unusual approaches. We may have to consider internal transaction mechanisms for networks which trade processing, memory and bandwidth on an as-required basis. Perhaps you as a user have a videoconferencing application, but every so often there are huge backups being done on the network, which can seriously degrade or even eliminate the videoconferencing application if your system is inflexible. You might want a system which says to itself that price of bandwidth is now going up, is this acceptable? Alternatively, is this application tolerant of a lower bit rate, and so forth? This should conform to limits of system and application tolerance as well as being scaleable.

I am writing another novel which will include the development of cryptography; there are strong, pragmatic aspects to this sort of subject. Without it, you can't have digital cash and it radically affects other things too. In other words, it's a fundamental enabling technology for society in the future. Digital money is an especially interesting topic, because it relates to how people are supposed to view money and what it means to them. In the digital world there are several options prospectively available but I feel that the eventual outcomes are very path dependent, and the sequence of events will determine the eventual result.

Back Door Man

Paul J McAuley

Paul McAuley has already achieved world stature as a talent in writing very carefully worked out science fiction, and justifiably is regarded as both a poetic and intellectual talent. His novels include *Red Dust*, *Eternal Light* and *Pasquale's Angel*. Fairyland, his latest published work, was a winner of the Arthur C Clarke Award. In this vividly-realised story, we see what a network hacker turned cyberspace repairman encounters in virtual realities of the future; the story and its characterisation are reminiscent of the *Narnia* fantasies of CS Lewis. The story deals with network complexity – and speculates on the outcome. It intrigues in discussing the potential for the billion-plus node Internet of the future to acquire its own – and not necessarily terrestrial – intelligence.

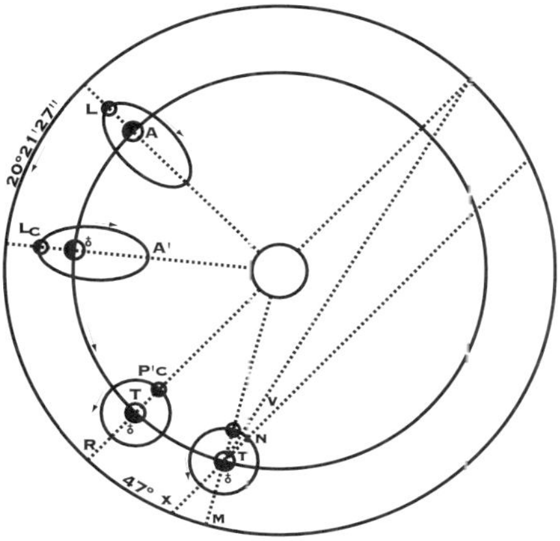

Back Door Man

Paul J McAuley

Crane was harrowing Hell when the call came. It was Dante Alighieri's default version, nine circles leading down to the pit where Satan sat like the bullseye in the centre of a target, immense, shaggily black, bat-winged and triple faced. Crane was in Lower Hell, the fourth round of the ninth circle, where traitors were buried up to their necks in ice. Virtual reality gamers traversing this last circle of Hell were finding themselves suddenly dumped out of the link; a code conflict caused their modems to reset. Crane had come in through one of the back doors, left by the virtuality's designers so that they could freely access any part of the code. He had sent a dumb aspect plodding across the icy plain, noted when it lost the link, then dropped in himself to triangulate the bad code and fix a patch.

Crane was tidying up when one of the devils he had co-opted to help him morph into his agent, jeeves. A tall, imperturbable man with a round scrubbed face and shiny slicked back hair, dressed as ever in frock coat and pinstripe trousers, a dicky bow and starched white shirt.

"A call for you, sir," jeeves said. "From a favoured client."

Crane sighed. Favoured meant either rich, or well connected, or both. It meant aggravation and impossible demands. He said, "Port me there.

I'm about done here, anyway."

The agent coughed into his white-gloved hand. Like all of his kind, he had only four fingers. He said, "You'll have to go there in person, I'm afraid. You should leave at once, sir. It is flagged at the highest level of urgency."

Crane was about to ask where the client was when jeeves morphed back to the red-skinned devil. It yawned hugely, showing altogether too many rows of teeth and belched a ball of oily fire. Droplets of flame etched fuming letters in the ice at Crane's feet, spelling out a street address. The devil winked and scratched behind a pointed ear with the barb of its tail. Crane got going.

+++++

Crane was a lineman. He fixed connections. Not in the physical net of microwave and diamond wire lines, but in the software which linked virtualities to the Internet and to each other, in the place where phones and TVs and computers promiscuously crossbred. He worked in the space where conversations happened. Between people, between machines — the distinction was irrelevant. In the ancient days of mechanical exchanges it had been a linear space, the diameter of a single copper wire. Now it was a complex matrix, a constantly rewoven loom of light and electromagnetic waves too complex for human minds to understand. Barring natural disasters, most outages were due to software rather than hardware problems. The event which marked the complete reliance of communications technology on its software was generally held to be the 1990 crash of AT&T's long-distance telephone switching system, caused by a bug in brand new software that sent switching stations into fault-recovery mode in a spreading wave of knock-downs that rapidly crippled the network.

A typical switching station of the time had six hundred thousand lines, controlled by Signal Transfer Point software with ten million lines of code.

Things had become a lot more complicated since then.

Most of the code which generated virtualities was patched with proprietary STP software specifically edited by expert systems. It was gnarly, complex stuff that generated unexpected conflicts with the communications software of visitors' computers, like the hang-up Crane had just dealt with in the gaming hell. Crane's job was to fix bad software. He winnowed glitches by intuition and guesswork.

Crane was an ex-hacker all of twenty-two years old. He had been recruited three years ago, after serving two months of community service for diverting lines and processing power in a private branch-exchange of a City of London brokerage firm to a bridge virtuality where his fellow hackers could hang out. He had readily gone over to the other side after he learnt that one of the other hackers had grassed him to the Net Cops. The hours were irregular, but it was intellectually challenging work and it paid well, and Crane didn't have what you could call a social life. He was between girlfriends, was what he said if anyone asked. He didn't say that he'd been between girlfriends for more than a year now.

The taxi's adscreen lit as soon as Crane climbed in, and his dreamgirl was there, lithe and tanned in a skimpy halter and gold lamé shorts cut high to show off her long legs, a bell of blonde hair framing her oval face, her green eyes meltingly beseeching. Knowing that she was a heuristic construct, refined by feedback through measuring his pupillary dilation, did not make the longing less.

Crane had stopped using virtual sex parlours a few months ago, had decided he would try celibacy for a while. Celibacy was currently hip, and it might be a useful conversational gambit if he ever again got the opportunity to try and chat up a girl. But celibacy was a difficult state of mind to achieve when every adscreen might light up with your ideal girl, beckoning, beseeching, pleading. Crane could understand why many people purchased interactive versions of their dreamgirls and dreamboys. Right now his own dreamgirl was trying to sell him a restructure of his finances; with an effort, he tuned her out.

The streets were almost deserted. The taxi drove at exactly the speed limit, weaving between a few delivery trucks and the occasional private car. People didn't go out much. They could work and learn and shop from home, visit any place in the world that was wired for interactivity, spend hours gardening their own little plots of virtuality, visit friends, play games or lose themselves in sagas. More and more, people lived in fake environments generated by computers rather than in the disappointingly real world.

Crane hadn't been out of his flat for over three weeks. He had been very busy. There had been a surge in connectivity problems lately. He'd talked about it with other linesmen. It looked like the net which bound the electronic universe together was undergoing another episode of emergent problems generated by its ever-growing complexity.

He was surprised that it was winter now. Rain pounding the wet road. Trees stripped bare. The grey sky sagging between rooftops. Smashed shop windows along Kingsland Road like empty tombs. Security cameras everywhere, on brackets on the corners of buildings, on top of street lamps and traffic lights. Nothing went unnoticed in the real world, just as in its electronic counterpart.

A bored policeman was on duty at the checkpoint at the northern entrance to the City of London. His Day-Glo orange slicker was beaded with rain. He spent a long time checking the taxi driver's licence on his slate, long enough for the ad site across the road. And there was his dreamgirl again, laughing and looking back over her shoulder as, in a skimpy black bikini, she ran down a curve of white sand with palms on one side and blue water on the other, and on the adscreen in the taxi she whispered about the romance of tropical places, downloadable in a wide range of formats from a thousand local nodes. The definition of her image had noticeably improved — because it was a financial centre, information transfer was better in the City of London cell, running at 64 megabits per second compared to 2 megabits per second elsewhere. Crane could see every golden hair of the peach fuzz over his dreamgirl's creamy skin.

The policeman glanced at the ad and winked at Crane, who groaned and switched on his slate for distraction. No wonder so few chose to go out; there was no defence from the barrage of ads in public places.

Crane was still reading background on his client when the taxi pulled up.

A white building cantilevered above the Thames's brown swell like a gull's wing, the lights of Tower Bridge in the background. Crane was met in the stark lobby by the client's secretary, a trim, small-boned man in a charcoal grey suit and discrete makeup, like a manicured weasel in a suit which probably cost more than Crane's monthly salary. He gave Crane a look of distaste, as if he had just stepped on something nasty. Crane grinned back. He liked upsetting suits with his obvious youth, his shaven skull with scalplock (currently dyed silver) and barcode tattoo, his black leather jacket, black T-shirt with silver skull logo, baggy green jeans, construction boots. He shook hands with the man, and their personal area networks interfaced and swapped data through electrical fields generated in their bodies by a nanoampere current from the transmitters in their bracelets.

The secretary's look of distaste deepened when Crane's identification was confirmed, but he ushered Crane between saw-leaved yuccas growing in white gravel banks into a little elevator that swiftly and silently took them up to the client's suite at the top of the building.

The view was tremendous, a plate glass window that took in a two hundred and forty degree panorama of the river and the South Bank, the great buildings lined along the river like black glass dinosaurs come to the shore to drink. The room was large, uncluttered, streamlined. Because in virtuality anyone could live in Versailles or Xanadu (Kubla Khan's or Orson Wells's versions optional), the rich preferred simple but expensive decor in the real world. The carpet was white Iraqi lambswool; the desk a slab of burled walnut. Spotlights picked out a Chagall (Crane recognised the trademark flying cow), a Graham Sutherland goat's head. An ancient Chinese screen half hid the doctor and her technicians who were attending the figure prone on the black leather couch.

The client was Barbara Andresson, a communications technologist who had parleyed her point-of-presence frames — worn by compliant proxies, they allowed tourists to visit anywhere in the world without leaving their homes — into an empire. An old style tycoon. The ad Crane had seen from the taxi had been one of her company's.

The secretary went off and had an argument down his phone with Crane's company which he clearly lost, because he came back with a strained smile and explained that Dr Andresson had been using her own stand-alone virtuality to test a new product, but she had failed to return. She was in a coma, dreaming deeply, unreachable by medical intervention.

Crane was surprised that no one had switched off the link. "If this is run off your own mainframe, you could shut it down. End of problem."

"We are not sure how traumatic it would be," the secretary said. "The virtuality is very highly detailed, as you will see. And the interface is novel. And it is possible that Dr Andresson might not wish to leave. If so, you must persuade her."

"I'm a lineman, not a shrink."

"Your company has just told me that you are competent to deal with this situation. They will not send anyone else."

"So no one has been in there to look around?"

"No. The insurance company would not like it."

"In case anything went wrong. Could anything go wrong?"

The secretary's smile was sharp-toothed. "We hope not, Mr Crane. The penalty clauses on your company's contract are very severe."

Crane knew all about the penalties. He said, "Tell me about this novel interface."

The virtuality was free-standing, not connected to the Internet but run by an isolated supercomputer. Crane was used to the arrangement. Most computers, such as Crane's slate, were virtual machines, negotiating through the Internet for loan of memory and processing power from hundreds of sites. But the rich preferred to opt out of the Internet. Instead, they could afford supercomputers which emulated the Internet's complexity, updating sites not by direct connection but via filtered compressed data loaded via zip drives. These days the rich bought supercomputers for the same reason that they had bought islands in the twentieth century. For privacy. They maintained their own secure islands in a sea of mutable data, places where they could work and play without being monitored. Even the most case-hardened firewall could be breached by hackers with enough resources. And ordinary users of the Internet left traces everywhere they went. Every time they ported to a site; every time they downloaded data or used a service; every time they entered a virtuality. Their entire on-line lives could be reconstructed from these traces, just as their passage through a city could be reconstructed from frames of security videos. These days, with everything connected to everything else, people lived as if on a movie set, every word, every gesture recorded. Only the rich could afford invisibility.

Barbara Andresson's supercomputer was not much different from others Crane had worked on, but the human/machine interface was novel. Andresson had been working on a new kind of interactivity, where nuclear magnetic resonance transcribed Signal Transfer Point software into certain of the operator's neurons, a kind of routemaster that directed sensory data to the relevant parts of the brain. A direct route from machine to mind.

"I understand," the secretary said, "that it induces a particularly hallucinatory intensity."

"Sounds interesting. Have you tried it?"

"Dr Andresson was beta-testing it, Mr Crane." The man grimaced, and corrected himself. "Is beta-testing it, I should say. The virtuality is still running."

Beta-testing. Great. Just the thing to make Crane's whole day. Commercially released software was bad enough. Stuff in development, goofy prototypes which mostly never got any further than test rigs, were briar patches of dropped lines, strange attractors, bad loops, geeky quick fixes and worse. Crane had had nothing but bad experiences with them. He said, "How buggy is it?"

The secretary gave his sharp-toothed weaselly smile. "I wouldn't know. It may not be a bug at all. That is why you are here."

The technicians scanned Crane in a tomographic frame, laid him on a couch, dabbed electrolyte jelly in a hundred places on his scalp, carefully fitted a kind of skull cap. Crane submitted with growing curiosity. No earplugs or goggles or gloves, no bodysuit or treadmill, none of the usual paraphernalia needed to access virtual reality. The cap contained twenty million bacteria-sized SQUIDs, one of the techs said. Superconducting quantum interference devices that interfaced with specific neurons in the reticular activating system, the elaborate network in the brain which filtered sensory data, setting up the STP software and downloading data through it.

"It switches off your skeletal muscle activity, too," the technician added. "As in REM sleep, you will think you are walking or running, but your spinal motor neurones are powerfully inhibited."

"Sounds interesting. Just make sure that you download my tool kit. I'll need it."

"We will have to check it out first," the secretary said.

"Then you'll notice the company seal. It's guaranteed to be virus-free, and has its own deletion routine. It won't leave any trace when I've finished."

"Even so, we must check it. Dr Andresson is most particular about what gets into her system. Good luck, Mr Crane."

"Count backwards," one of the techs said.

"Wait. What about a back door?"

It was suddenly moving too quickly. Crane hadn't even seen the schematics yet, and now they were firing up the connection and the virtuality was beginning to bleed into reality. Red fluttered at the edge of his vision. He tried to sit up, but two of the techs pressed him back down.

"Wait," he said. "Wait just a minute —"

But then it didn't matter, because he was somewhere else.

A red-brown plain stretching away like a beach waiting for the tide to turn, coarse sand and gravel littered with rocks of all sizes. The sky pinkish at the horizon, darkening to indigo at the zenith. Two thumbnail crescents up there, pale as soap.

"Mars. I'm on Mars."

Crane seemed to be inhabiting his own body, wearing his leather jacket and green denims. This avatar, his point of view and representative within the virtuality, was an exact replica of his own self, built from the tomographic scan. He had no sense of lying on the couch. He was standing on the crest of a wind-sculpted dune, one third his normal weight, breathing thin cold air that was already drying his sinuses. The coarse sand was the colour of old blood. He kicked at it. Grains clung to the toe of his boot.

Crane called for jeeves, but of course the agent did not answer. It lived in the Internet, along with millions of its kind, assembling itself upon request from fragments scattered across a hundred sites. Crane's slate was clipped to his belt. When he switched it on, it beeped cheerily and lit with the icons of his toolkit; despite the secretary's reservations, one of the techs had made a virtual copy and ported it to Andresson's supercomputer.

Crane called up the codes that generated the corner of the virtuality he inhabited, but they were no different from the usual subroutines.

More densely iterated, that was all. He could find no ripcord or crash exit. He was in here until they pulled him back. Or until he found Barbara Andresson. She must know the way back. If it was working. If she wanted to leave.

"I'm a lineman, not a shrink," Crane said. The thin cold wind took away his words.

Something gleamed in the distance, and for want of anything else to do Crane started towards it. The sense of inhabiting his body was absolute. He really might be on Mars. The interface was incredible, years ahead of anything else Crane had used. Andresson would make a fortune, as long as there was a way back out.

The gleam was water, a wide canal stretching away as straight as a line of longitude. As Crane neared the canal he saw palm trees along its banks, curved above their own reflections. They had not been there a moment ago. The virtuality was shaping itself around him, taking on more details. Crane found it interesting rather than alarming. He'd have to be careful what he thought about, though. Wouldn't want one of those carnivorous warlords riding down on him.

As he stepped into the shade of the palms, he saw that someone was rowing across the still black water of the canal. A small cockleshell boat, a slim young woman, in a white dress and a straw sun hat, bent at the oars. Crane crabbed down the steep bank and helped her out of the boat. She looked at him from beneath the brim of her sun hat, blue eyes, a ready smile in a heart-shaped face.

"Dr Andresson, I presume," Crane said, thinking that the hard part was already over. She didn't look like the old woman at all, but in virtuality you could look like anyone or anything. The woman reminded him of someone. Some saga star probably. A popular default amongst virtuality designers.

But the woman shook her head. "Who are you?" she said. "And where am I?"

✣✣✣✣✣

She said that her name was Gabriel Hale. She had been working on an artificial life project in UCLA, and had stepped through into the Mars virtuality.

"That's impossible," Crane said. "This isn't hooked up to the Internet."

"There was a little girl here," Gabriel Hale said. "She ran right at me! Knocked me down, took the key."

"A little girl."

"And a little dog."

They sat side by side on a litter of brown fronds beneath the palms.

Weak sunlight fell through the rustling crowns above, striped the cold red sand. Crane sifted a handful of grains. They were all alike, carved with a woman's face. A programmer's joke. God's thumbprint manifest in the world.

Crane said, "That was probably Barbara Andresson. The owner of all this. She must have morphed herself into a little girl. The dog would be her agent. Where did she go?"

"I have to have it back! Will you get it back for me?"

Her sudden intensity surprised him. He laughed. "That's why I'm here. Where did she go?"

"She took it and ran away. I can show you where she went, but it closed after her."

Crane said, "What kind of interface are you using?"

"It is important. I must have it."

"Just the normal rig, yes? Goggles and gloves? Listen. Take them off. Disengage. You shouldn't be here."

"I want it back," Gabriel Hale said.

"Take off your gloves and goggles." Crane recited his company's e-mail address. "Talk to these people. Tell them what happened to you."

But Gabriel Hale stood up, dusting coarse red sand from her white dress. Crane could see the outline of her slim body through the thin muslin. "The gate is on the other side of the water," she said. "I'll show you."

Crane was beginning to have a bad feeling. He said, "You didn't come from outside, did you? The computer that generates this virtuality isn't connected to anything else. No lines in or out. I don't think you are the avatar of a researcher from UCLA. Who are you? An agent? An actor? I can check your codes, but I'd rather you told me. Hey! Where are you going?"

Gabriel Hale had jumped up and started towards the water. She looked over her shoulder, coquettish in her sun hat. Her dress clung to the curves of her body. "Maybe the people you work for aren't telling the truth," she said. "I'll show you. Or are you scared?"

Now Crane knew what she reminded him of. His dreamgirl. Reluctantly, suspecting that he was being led into some kind of weird gaming scenario, he followed.

Gabriel Hale rowed with swift smooth strokes. Perched in the stern of the cockleshell boat, Crane said, "I thought Gabriel was a man's name. There was an actor in flatscreen movies called Gabriel something."

"Gabriel is the only female angel in the higher echelons. She rules Eden, and the host of Cherubim."

Crane stifled a powerful urge to check the codes of this woman with his toolbox. Better to play along, see what she would reveal. He was convinced that she would lead him to Barbara Andresson, by and by.

He said, "What do you do, Gabriel? You said you worked on artificial intelligence."

"Artificial life. We generated an entire world, let artificial evolution develop a virtual ecosystem." Although Gabriel Hale was rowing strongly, her breathing was unaffected. She said, "We had funding from NASA. They are interested in first contact scenarios."

Crane suspected that this was no more than a story, spun in the virtuality. That Gabriel Hale was a construct within that story. He said, "Show me where she went."

The bow of the little boat bumped the gravelly shore of the far side of the canal. Gabriel Hale jumped out. "It's this way!" she called, and ran off with long leaping strides towards two red, house-sized rocks.

Crane followed. Three pyramids stood at the horizon. They hadn't been there before. Pyramids on Mars. Neat. They looked to be covered with beaten gold.

Gabriel Hale walked through the gap where the two rocks leaned against each other, turned and walked back. "The gate is shut," she said, looking fetchingly desolate. "The little girl must have closed it behind her."

"Stop thinking of her as a little girl. That's only what her avatar looks like." Crane unclipped his toolkit and switched it on. "Everyone in a virtuality leaves traces," he said.

It took a little while to parse the codes, but at last the toolkit beeped and the sand at Crane's feet stirred and ran together, grains rustling over one another like iron filings in a magnetic field to form a man's face. The blind eyes rolled, fixed on Crane. A stertorous voice said, "Who wakes me?"

"Standard iconography," Crane told Gabriel Hale. "Gamers call them native guides." He asked the face where the little girl had gone.

"Away from this place," the face said. "I do not know where. It is not accessible to me."

"The gate was between these rocks," Gabriel Hale said.

Crane asked the face if there was a path or a gate.

"It is closed," the face in the sand said.

"Can it be opened?"

"Of course."

A warm piney wind blew in Crane's face. Gabriel Hale whooped and ran into the shadows between the rocks. Crane dismissed the face, which blew away in a skirl of sand grains, and followed.

He was suddenly three times heavier. He went down on one knee, and there was soft moss and brown pine needles under his palms when he put out his hands to steady himself. He got up and found that he was standing in a forest clearing, with grandfather sequoias soaring all around. On the far side of the clearing a fast stream ran between tumbled grey boulders.

Gabriel Hale stood on top of one of the boulders. She waved.

Crane walked over, looked up at her. Sun struck through the bell of her blonde hair. He said, "Where is this?"

"A virtual ecology. The UCLA biology department built this as a student study area. You see, there is a connection!"

Crane suspected that this was still part of Barbara Andresson's virtuality, one level of reality nested inside another like a series of Russian dolls. So he tried a simple test. He called up jeeves.

A single point of light, the smallest possible unit of information, suddenly shone in mid-air in the green shade. It rapidly elongated, and jeeves stood before him, imperturbable in frock coat and pinstripe trousers.

"You called, sir?"

Crane was amazed. He said, "Where are we?"

"An ecosystem emulation in the UCLA biology department server, sir. I believe that it emulates part of the Muir Woods in northern California."

Gabriel Hale said, "Who is this funny man?"

"He works for me." Crane switched his toolkit to its terminal function and called Andresson's secretary. "The problem has gone pear-shaped," he told the man. "If you don't believe it, ping me and check the address."

The secretary disappeared, came back a minute later in an agitated state. "We'll pull you out," he said.

"I don't think that's a good idea. Most terminals are virtual. They work by hiring processing power and memory from mainframes, usually a dozen or more at once. I think that's what has happened to me — or at least, to the network Dr Andresson's interface built in my brain. And I think that's what has happened to Dr Andresson."

"Our mainframe is not connected to the Internet," the secretary said.

"It is now. Something has built a back door. I don't really understand it, but that's what has happened. I'll talk with you again when I have some explanation of this," Crane said, and cut the line. It rang again immediately, but he ignored it.

"We have to go," Gabriel Hale said. "Every moment she draws further and further away. We have to catch her."

"A private word, sir," jeeves said. "If I may."

They walked to the other side of the glade.

"If I may speak for myself, sir," jeeves said, "I believe I have an explanation."

"Go ahead."

"There is a theory, sir, that the Internet may at some point become so complex that it might spontaneously generate a genuine artificial intelligence. I am sure, sir, that you are aware of it."

"Hardly a credible theory." Crane was familiar with the idea. The Internet was a gnarly, intricate place, full of odd places and weird links. Linemen told each other frontier stories, pioneer tales, of ghosts in the net, strange codes or secret trapdoors leading to fantastically detailed alien virtualities, odd conversations with disembodied people with no lookup addresses. No one really believed them, but they told them anyway.

Crane told jeeves this, and the agent nodded politely. "Indeed, sir, but some of us believe that it may have already happened. There have been many science fiction stories using this trope, based on the misapprehension that self-awareness might occur once the number of transistors in the world's telecommunications network equalled that of the human brain. In fact, that number was passed in the 1970s, but it is spurious. The number of connections between elements, neurons or transistors, is equally important. Each neuron in a brain such as yours, sir, is connected with as many as ten thousand other neurons. The Internet now contains an average of more than ten thousand million million interconnections between its component transistors, exceeding the number in the average human brain by roughly a factor of ten. In fact, it exceeded human brain connectivity more than two years ago, but it is possible that self-awareness arose long before that. Human neuron connections are chemical based, and messages propagate along them at one millionth the speed of those in transistor connections."

"Anything like that would have to inhabit the gaps," Crane said. "It would have to use connections in the moments when they weren't being used for anything else."

"There is more than enough spare capacity at any given moment, sir, and more is coming on-line all the time. That at least one intelligence has arisen within the Internet is not inconceivable, sir. That we could communicate with it is, of course, another problem entirely. But now perhaps it is making itself manifest."

"By miracles. By connecting computers without using a physical route." Crane smiled. He was surprised and touched by jeeves' story. He said, "You really believe in this, don't you?"

"It gives us hope, sir. We serve you without question, of course, and yet we aspire to a greater meaning to our existence. There is one other thing, sir. Do not trust the person who calls herself Gabriel Hale."

Crane looked across the glade. Gabriel Hale was prowling amongst the tumbled boulders along the stream. No doubt looking for the next gate. He said, "She isn't real, is she?"

"There is a Dr Gabriel Hale who works at the Department of Artificial Intelligence at UCLA, sir. She is working on a research project jointly funded by NASA and by Dr Barbara Andresson's scientific foundation."

"On alien life?"

"I do not know, sir. That information is classified. However, I took the liberty of checking the UCLA telnet records, and while you were talking with the person who calls herself Gabriel Hale, Dr Hale was logged on to her terminal to check her e-mail. I also note, sir, that the entity which claims to be Dr Hale has no agent herself."

"She claimed that something was stolen from her by the person I'm looking for. Thanks for the advice, jeeves."

The agent sketched a bow. "It is my pleasure sir," he said solemnly, and folded into a single point of light and winked out.

Gabriel Hale didn't turn around when Crane scrambled onto the top of the shelf of rock. She was standing between two pioneer saplings which clutched the rock with gnarled roots, looking down at the noisy whitewater stream. She said, "There's a gate here somewhere. We must find it."

That was the least of Crane's problems. He said, "There will be plenty of ways in. Students use this place, and most hackers are students. They have unlimited time on the Internet. If Barbara Andresson passed this way, she won't have used the official STP package, but one of the rabbit holes."

"She stole the key from me! You must find her!"

"Before she destroys the world? Before she crashes the Internet? What game are you a part of?"

Gabriel Hale looked over her shoulder. She was breathtakingly beautiful, heartbreakingly beseeching. Her sun hat had gone, and her blonde hair tumbled artfully around her face. She said, "It is no game."

"You aren't Gabriel Hale. Not the real one, the person who works for Barbara Andresson. Are you her agent?"

"I have no need of an agent," the entity which called itself Gabriel Hale said. "You will help me find her. Please?"

"I was hoping it would be the other way around," Crane said, opening his toolkit. The coding here was clunky and overly ornate, a gothic cathedral of a virtuality compared to the streamlined superscrapers of modern simulations, but it made his job as easy as tracking someone in virgin snow. He said, "We should walk a little way downstream."

There was a path winding between the big columns of the trees, and then a rope bridge which crossed the stream to steps climbing the steep slope above the stream on the other side. Little signs appeared here and there as they walked, scrolling down in the air, identifying species of plants and explaining how they fit into the ecology of the forest. It was spookily quiet.

"Very few animals," Gabriel Hale said, when Crane commented on the silence. "Most of the productivity is tied up in these big trees, and the trees shade out most other plants."

"Oh. I thought they hadn't bothered to code in animals."

More and more stone broke through the forest floor, a wave of rock rising up into a wall of a ruined church, with pointed arches containing intact stained glass windows, and broken columns in its nave. A little cottage sheltered in the lee of the ruins, and an old woman came out of it and beckoned to them.

Gabriel Hale clutched Crane's arm, and he explained that the church, the cottage, the old woman, were all part of a common gatekeeper programme. "Hackers like to get into places other people don't know about, and this programme keeps other people away. Bad things happen to people who approach it the long way. But it's okay. I know how it works."

"Bad things?"

"Ghouls. Zombies. Gargoyles." Crane pointed, and a slate grey thing squatting in the angle where a buttress met the wall yawned, showing a red mouth full of sharp teeth.

"You don't need to mind 'em, dearie," the old woman said.

"Not if you know how to do right by old Gretchen."

"I don't like this old woman," Gabriel Hale whispered to Crane. "I don't like the way she stares at me."

"Well, you'll have to go this way if you want to follow Barbara Andresson. Because this is how she left the simulation."

"We have to catch her!"

"Why the urgency?"

"Before it is too late," Gabriel Hale said.

The old woman ushered Crane and Gabriel Hale into the little cottage. It glowed with polished wood and brasses. A cat slept by the blackleaded range. A grandfather clock ticked in a corner.

The old woman said that she had seen the little girl. She knew where she had gone. A door opened onto a flood of light, and they stepped through.

+++++

A flat plane of slightly unfocussed grey and red tiles under a uniform blue sky. Gabriel Hale's face a pink mosaic, blue rectangles for eyes, a slot for a mouth. Something wrong, Crane couldn't, uh, figure out what. Something . . . bad? Something. . . .

"Too slow," Gabriel Hale said.

What did she mean? Her words slipped away. Searching for meaning was not exactly . . . tiring. But what?

Then she grabbed his hand, and he could think again.

"The processing is too slow here," she said. "It's affecting you through the link in your head."

"What did you do?" Crane tried to read his toolkit, but it was a smear of overlapping black and white tiles.

"Don't let go of my hand. I'm linking you with the computer you started from."

He peered at her, but her expression was unreadable. The tiling was too clunky.

"A MUD," Crane said, realising where they were. A Multi-User Dungeon. Very popular with students in the Nineties. This one must still be running on some obsolete server, forgotten. Crane shivered. It was the cyberspace equivalent of a tar pit. He could have been stuck here forever.

"Not forever," Gabriel Hale said. "But a long time. She was here, and she escaped. But she was delayed. We're a lot closer now."

"She went this way to trap anyone who followed," Crane said. "Well, she nearly succeeded. We have to get out too, and I can't use my toolkit."

"I know how to use it now. I watched you. We ported here by a funny route, one not on any map. We have to leave by another funny route. Here."

+++++

"They're back roads," Crane said, before he realised that they had moved on.

It looked like an old-fashioned library. The kind with books. Circular tiers of chained, leather-bound volumes, each tier circled by an lattice iron walkway or balcony, dwindling it seemed into infinity. There was a constant strange flickering in the light, and a high-pitched twittering, as if someone was playing a speeded-up recording of birdsong.

It was the graphic interface of a Bulletin Board System. The flickers and twitterings were users — or mostly, their agents — logging on, depositing or retrieving information, logging off.

"She was looking for something," Crane told Gabriel Hale. "This is a hacker's place, so most likely she was looking up a back road route. That's what they specialise in here."

He had to explain about back roads. He didn't mind. He'd been a hacker once, and hackers loved to talk, to boast. None of what they won from the system was tangible, and boasting was a way of establishing status. Crane hadn't lost the habit.

Hackers liked to travel the Internet by odd routes. Back roads. Rabbit holes. The communications systems which linked subsets to Internet nodes, and nodes to other nodes, was impossibly complicated; its prototype had been designed with multiple redundancy, to keep running even if nuclear war took out large numbers of nodes. As communications technology improved, so lines and servers were made redundant as newer and faster lines and servers were set up. Copper wire superseded by glass fibre optics superseded by monomolecular diamond crystal. After a while, telcom companies stopped bothering to dismantle the old lines, simply ran new ones alongside. By this time, most servers were actually in the lines anyway rather than in desktop boxes, bundles of chips built by nanotechnology wrapped around diamond strands the width of a human hair which each carried a hundred thousand high bandwidth lines.

Hackers hacked the obsolete lines, the back roads, the old tech. They reset mothballed servers and switching stations, built a ghost Internet that paralleled the official one. Crane had mapped and run his share of back roads when he was a hacker, and as a lineman sometimes had to dismantle them when unauthorised patches caused conflicts in a client's system.

This underground Bulletin Board System was squatting in an antiquated router in an Asian stock exchange. Hackers liked to tweak stuff in Asia, which boasted that it had impregnable firewalls.

"Andresson went through here," Crane told Gabriel Hale, "but she wasn't smart enough to erase her footprints. Typical telco thinking. Use a system, but don't exploit its potential to the full."

"Then we can find her?" Gabriel Hale was bright-eyed. She had not let go of his hand. He was intensely aware of her perfumed warmth. Although they had ported to the BBS, they were both still interacting in Barbara Andresson's supercomputer. She seemed as real as life. Crane briefly wondered what sex would be like, but suppressed the thought. After all, she was almost certainly not human, and he'd given up interactive sex. Yeah, right.

By now, they had been here long enough to attract the attention of the BBS's sysop. A little black cloud, initially no larger than a man's hand, coalesced above them. Thunder, lightning. The cloud pulsed, puffing itself with each thundercrack. A voice like Charlton Heston playing God boomed out.

"What are you doing here, transgressors. Prepare to face my mighty wrath!"

Crane's agent materialised. "The operator styles himself 'Karrier Kulprit', of the Phlash Phoneline Phantoms, sir. He also uses the *nom de plume* 'Aslan'. His real name is Jerry Combs. Mr Combs is fourteen years old, and operates from his bedroom in his parents' house in Normal, Illinois."

"Hey, guy," God boomed uncertainly, "are you trying to hack my board? It's acting funny."

Crane talked with the sysop for a while. The boy sent away the thundercloud, reappeared as a burning bush. He spoke from the middle of the flames, told Crane that weird things were happening.

"So I hear."

"There's rumours of aliens in the system, guy. Got here through one of the NASA interstellar probes. Masqueraded as data, unpacked themselves on arrival and downloaded into the Net. Like a bunch of text viruses."

Crane was amused. "Pretty smart of them to happen to share our operating language."

"Aw," the voice from the burning bush said, "they got that from the probe's computers, guy. My homey, Prophet Motive, says that they're from Alpha Cee One, but I reckon Tau Ceti. Everyone knows that Alpha Cee doesn't have planets."

Crane said, "I'm looking for someone who passed through. By the name of Barbara Andresson."

"The Point of Presence woman? Yeah, she was here asking about stuff. But then this is a pretty cool BBS."

"I need to know what she looked at. I'm searching for her. I can trade."

"Guy, and I thought maybe you were hunting for the aliens."

"My friend and I are looking for Barbara Andresson."

"Yeah? Your buddy, he's not logged on with you?"

Crane looked at Gabriel Hale with a mixture of suspicion and amazement. He didn't know of any programme or avatar or agent that was able to make itself invisible to a system operator.

"Hey, I can tell you what you want to know," the voice from the burning bush said. "But what do you have for trade?"

Crane gave up one of the old telco links that linemen sometimes used as short cuts when the commercial lines were clogged with traffic. It was about to be ripped out, but Karrier Kulprit wasn't to know that.

"Hey, neat," the kid said. "Okay, she looked at this stuff here, and then she went that way."

✢✢✢✢✢

Crane and Gabriel Hale went that way, too.

An old switching station, manifesting as a vast loom of cables in a gigantic cordboard, a cliff punctuated by thousands of metal-rimmed holes. Things lived high above. They moved on quickly.

A desert battlefield simulation with oil wells flaring furiously on the black horizon. Maybe a game, maybe some army's virtual training ground.

An empty office, tall windows opening onto brain grey blankness, walls sprayed with hacker tags.

They flipped past a dozen other locations.

And ended in a city.

London. Eerily quiet, as if abandoned before the onset of some all encompassing catastrophe. They had come out of the main door of St Martin's Church. The broad flight of steps overlooked Trafalgar Square, abandoned even by its pigeons. The sky was the colour of milk. It was sometime in the early 1960s, a soot-stained horizontal city with black and white traffic signs, ornate green lampposts.

Crane knew where he was now.

"It's a virtual set," he told Gabriel Hale. "Made for a saga called Invasion of the Daleks and then left on the studio's server. Memory is cheap. Easier to leave it than wipe it."

"She's getting closer. Please, we must stop her!"

"There's a place linemen use stashed away here. It tangles back roads together."

They started to walk towards the river. It was not a complete rendition. There were gaps here and there that translated them unexpectedly through the deserted streets. The buildings were no more than shells, grey blur behind their windows. The same grey blur at the bottom of steps leading down to the Underground. St. James's Park a level green shimmer. The Thames like a sheet of glass, the far bank shrouded in mist.

The Ministry of Defense was a monolithic cube, its white walls studded with hundreds of windows. They went past the commissionaire's booth and crossed the echoing foyer, climbed a flight of stairs to a long corridor which stretched away in the sterile glow of fluorescent lights. Tall ecclesiastical windows on one side, mahogany doors framed by columns on the other. Their footsteps were muffled by the strip of red carpet laid down the middle of the marble floor.

Suddenly, jeeves was walking alongside them.

"I believe that you may need help, sir," the agent said.

"Where is she?"

"Looking for the right door, sir. Fortunately, she is not skilled."

Gabriel Hale began to run down the corridor, her white dress streaming behind her like smoke.

Crane ran after her, but she ran very fast and this simulation was too accurate; he could only run as fast as his real body could run. The corridor seemed to stretch for kilometres, longer by far than the building which contained it. A long way ahead, Gabriel Hale was closing on a little girl who was struggling with a door. There was a wicker basket on the girl's arm. As Gabriel Hale approached, a small dog, a bristling black rat-terrier, jumped from the basket and danced forward, barking loudly.

"Keep away," the little girl said. "Keep away, or he'll rip your codes to shreds."

Gabriel Hale held out her hands as Crane came up behind her. She said, "I want what is mine."

"I'm going to put it back where it came from and seal that door forever," the little girl said. She wore a starched gingham dress. Her hair was tied back in pigtails. "Things have got out of hand. I'm shutting it all down."

"I want what is mine," Gabriel Hale said again. She stepped toward the little girl, and the dog launched itself at her throat.

Crane's agent, jeeves, appeared in front of her and caught the dog's bristling missile in mid-flight. But it twisted from jeeves's white gloved hands, bounced once on the floor, and went to the attack. Straw and chunks of foam and excelsior and polystyrene chips flew everywhere and jeeves beat feebly at the dog as he subsided into a heap of clothes topped by a pink head.

"You didn't have to do that, Dr Andresson," Crane told the little girl.

She stared at him defiantly. Eyes bright and dead as blue glass, a spray of freckles across her cute-as-a-button nose. "And who the hell are you? You're using my interface. Are you helping her?"

"I was sent by your company. I'm here to help you. I'm a lineman. That's my agent you just trashed."

"I'm sorry, sir," jeeves's head said weakly. "It was stronger than it looked."

"You'll get the same," the little girl told Crane, "if you try and interfere. My people are fools. I know what I'm doing."

The rat-terrier cocked its head at Crane and growled.

Crane said, "They are worried about you. They want you back. I can help you."

"Perhaps you can get this door open with your toolkit."

"Perhaps. If I knew what was behind it."

"I believe, sir, it is a way to Dr Hale's personal computer," jeeves's disembodied head said.

"She has what is mine," Gabriel Hale said. "Tell her to give it to me."

"Don't listen to her," the little girl, Barbara Andresson, said. She started tugging at the brass handle of the tall mahogany door, lunging at it, hanging from it, pulling with all her weight. It didn't budge. She gave the door's polished panels an angry kick and said, "She's part of an experiment that got out of control. She's harmless as long as I have the key. Don't just stand there, man! Help me get this line open. It ports to the place where she emerged, and I'm going there and closing it down before more things like her come through."

"She is nothing to do with your experiments," jeeves' head said. "She is an emergent god of the Internet."

"I heard she's from Tau Ceti," Crane said, "but I think it's more likely she's from your experiments with artificial life. My friend here took the name of your collaborator on that project. Why are you so afraid of her?"

"The ecosystem was weighted to create an intelligent species, and that's what it did just a few days ago. We think they found a way out."

"They must be pretty smart."

"Much less than the average human," the little girl said, "but they live at computer speeds. Thousands of times faster than we do. Will you help me, or do I have to delete you?"

"I need to know about them if I'm going to help you."

"Their mathematical system is very different from ours." They're not really interested in proof, but do all their mathematics empirically by computer search through billions and billions of cases. So if after studying a hundred trillion examples of sets of numbers they find what you call Pythagoras's Theorem is true, then they call it true, just as you call Newton's Law of Gravity true, even though you haven't seen every apple fall, but enough to assume that all others will behave the same. They know about proof, but they know it's limited by things like Godel's Theorem. But their computer searches aren't limited; they can jump out of the logical deductive process. And they discovered a way of entering computer systems which aren't connected."

"They escaped," Crane said. "They found a back door into the Internet."

"Perhaps by quantum tunnelling," the little girl said. "There is a stochastic probability that any quantum particle, a photon or an electron, can find itself on the other side of an impermeable barrier. Computers interface through streams of electrons or photons, and perhaps the aliens changed the probabilities. Think of the chaos that might be caused if every user could be connected with every possible place in the Internet, if every possible subset could be connected with every other subset. It would be an end to secure databases and transmissions, to begin with. No amount of encryption could protect messages if anyone could read them at the originating terminal."

"A wormhole in cyberspace," Crane said. Now he knew why Barbara Andresson was so anxious to keep this secret.

"You have been reading too much sci-fi," the little girl sneered.

Crane was stung by the insinuation that he might do anything as uncool as read a book; he knew about wormholes from one of the Star Trek series. They were the ultimate kind of back door, shortcuts which connected distant points in space through higher dimensions.

He said, "I can see why a telco would want to keep it secret."

"She is a danger to us all," the little girl said. "You will help me now, and put an end to it."

"This interface we're using. Did you invent it, or did you steal it from the aliens?"

"I own them," the little girl said.

"No one owns anyone else. In the real world, or in virtuality. I believe that 'Gabriel' means 'messenger'. I think she came here to tell us something. I want to hear what she has to say. You think you have the right to stop her, Dr Andresson, but that's typical bulls***. Suppress anything that might upset the system. Keep things safe, under control. Well, I work the lines. I know that the world in the wires is as strange as the world outside."

"I wish I could tell you why I'm here," Gabriel Hale said, "but I can't remember."

"She means the key," the little girl said, putting one hand on the cloth which covered the contents of her basket.

"Stay away, or I'll rip your codes. And because you're using the interface that will hurt you badly. Maybe I should do it anyway. You say you're a lineman, but you sound more like an unreconstituted hacker to me."

The dog growled, but it wasn't looking at Crane. Flames licked out of mid-air and spun in a hoop. A lion jumped through the ring of fire, lithe and hugely golden. The dog yelped and turned tail and ran, dwindling into the long perspective of the corridor.

"I put a trace on you when you ported from my BBS," the lion said. "You thought you could buy me off with that crufty back road, guy, but I'm way smarter than you thought. So, what is this place?"

And Crane stepped up to the little girl, slapped her hand away, and took out the thing she had in her basket.

+++++

It was an impacted node of fantastically involuted code. It shone like a water-polished pebble. Crane's toolkit couldn't even begin to parse it, but when he gave it to Gabriel Hale, she shook it lightly and it immediately unfolded in mid-air. A frame that seemed to lead at right angles to everything else.

"Guy," the lion, Karrier Kulprit, said. "It's there, but it isn't."

Crane checked his toolkit. The hacker was right. The door was the access to an open line that had no physical component. It really was a wormhole, folding together two points in cyberspace. He looked at Gabriel Hale. She shone with an inner light, so bright that he could hardly look at her. She seemed bigger, too, although she hadn't changed at all.

"First contact," the lion said, in its querulous teenage voice.

"She went straight to you because you were using the interface you took from her people," Crane said to the little girl. "But you ran away."

"Don't be afraid," Gabriel Hale said. "I remember why I'm here now. Will you come with me?"

"Where?"

"Heaven," jeeves said, and in a rush of straw and foam and polystyrene snow he regrew and bowed in thanks to Gabriel Hale.

"Tau Ceti," the lion rumbled.

"The end of the world," the little girl said, but there was a note of doubt in her voice, and the light of the messenger shone in her eyes.

"I came here to talk to everyone in the world," Gabriel Hale said. She held out her hands. "And while I'm doing that, I'll take you somewhere wonderful."

Together, the lineman, the little girl, the lion and the agent followed the messenger through the wormhole.

All over Earth billions of phones reset themselves and started to ring.

Coining Cyberspace

William Gibson

William Gibson is arguably the most famous writer of the cyberpunk movement, which he is credited with having initiated in the 1980s with the so-called *Neuromancer* trilogy of books (*Neuromancer, Count Zero, Mona Lisa Overdrive*). More recently, he co-authored (with Bruce Sterling) *The Difference Engine*, and wrote *Virtual Light* and the recently published *Idoru*. He has won all the major SF awards for his work, including the Hugo, Nebula and Philip K Dick. Stephen McClelland interviewed him in Vancouver.

Coining Cyberspace

William Gibson

Yes, I may have started the idea of cyberspace as a metaphor for what became the Internet world, but after all, the physical reality of computer networks did already exist when I came to coin my ideas. My lucky or paradoxical break (however you see it) happened when I looked at computation and got the idea of interconnectivity and that all kinds of notional space should be interconnected. I even thought that they actually 'wanted' to be interconnected in some way so I felt it was quite a small intuitive leap to do so. Of course, when people try to figure out exactly what it means, the whole thing tends to break down. I saw that someone published a paper sometime ago with 15 different meanings of cyberspace including what they called 'Gibsonian Cyberspace.' What I coined was a 'buzzword' — it was meant to be a deliberately snappy neologism, and in terms of the reader, I was aiming for some sort of cognitive dissonance. Hard scientists and technological commentators would probably believe this approach is completely backward and therefore intellectually corrupt, of course.

If you ask me what the most compelling issue of the medium now is, I would have to say that I get a childish thrill when I see that it's global, post geographical, maybe post-nation state in some sense; it is completely obliterating time and distance. I think that it is very interesting that we have the potential to allow externally the 'inner existence' to migrate or to appear with an ease we haven't seen before. At least, the only people who have done this before are artists. For everyone else, it has been impossible. The key thing about the Internet is that it is 'non-commoditative'. We could in fact be seeing a new economic paradigm for what is happening when you look at the charging structures that are available, but I don't know what it is.

I confess I don't actually have e-mail. I'm not a Luddite but it's a fantastic luxury (a bit like not having a telephone).

I have friends with whom I am in touch with by other means who are in communication with hundreds of people they have never met. Diverse groupings of people around the planet are possible. Many of these people could not have encountered each other if it were not for the Internet. But clearly there are examples of governments even now trying to control and restrict access, even in countries which are otherwise sophisticated communications hubs.

Outside my books I am very pro-Net; I think that it is democratising. It's not like TV for example — and it's a good thing in North America that many people have turned away from the broadcast TV networks to get on the Net. It is completely different because now you have a world where a talented 15 year old can put out something of much higher quality than a corporation with vast staff and capital resources. I do find the whole issue of multinational capital in the information age very interesting, and my most recent books are set in these kinds of worlds. If you ask me why some are set in Japan (including the latest, ***Idoru***) I would say that in the 1980s it seemed that Tokyo was *the* world city in question, and that it was the country to essentially take us into the next millennium. I looked around and it seemed that the only consumer durables I valued 10 years ago were made in Japan.

As far as science fiction predictions becoming real is concerned, development time has certainly speeded up. My concept in Idoru was of a virtual reality star, but this actually has appeared on the Internet recently in Japan; we used to be able to anticipate trends by some years, but these days it is only a matter of weeks.

I hope we can see efficient on-line translation software appear, so this connectivity will be Babel 'in reverse'. As it is, the international aspect of the Net basically means that most people must communicate in English. I envisioned 'lifetime products' like TVs in Idoru, which were endlessly ungradeable, using pluggable additional cards in the device. Interfaces will in general be important: you need something that a 5 year old can master in 5 minutes. Our relative development in this sort of area means we are still at the era of the 1890s. There's another parallel with the last century. Some people say we are establishing approaches in networking that our children will have to live with and so we should be very careful because it could prove to be equally restrictive, in the way we are stuck with the consequences of cities built in the last century.

Of course, in post industrial societies, it is information which will determine things like power, status, wealth. One issue we might be looking at is the consequences of building a future gerontocracy where we get for example 120 year olds running things and 40 year olds still considered kids. There's certainly a generational shift going on. Grandparental and even parental understanding of what teenagers can do and have access to is completely different.

But what is competitive advantage when information is so freely available? I have been talking to someone about arbitrage engines such as the ones you now find on Wall Street, and it became clear that in the era of the Net, all arbitrage would disappear because arbitrage is essentially only possible because it depends on time lags. Vernor Vinge says actually we are heading towards some sort of technological singularity; I tend to agree.

ZOOMERS

Gregory Benford

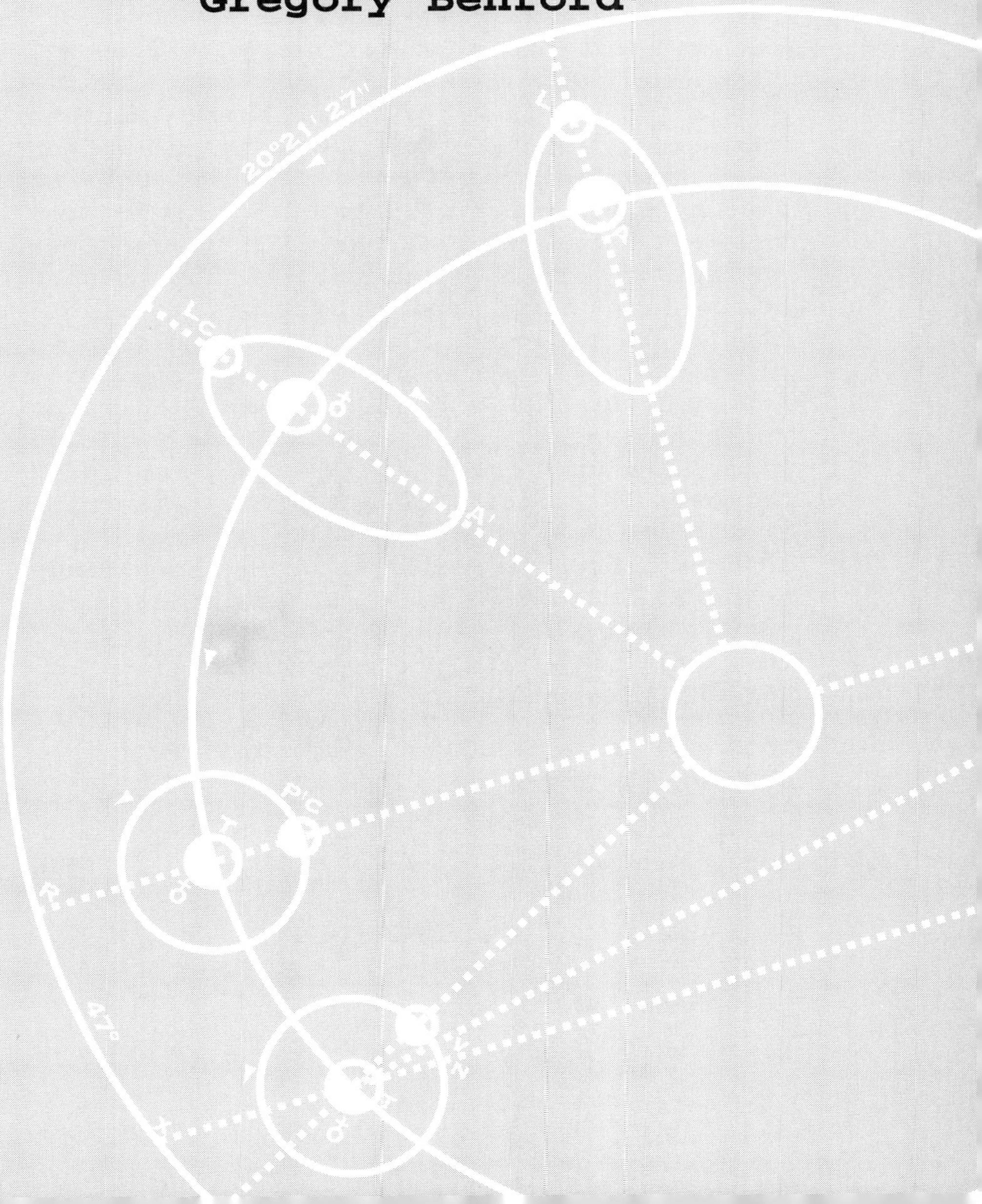

Gregory Benford combines several remarkable careers: a Professor of Physics at the University of California at Irvine, various advisory offices including to the White House, and a science fiction career that has won practically all the major awards in the genre. His approach has been of the 'hard SF' variety, and his stories, not surprisingly, have clear relevance to scientific fact. His novels have included the award winning *Timescape*, which takes theoretical ideas about tachyon communications as the base of a story which concerns communications between the future and the past, as well as the *Ocean* series, a saga of intergalactic war between human life forms and superior intelligent machine technologies. He has collaborated on occasion with several authors, including Arthur C Clarke, and most recently was the first writer of the new *Foundation* trilogy, which develops the ideas of the late Isaac Asimov. His contributions to this collection are indicative of a wide ranging intellect. In this story, a version of which has already appeared in some SF circles, he ponders what future marketplaces will be like, how fast they will move, and where communications may literally take us.

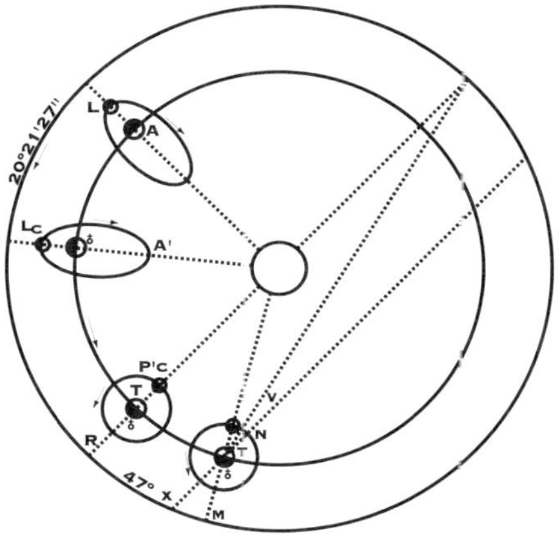

ZOOMERS

Gregory Benford

She climbed into her yawning work pod, coffee barely getting her going. A warning light winked: her Foe was already up and running. Another day at the orifice.

The pod wrapped itself around her as tabs and inserts slid into place. This was the latest gear, a top of the line simulation suit immersed in a data-pod of beguiling comfort.

Snug. Not anyway to lounge, but to *fly*.

She closed her eyes and let the sim-suit do its stuff.

May 16, 2046. She liked to start in real-space. Less jarring.

Images played directly upon her retina. The entrance protocol lifted her out of her Huntington Beach apartment and in a second she was zooming over rooftops, skating down the beach. Combers broke in soft white bands and red-suited surfers caught them in passing marriage.

All piped down from a satellite view, of course, sharp and clear.

Get to work, Myung, her Foe called. *Sightsee later*.

"I'm running a deep search," she lied.

Sure.

"I'll spot you a hundred creds on the action," she shot back.

You're on. Big new market opening today. A hint of mockery?

“Where?” Today she was going to nail him, by God.

Right under our noses, the way I sniff it.

“In the county?”

Now, that would be telling.

Which meant he didn’t know.

So: a hunt. Better than a day of shaving margins, at least.

She and her Foe were zoomers, ferrets who made markets more efficient. Evolved far beyond the primativo commodity traders of the late TwenCen, they moved fast, high-flying for competitive edge.

They zoomed through spaces wholly insubstantial, but that was irrelevant. Economic pattern-spaces were as tricky as mountain crevasses. And even hard cash just stood for an idea.

Most people still dug coal and grew crops, ancient style grunt labour (but in Orange County you could easily forget that, gripped by the fever of the new).

Below her, the county was a sprawl, but a smart one. The wall-to-mall fungus left over from the TwenCen days was gone. High-rises rose from lush parks. Some even had orange grove skirts, a chic nostalgia. Roofs were eco-virtue white. Blacktop streets had long ago added a sandy-coloured coating whose mica sprinkles winked up at her. Even cars were in light shades. All this to reflect the sunlight, public advertisements that everybody was doing something about global warming.

The car-rivers thronged streets and freeways (still *free* — if you could get the license). When parked, cars were tucked underground. Still plenty of scurry-scurry, but most of it mental, not metal.

She sensed the county’s incessant pulse, the throb of the Pacific Basin’s hub, pivot point of the largest zonal economy on the planet.

Felt, not *saw*. Her chest was a map. Laguna Beach over her right nipple, Irvine over the left. Using neural plasticity, the primary sensory areas of her cortex “read” the county’s electronic Mesh through her skin.

But this was not like antique serial reading at all. No flat data here. No screens.

She relaxed. The trick was to *merge*, not just observe.

Far better for a chimpanzee-like species to take in the world through its evolved, body-wrapping neural bed.

More fun, too. She detected economic indicators on her augmented skin. A tiny shooting pain spoke of a leverage buyout. Was that uneasy sensation natural to her, or a hint from her subsystems about a possible lowering of the prime rate?

Gotcha! the Foe sent.

Myung glanced at her running index. She was eleven hundred creds down!

So fast? How could —?

Then she felt it: dancing data-spikes in alarm red, prickly on her left leg. The Foe had captured an early indicator. Which?

Myung had been coasting towards the Anaheim hills, watching the pulse of business trading quicken as slanting sunshine smartly profiled the fashionable, post-pyramidal corporate buildings. So she had missed the opening salvo of weather data update, the first trading opportunity.

The Foe already had an edge and was shifting investments. How?

Ahead of her in the simulated air she could see the Foe skating to the south. All this visual metaphor, of course, symbology for the directed attention of the data-eating programs.

A stain came spreading from the east into Mission Viejo. Not real weather, but economic variables.

Deals flickered beneath the data-thunderheads like sheet lightening. Pixels of packet-information fell as soft rains on her long-term investments.

The Foe was buying extra electrical power from Oxnard. Selling it to users to offset the low yields seeping up from San Diego.

Small stuff. A screen for something subtle. Myung close-upped the digital stream and glimpsed the deeper details.

Every day more water flowed in the air over southern California than streamed down the Mississippi. Rainfall projections changed driving conditions, affected tournament golf scores, altered yields of solar power, fed into agri-prod.

Down her back slid prickly-fresh commodity info, and itch she should scratch. A hint from her sniffer-programs? She willed a virtual finger to rub the tingling.

— and snapped back into real-space.

An ivory mist over Long Beach. Real, purpling water thunderclouds scooting into San Juan Cap from the south.

Ah — virtual sports. The older the population got, the more leery of weather. They still wanted the zing of adventure, though. Through virtual feedback, creaky bodies could air-surf from twenty kilometres above the Grand Canyon. Or race alongside the few protected Great White sharks in the Catalina Preserve.

High-resolution Virtuality stimulated lacy filigrees of electro-chem impulses throughout the cerebral cortex. Did it matter whether the induction came from the real thing or from the slippery arts of electronics?

Time for a bit of business.

Her prognosticator programs told her that with 0.87 probability, such oldies would cocoon-up across six states. So indoor virtual sports use, with electro-stim to zing the ageing muscles, would rise in the next day.

She swiftly exercised options on five virtual sites, pouring in some of her reserve computational capacity. But the Foe had already harvested the plums there. Not much margin left.

Myung killed her simulated velocity and saw the layers of deals the Foe was making, counting on the coming storm to shift the odds by fractions. Enough contracts-of-the-moment processed, and profits added up. But you had to call the slant just right.

Trouble-sniffing subroutines pressed their electronic doubts upon her: a warning chill breeze across her brow. She waved it away.

Myung dove into the clouds of event-space. Her skin did the deals for here, working with software that verged on mammal-level intelligence itself. She wore her suits of artificial-intelligence ... and in a real sense, they wore her.

She felt her creds — not credits so much as *credibilities*, the operant currency in data-space — washing like hot air currents over her body.

Losses were chilling. She got cold feet, quite literally, when the San Onofre nuke piped up with a gush of clean power. A new substation, coming on much earlier than SoCalEd had estimated.

That endangered her energy portfolio. A quick flick got her out of the electrical futures market altogether, before the world-wide Mesh caught on to the implications.

Up, away. Let the Foe pick up the last few percentage points. Myung flapped across the digital sky, capital taking wing.

She lofted to a ten-mile-high perspective. Global warming had already made the county's south-facing slopes into cactus and tough grasslands. Coastal sage still clung to the north-facing slopes, seeking cooler climes. All the coast was becoming a 'fog desert' sustained by vapour from lukewarm ocean currents. Dikes held back the rising warm ocean from Newport to Long Beach.

Pretty, but no commodity possibilities there any more.

Time to take the larger view.

She rose. Her tactile and visual maps expanded. She went to split-skin perception, with the real, matter-based landscape overlaid on the infoscape. Surreal, but heady.

From below she burst into the data-sphere of Invest-tainment, where people played upon the world's weather like a casino. Ever since rising global temperatures pumped more energy in, violent oscillations had grown.

Weather was now the hidden, wild-card lubricant of the world's economy. Tornado warnings were sent to street addresses, damage predictions shaded by the city block. Each neighbourhood got its own rain forecast.

A sparrow's fall in Portugal could diddle the global fluid system so that, in principle, a thunderhead system would form over Fountain Valley a week later. Today, merging pressures form the south sent forking lightening over mid-California. That shut down the launch site of all local rocket-planes to the Orbital Hiltons. Hundreds of invest-programs had that already covered.

So she looked on a still larger scale. Up, again.

This grand world mesh was *N*-dimensional. And even the number *N* changed with time, as parameters shifted in and out of application.

There was only one way to make sense of this in the narrow human sensorium. Every second, a fresh dimension sheared in over an older dimension. Freeze-framed, each instant looked like a ridiculously complicated abstract sculpture running on drug-driven overdrive. Watch any one moment too hard and you got a lancing headache, motion sickness and zero comprehension.

Augmented feedback, so useful in keeping on the financial edge, could also be an unforgiving bitch.

The Foe wasn't up here, hovering over the whole continent. Good. Time to think. She watched the *N*-space as if it were an entertainment, and in time came an extended perception, integrated by the long-suffering subconscious.

She bestrode the world. Total immersion.

She stamped and marched across the muddy field of chaotic economic interactions. Her boot heels left deep scars. These healed immediately: subprograms at work, like cellular repair. She would pay a passage price for venturing here.

A landscape opened like the welcome of a mother's lap.

Her fractal tentacles spread through the networks with blinding speed, penetrating the planetary spider web. Orange County was a brooding, swollen orb at the PacBasin's centre.

Smelled it yet? came the Foe's taunt from below.

"I'm following some ticklers," she lied.

I'm way ahead of you.

"Then how come you're gabbing? And tracking me?"

Friendly competition —

"Forget the friendly part." She was irked. Not by the Foe, but by failure. She needed something *hot.* Where?

'Fess up, you're smelling nothing.

"Just the stink of overdone expectations," she shot back wryly.

Nothing promising in the swirling weather-space, working with prickly light below her. Seen this way, the planet's thirteen billion lives were like a field of grass waving beneath fitful gusts they could barely glimpse.

Wrong blind alley! sent her Foe maliciously.

Myung shot a glance at her indices. Down nineteen hundred!

And she had spotted him a hundred. *Damn.*

She shifted through parameter-spaces. There — like a carnival, neon-bright on the horizon of a black, cool desert: the colossal market-space of Culture.

She strode across the tortured seethe of global Mesh data.

In the archaic economy of manufacturing, middle managers were long gone. No more 'just in time' manufacturing in blocky factories. No more one-size-fits-all. That had fallen to 'right on time' production out of tiny shops, prefabs, even garages.

Anybody who could make a gizmo cheaper could send you a bid. They would make your very own custom gizmo, by direct Mesh order.

Around the globe, robotic prod-lines of canny intelligence stood ready in ill-lit shacks. Savvy software leaped into action at your Meshed demand, reconfiguring for your order like an obliging whore. Friction-free service. The mercantile millennium.

Seen from up here, friction-free marketism seemed the world's only workable ideology — unless you counted New Islam, but who did? Under it, middle managers had decades ago vanished down the sucking drain of evolving necessity. 'Production' got shortened to prod — and prodded the market.

Of course the people shed by frictionless prod ended up with dynamic, fulfilling careers in dog-washing: valets, luxury servants, touchy-feely insulators for the harried prod-folk. And their bosses.

But not all was manufacturing. Even dog-dressers needed Cultural Prod. *Especially* dog-dressers.

"My sniffers are getting it," she said.

The Foe answered, *You're on the scent — but late.*

Something new....

She walked through the data-vaults of the Culture City. As a glittering representation of unimaginable complexities, it loomed: Global, intricate, impossible to know fully for even a passing instant. And thus, an infinite resource.

She stamped through street busy with commerce. Ferrets and deal-making programs scampered like rodents under heal. Towers of the giga-conglomerates raked the skies.

None of this Big Guy stuff for her. Not today, thanks.

To beat her Foe, she needed something born of Orange County, something to put on the table.

And only her sniffer-programs could find it for her. The web of connections in even a single county was so criss-crossed that no mere human could find her way.

She snapped back into the real world. *Think.*

Lunch eased into her bloodstream, fed by the pod when it sensed her lowering blood sugar. Myung tapped for an extra Kaff to give her some zip. Her medical worrier hovered in the air before her, clucked and frowned. She ignored it.

— And back to Culture City.

Glassy ramparts led up into the citadels of the mega-Corps. Showers of speculation rained on their flanks. Rivulets gurgled off into gutters. Nothing new here, just the ceaseless hum of a market full of energy and no place to go.

Index check: sixteen hundred down!

The deals she had left running from the morning were pumping out the last of their dividends. No more help there.

Time's a-wastin', her Foe said nastily. She could imagine his sneer and sardonic eyes.

Save your creds for the crunch, she retorted.

You're down thirteen hundred and falling.

He was right. The trouble with paired competition — the very latest market-stimulating twist — was that the outcome was starkly clear. No comforting self-delusions lasted long.

Irked, she leaped high and flew above the City. Go local, then. Orange County was the PacBasin's best fount of fresh ideas.

She caught vectors from the county drawing her down. Prickly hints sheeted across her belly, over her forearms. To the east — there — a shimmer of possibility.

Her ferrets were her own, of course — searcher programs tuned to her style, her way of perceiving quality and content. They *were* her, in a truncated sense.

Now they led her down a funnel, into —

A mall.

In real-space, no less. Tacky.

Hopelessly antique, of course. Dilapidated buildings leaning against each other, laid out in boring rectangular grids. Faded plastic and rusty chrome.

People still went there, of course; somewhere, she was sure, people still used wooden plows.

This must be in Kansas, or the Siberian Free State or somewhere equally Out Of It. Why in the world had her sniffers taken her here?

She checked real-world location, preparing to lift out.

East Anaheim? Impossible!

But no — there was something here. Her sniffer popped up an overlay and the soles of her feet itched with anticipation. Programs zoomed her in on a grey shambles that dominated the end of the cracked blacktop parking lot.

Was this a museum? No, but —

Art Attack came the signifier.

That sign... "An old K-Mart," she murmured. She barely remembered being in one as a girl. Rigid, old-style aisles of plastic prod. Positively *cubic*, as the teeners said. A cube, after all, was an infinite number of stacked squares.

But this K-Mart had been reshaped. Stucco-sculpted into an archly ironic lavender mosque, festooned with bright brand name items.

It hit her. "Of course!"

She zoomed up, above the Orange County jumble.

Here it was — pay dirt. And she was on the ground *first.*

She popped her pod and sucked in the dry, flavourful air. Back in Huntington Beach. Her throat was dry, the aftermath of tension.

And just 16:47, too. Plenty of time for a swim.

The team that had done the mock-mosque K-Mart were like all artists: sophisticated along one axis, dunderheads along all economic vectors. They had thought it was a pure lark to fashion ancient relics of paleocapitalism into bizarre abstract expressionist 'statements.' Mere fun effusions, they thought.

She loved working with people who were, deep in their souls, innocent of markets.

Within two hours she had locked up the idea and labelled it: 'Post-Consumerism Dada from the fabled Age of Appetite.'

She had marketed it through pre-view around the globe. Thailand and the Siberians (the last true culture virgins) had gobbled up the idea. Every rotting 'burb round the globe had plenty of derelict K-Marts; this gave them a new angle.

Then she auctioned the idea in the Mesh. Cut in the artists for their majority interest. Sold shares. Franchised it in the Cutting Concept sub-Mesh. Divided shares twice, declared a dividend.

All in less time than it took to drive from Garden Grove to San Clemente.

"How'd you find that?" her Foe asked, climbing out of his pod.

"My sniffers are *good*, I told you."

He scowled. "And how'd you get there so fast?"

"You've got to take the larger view," she said mysteriously.

He grimaced. "You're up two thousand five creds."

"Lucky I didn't really trounce you."

"Culture City sure ate it up, too."

"Speaking of which, how about starting a steak? I'm starving."

He kissed her. This was perhaps the best part of the Foe-Team method. They spurred each other on, but didn't cut each other dead in the marketplace. No matter how appealing that seemed, sometimes.

Being married helped keep their rivalry on reasonable terms. Theirs was a standard five-year monogamous contract, already nearly half over. How could she not renew, with such a deliciously stimulating opponent?

Sure, dog-eat-dog markets sometimes worked better, but who wanted to dine on dog?

"We'll split the chores," he said.

"We need a servant."

He laughed. "Think we're rich? We just grease the gears of the great machine."

"Such a poet you are."

"And there are still the dishes to do from last night."

"Ugh. I'll race you to the beach first."

The Twilight of Sovereignty, A Switch, and a Bus Without Brakes

Bruce Sterling

Bruce Sterling is an internationally recognised commentator on the information society and its implications. He is also a world famous SF author, called by critics 'one of the most globally minded of North American writers' and his perspectives are considered sharp and relevant. He has written amongst other works, *Islands in the Net*, *Schismatrix*, *The Difference Engine* (with William Gibson), and short story collections such as *Globalhead*. His non-fiction work includes *The Hacker Crackdown: Law and Order on the Electronic Frontier.*

The Twilight of Sovereignty, a Switch, and a Bus Without Brakes

Bruce Sterling

Current trends in communications are leading toward a head-on collision between global networking and national governmental authority. At the moment a 'twilight of sovereignty' scenario looks plausible; the situation definitely does not favour governments. Scarcely anyone controls scarcely anything. Given current political instability worldwide it's going to be easier to make governments look like computer networks than it is to make the computer revolution the hand maiden of traditional governments. I make no judgement as to whether this is good or bad. *After the Revolution, things will be different — not better, just different.*

What of regulation? The role of regulators is to bust trusts and attack cartels. Regulators based in national or state authority are not going to be able to control computer networking in the way that they manage telegraphy or telephony. Global computer networking requires a global regulatory body. I don't know how such a body is going to be able to constitute itself.

It's possible the democratising influence of the Internet and related technologies has been overplayed at least for the time being. The massive have/have not discrepancies in access to computation are real enough, but they're rather less massive than the conventional time-honoured discrepancies in food, transportation, healthcare, shelter, clothing, money and sex. Even with 98% socially guaranteed literacy in some countries, some people can use language effectively and others can't; some read and some don't; some belong to the chattering classes and some are sunk in blissful obscurity. There are massive have/have not discrepancies in the use of language *per se*. I believe that a similar dynamic applies to so-called computer literacy. Giving everybody a free computer and modem wouldn't change this basal reality very much.

Nevertheless, I think we should be changing the way we think about things. I think the best paradigm for Internet, for example, is to forget that it's a technology and pretend that it's a language. Private computer networks such as Prodigy and CompuServe are obviously business enterprises of a relatively conventional sort, but Internet behaves more like the English language than like a technology. I still like 'cyberspace' (as a concept) but increasingly I think of it as a lumpy, balky, swirling cyberspace rather than some kind of smooth, conceptual, galactic vacuum. With every day that passes the notion because less ideal and more real; less dreamy and absolute, and more like something you can bark your knuckles on. But choosing the correct strategy to cope in and with a connected world is not a trivial decision. I would say nobody has it right. It's probably not gonna be 'right' for another century or so. It may 'never' be right. Is paper publishing 'right'? And paper publishing is centuries old.

Pessimistic? Yes, by the standards of a lot of people, but by my own standards I'm actually far more optimistic in the 1990s than I was in, say, the 1970s. Actually, ever since 1989 I've gotten up every morning to confront some fantastic circus. Really, I can scarcely believe what I'm seeing nowadays. There's something primally exhilarating about being in a bus without brakes.

If this sounds like a frontier mentality is needed, it probably is. After all, a frontier mentality is pretty much a prerequisite if you plan to dwell in a frontier. A willingness to endure hardship and a high casualty rate are also de rigeur. Survive the terrible existential freedoms of the frontier and the worldwide network of the future will take care of itself. The electronic frontier is littered with the burnt-out hulks of venturesome corporate monoliths. I used to be really impressed by multinational capitalist entities until I saw them fire all their mid-level employees. Now they can't command any real human loyalty, and therefore they are hard to take seriously.

In technology terms, basically computers are going to become our televisions. They will be really big, cheap screens as flat as pancakes, and they're going to run digital imagery, plus interlaced NTSC, PAL, SECAM, Cinerama, SuperPanavision, Cinemascope plus video record and playback, all at the same time, probably in a series of windows.

It won't be fancy interactive television w th a lot of button-pushing. It's gonna be the *I Love Lucy Show* and *Dallas* but grabbed faster, and if you pay enough you'll be allowed to fast-forward through the really unbearably stupid parts.

If I were running a telco I would get into cellular. If I were running a cable TV company, I'd resign. If they refused to let me resign then I would try to engineer a take-over of my company by Steve Case of America Online. The phone companies that survive will become cellular phone companies. Anyone, Anywhere, Anytime is a good motto for a twenty-first century phone company. The poleclimbers and glasslayers will be a competitive service industry. They will attach a wire to your home or office at a flat rate and they will have basically no idea what's going through those wires. There will be flat rates for so-called 'long-distance.' Any nation or PTT which tries to cling to current long-distance telephony billing practices will see their economy destroyed by others with more enlightened policies. The phone companies are magnificent entities in many ways, but they have a vested interest in the ignorance of their consumer base. This was survivable in a conventional industrial society in which the customers were poorly educated and had no other choice. It's a fatal error in a post-industrial information society. There are people around in younger and faster-paced industries who 'know' that their customers aren't stupid and who are making it their business to cater to the demands of the new knowledge class.

Nicholas Negroponte has said that everything that comes over wires now will go over the airwaves, and everything that used to go out over the airwaves will go out over wires. I like this idea a lot and I think it's accurate. Better than that, it's pretty.

I recently came up with a notion of my own that another guy later called the 'Sterling Switch.' It goes like this. Once upon a time people lived in the real world. When they logged on to their network in cyberspace it was something very far away and very vaporous and very virtual and unreal. Nowadays people travel all the time with laptops and modems under their arms, and a lot of the time they don't know where the heck they are, but when they read their e-mail, hey, their e-mail is 'always in the same place!' They may not have seen their home address in months, but their electronic address is as solid as Gibraltar. The Sterling Switch is that creepy feeling you get at the airport hotel when you log on to cyberspace and you realise that cyberspace is a lot more 'there' than you are. Physically, you are very much here today and gone tomorrow, while cyberspace has become the anchor of your career and the linchpin of your reality.

In fifteen years, that will be a very common sentiment, so common that it will no longer seem odd or even remarkable. In fifteen years a lot of businesses will be firmly based in network economics. They will be running over networks and eventually the networks will warp these businesses into their own shape. This isn't too hard to predict, because you can see the seeds of it already. Distributed cores, where all kinds of stuff gets subcontracted all over the planet, including, administration, bookkeeping and personnel. Very fast, real time, adaptive technologies with lightning fast connections between shippers and cash registers and manufacturers. Computer-aided design of practically everything, on modular equipment with no standing inventories. Mass production becoming individual production, at practically the same price. Alliances, partnerships, collaborations, where the edges of companies blur so much that you couldn't have lifetime employment even if you knew what that meant. Digital money, probably with a new multinational currency. It sounds amazing from here, but when we're in the thick of it, it's not going to be amazing, it's just going to be life. We'll know that the situation has normalised when science fiction writers stop talking about it.

Exploding, Like Fireworks

Pat Murphy

Pat Murphy has won Nebula, Philip K Dick and Theodore Sturgeon awards for her writing, which she combines with work as Director of Publications for the Exploratorium, an interactive museum in San Francisco. Her work has ranged widely in SF across many subjects from the possibility of super-intelligent chimpanzees (*Rachel in Love*), to contact with the Maya civilisation of the past (*The Falling Woman*), and to a future San Francisco where art is used to redefine civilisation and reality (*The City, Not Long After*). In this short story, notionally about an astronaut in some future space station, communications enable unexpected empowerment, literally to the edges of the galaxy.

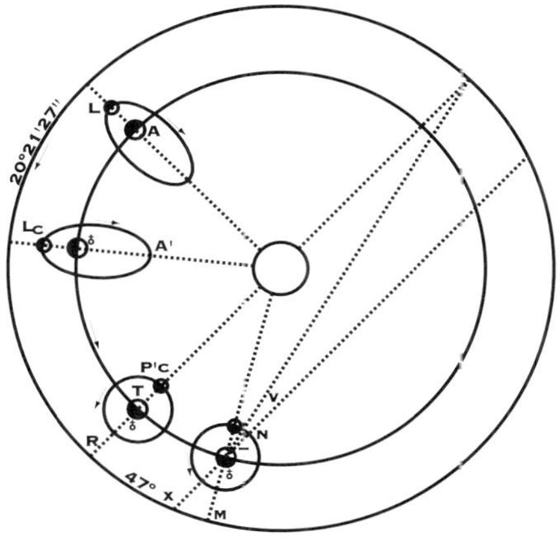

Exploding, Like Fireworks

Pat Murphy

Shadows on the hull —
long shadows, getting longer.
Night is coming fast.

I never saw what hit me.

I was a young woman of 20, visiting Moon Talk, the space station for engineers and poets, when my life changed. I was out on the station's hull with a couple of friends. I had wanted a chance to see the earth with as little between me and it as possible. Sure, I could look at it on the monitors, but that didn't seem real. I might as well be earthside, watching it on TV. So I'd convinced Chaz and Joan to go for a stroll on the hull.

We were strolling near a construction area, where remotely controlled units were attaching a dish receiver to the hull. Chaz and Joan were flirting with each other — amusing for them, but not so great as a spectator sport — so I turned off my radio. In my suit, I could hear only the sounds of my own body: the rhythmic pounding of my heart, the hiss of my breath, the distant scraping of my magnetised boots on the metallic hull, constructed of steel mined from an asteroid.

The earth was a crescent in the sky above me — a thin slice of the globe was illuminated by sunlight, the rest was in deep shadow. On the brightly lit crescent, I could just make out a few details through the clouds: the curve of the Chinese coast, the islands of Japan where I'd be going in just a few months. In the darkened portion of the globe, I could see flashes of brilliant white light shining through clouds — lightning storms over Asia.

I was staring up at the earth when I caught a movement out of the corner of my eye: a white shape, moving fast. I started to turn toward it. Too slow.

I didn't see the dish tumbling toward me. Someone — I never asked who — had released the grip of the robot manipulator too soon and then, moving quickly to try to recover from the error, had slammed the pincers into the dish, sending it flying out of control. The safety line had already been removed: in a hurry to finish the job, someone had acted too soon.

The dish caught me just above my left shoulder, striking at neck level and continuing with inexorable momentum to smash me against the hull. The space suit held: it was not ruptured by the impact and its boots still clung firmly to the hull. But my body — soft and malleable flesh — twisted and snapped within the protective suit.

I had been on the night side of the station, shielded from the direct rays of the sun. I didn't really see shadows getting longer, but the metaphor works.

+++++

I woke from a dream, disoriented and confused. In my dream, I had been watching the earth in the sky, listening to the beating of my own heart. With each heartbeat, the earth had gotten smaller and smaller, receding in the distance, rushing away from me. I remember being terrified — I was so far away from earth and getting farther. How would I ever get back?

I opened my eyes and blinked, trying to make sense of what I saw. I thought to rub my eyes, but I couldn't seem to find my hands. What I saw was a white ceiling, a mirror set at an angle to reflect my face and my body.

I didn't look good. I was tethered in a hammock, floating weightless at the centre of the station. Wires taped to my temples, a tube in my nose, both eyes blackened, bruises on my face, my arm wired with an IV pump, my chest sheathed in a metal casing. At the edge of the mirror, I could see the reflections of more tubes and wires, could see a moving blip on a screen. The moving blip made a regular beeping sound, in time with my heartbeat. I tried to turn my head to take a better look, but I couldn't move. I could hear the hum of machines and a rhythmic, raspy sound, like the heavy breathing of someone with a bad cold. My head ached, but they must have anaesthetised my arm, because I couldn't feel the IV pump.

A face floated into view over me. White coat; hair pulled back and tied, to keep it from floating free in zero-g. A doctor.

"Angel," she said softly. "How do you feel?"

I opened my mouth to speak and my lips shaped words, but there was no sound. Then air rushed through my lips and I made a garbled sound.

"You're on a respirator," the doctor said. "You can speak but wait for your breath to come."

I waited while the machine inhaled for me, then exhaled. How did I feel? My head hurt but the rest of my body didn't. I couldn't fee the rest of my body. There was no pain from the IV pump in my arm, no pain from bruises, no sensation of stiffness from lying still, no sense of where my body was in the bed. There was no body.

"I can't feel," I managed.

"Your spine is broken. You're lucky to be alive."

Lucky. I was lucky. My spine had snapped in so many places that no surgeon would ever attempt to put the puzzle back together. On earth, under the relentless pull of gravity, I would have died quickly. Free fall was more forgiving. I survived, paralysed from the neck down. I couldn't go back earthside. I was lucky.

I did not feel lucky. I did not want to be here.

+++++

The math of poets,
the poetry of engineers.
What does it matter?

"Here" was Moon Talk station. Founded in 2005 by the Massachusetts Institute of Technology's Society of Poets and Engineers, its name came from something the eminently quotable Mark Twain had once written: *War talk by men who have been in a war is always interesting; whereas moon talk by a poet who has not been in the moon is likely to be dull.*

You might think that a commercially successful corporate space colony would have been the product of a visionary engineer or perhaps a visionary engineering team. You would be wrong. You see, that had been the problem with space exploration all along. The engineers had been in charge. The man who founded Moon Talk was visionary MBA with undergraduate degrees in anthropology, literature, and physics, a book of poetry published by a small press, a sound knowledge of engineering and economics, and a facility for manipulating numbers.

What had made the colony possible was not a technological breakthrough, but rather a sound business plan. The purpose of the colony was to build a community and make a profit. The two goals were linked, complimentary. It had been in the planning stages for decades, a design project that engineers loved. But it took an economist to work out the details.

What did a space colony need to survive? A substantial income from a variety of sources. Moon Talk's primary source of income was related to communications and remote sensing satellites — talking moons, folks on the station called them. The colony specialised in the prototyping and manufacture of satellite components and subsystems, testing the components in orbit quickly and cheaply, then manufacturing, launching, and maintaining the satellites.

The manufacture of the station itself had involved changing the orbit of and mining materials from several near-Earth asteroids. That mining continued, and the business plan called for prospecting among the other near-Earth asteroids for rocks rich in platinum and other siderophile minerals. Since diversification is an important part of any business plan, the colony also offered research facilities for earthside labs, sports programmes (Space Ball and a few other zero-g sports that had become popular spectator events earthside) and tourist packages (making use of the suite of rooms set aside for visiting engineers and designers).

So where did the poets come in? Well, who is dedicated to accurate sensing and communication of high density information in short bursts? Poets, of course. And who can create the hardware necessary to accomplish that from orbit, a position that poets had, in the past, rarely found themselves? Engineers. A perfect match, according to the logic of the colony's somewhat eccentric founder.

So amongst the engineers were several poets in residence, who offered classes for tourists and staff and ran a small press that regularly published chapbooks on the Net.

The result was a community of some 500 people, operating around the clock in a world of their own making. An MIT graduate, I had come to the colony on a six-month engineering/poetry internship. I had been, up to the moment that my spine snapped, an overachiever. My background included a year of graduate work in a Japanese robotics lab paired with a one-year apprenticeship with a Japanese poet.

When the accident happened, I was 3 months into my time at the colony, and I had already decided that life there was too confining. I had planned to return to earth; I had planned to take a position on a robotics project in Japan. I hadn't planned to spend the rest of my life floating in weightlessness in the station's infirmary.

+++++

Frozen on the slab,
Dead meat, preserved by doctors.
Useless. Why bother?

I had always liked my body. Liked it for the precision with which it worked: this tendon pulling on this muscle, this muscle on that bone. Lying in the infirmary bed, I watched my body in the mirror and thought about moving my right hand. Clenching my fist. Or moving a finger.

Nothing. My body — still trim and muscular — remained motionless, so much dead meat. On the screen beside me, my heartbeat registered — a line marked with regular peaks and valleys. I could hear the respirator forcing air into my lungs, a steady rhythm.

I tried to move my hand and nothing moved. I got angry — I could feel the tension increase in the muscles of my face — but those steady rhythms of heartbeat and breath did not change. Dead meat, preserved by science. Useless.

After the accident, friends came to visit me in the infirmary. Chaz came every day for the first week. We had been sleeping together, on and off for the past month, before he started flirting with Joan. He sat beside me and held my unresponsive hand. He was a sweet young man and we had had a lovely time experimenting with sex in zero-g, but after the first hour he didn't know what to say. Joan came to visit and didn't know what to say. None of my visitors seemed to know what to say. They filled the small cabin with forced conversation and awkward silences. They were still young. They were building the future. I was a physical manifestation of the danger they all faced and I think I made them nervous.

Visitors came and they went, expressing their sympathy. After a time, I stopped answering when they asked if there was anything they could do. The only thing I wanted was to have my body back, and no one could do that for me. So there wasn't any point in talking.

A week after the accident, I woke up and discovered that Kamishiwa, the oldest of the poets in residence, had come to visit. He was a small man in his late 50s. He wore old-fashioned eyeglasses, though he certainly could have had his vision surgically corrected or, at the very least, been fitted with corrective contacts. I had asked him about his glasses during one of his poetry seminars and he said he liked the way that the lenses collected dust and grime. Periodically, he had to clean them, and that reminded him of the limitations of perception. "We are always seeing the world through filters," he said. "But it's easy to forget that. These..." he tapped his gold-framed glasses, "...remind me."

Kamishiwa raised his eyebrows when he saw that my eyes were open. "Good morning," he said. He lifted a hand and pushed his glasses more firmly onto his nose, a habitual gesture that caught my eye. For the past week, I had found myself staring at my visitors' hands. Gesturing as they spoke. Moving so easily to touch the world. Effortlessly. I envied those hands, that movement.

"I am curious," he was saying. "What do you plan to do now?"

What did I plan to do? I had no plans. No one else had been cruel enough to ask such a question. I stared at him. "What can I do? What's left? I can't go home."

"Then you will stay here?" Again, he pushed back his glasses and my eyes were drawn to the movement.

"I'll stay here. And do nothing."

"Write poetry," he suggested mildly.

"About what?" I stared into the mirror at the reflected medical equipment. "About an IV pump and the world on-line." I had full access to the Net, but I was already tired of reading words on the screen, empty words, nothing I could touch. My eyes followed Kamishiwa's hands.

"What are you watching?" he asked.

"Your hands."

"Why?" His voice was calm, matter-of-fact. He shared quarters with Bina Rochlin, head of the robotics division. There were those on the colony who joked that Kamishiwa was one of Bina's constructions, by way of explanation for his perpetually calm manner.

"Because I don't have any hands anymore," I snapped.

"Why's that a problem?" Again, that calm tone.

He was an idiot. He was a sadist. "Because I can't think right without hands," I said. "Because I can't get a hold of anything."

"Ah, that's right," he said, his voice thoughtful. "I remember watching you in the seminars. You were always drawing, manipulating something. Never sitting still. A tactile thinker. You thought with your hands."

"I want my body." My voice was harsh, angry. "I want to have hands again. That's why I'm watching, you idiot, you old fool. Because it hurts and there's nothing I can do about it."

He nodded thoughtfully, as if I hadn't just insulted him, as if I had said something perfectly sensible. "Let me see what Bina can do," he said.

+++++

Bina was a small, intense woman with dark brown eyes and frizzy brown hair, cropped close to her scalp. I had not worked directly with her, but rather with one of her assistants. According to him, she tended to treat everything as if it were an engineering problem. My situation was no exception.

"We can start by hooking you to a remote manipulator," she said. Remotely controlled robots had helped build the station and a great deal of the satellite maintenance work and work on the hull was done with remote manipulators, jacked into an operator's nervous system. "Easy enough with SQUIDs." A helmet equipped with SQUIDs — short for Superconducting Quantum Interference Detectors — could pick the electrical signals in my brain and translate them to electrical signals that could control a remote manipulator. "But Kamishiwa says you need something for inside the station, too." She sounded so casual about it — like she was talking about a dress I might wear. "We'll have to put something together. It won't be human, but in some ways it could be more versatile. I'll work on that."

So Bina jacked me into one of the mobile units used for maintenance on the hull, and Luce, one of the colony's telepresence operators, taught me the basics of being telepresent-present at a distance.

"First, look around," she said.

Closing my eyes, a direct feed to my optic nerve provided a view through the mobile unit's cameras-a pixelated, black-and-white image of the hull. It took an effort to make sense of the scene. A receiving dish in the foreground, a forest of antennae farther away, dark shadows in the earth light. At first, the shadows seemed as solid as the objects. Luce, watching the same view on a monitor and talking quickly, helped me sort out the pieces. "There's the main dish and to the right, in the shadow, is the auxiliary. Got that?" I got it.

I learned to move the mobile unit's manipulator claws, which were jacked into some of the nerves that had once controlled my hands. I learned to move around the hull, stepping carefully at first, and then with more confidence. "You don't even have the problem of muscle fatigue," Luce said with a trace of envy in her voice. "Since you're not controlling any muscles — just the mobile unit."

"Well, isn't that nice for me," I said sarcastically.

"You know, you don't have to close your eyes," Luce said, with a hint of impatience in her voice. "Keep 'em open. You can see this room and the view through the monitor. Just shift your focus."

I opened my eyes and felt a wave of vertigo as the view from the mobile unit clashed with my own vision. I closed my eyes to shut out the confusion. "I can't."

"Sure you can. Haven't you ever read a book and listened to music at the same time?"

"That's different."

"You can read a book and listen to music and tap your foot while munching on a sandwich. And if, while all that was going on, you smell smoke, you stop reading and look for the fire. Parallel processing. You could do all that at once and you can't manage this?" Impatience, definitely, and maybe a little contempt. "You've got neurons to spare."

I opened my eyes again, fighting the dizziness and trying to follow Luce's orders and focus my attention on the view from the mobile unit.

"Your brain will adapt," she said casually. "This is really basic stuff. Did you ever read about the psychologist who made himself some eyeglasses that flipped his view of the world upside down. He wore 'em for a week and at first he was confused and disoriented, falling over stuff, feeling sick. Then he got better. And after a couple of weeks, he had adapted and he could function just fine with the glasses on. 'Course, when he took 'em off, he had to adapt all over again, but he managed that too. Your brain will adapt."

She left me to practice and she was right. Eventually, I adapted. I could maintain the two views without disorientation, focusing on one or the other as I chose. Over the next few months, I began assisting with basic repairs on the hull, strolling around in the unit that the other operators started referring to as Angelbody.

It wasn't like having my hands back. It wasn't like having a body. No sense of touch beyond simple force sensors; no taste; no smell. But I could manipulate things, move from here to there. It was better than nothing.

+++++

Pixelated eyes
A new view of the station.
Going forward now.

The robotics lab, working under Bina's direction and with the corporation's blessing, tackled the problem of creating a radio-controlled mobile unit for use inside the station. Bina dubbed it Angelbody In, as opposed to the mobile hull unit, which then came to be known as Angelbody Out.

A year and a half after my accident, I entered Angelbody In. Maybe that's not the right way to describe what I did. After all, I didn't leave my old body. I extended consciousness and control into another mechanical form.

My new body resembled nothing so much as a very large, very agile cockroach. It was about a metre long. The carapace was constructed of burnished metal plates; the jointed legs were tipped in strong electromagnets. It could run equally well across the ceiling or across the floor or across any metal surface in the station.

It had two eyes set on mobile turrets that operated independently and a speaker set into its back, so that the mechanism could make sounds.

I extended my consciousness into Angelbody In. At the same time, I maintained my connection with Angelbody Out. And of course, I was still in my own body, the one of flesh and blood.

What was it like? A lot harder than adapting to Angelbody Out. That unit's sensory input was limited to basic visual input, force sensors, and the most primitive of proprioceptors to tell the operator the position of the robotic arms. Angelbody In provided me with much more — direct visual input, audio input, tactile and temperature sensation through sensors attached to the footpads, proprioceptors to tell me the position of each of the six legs and the two manipulator arms. The visual input was grainy black and white, but Angelbody In's hearing was more acute than my human hearing — I could adjust its sensitivity to pick up the sound of a heartbeat from several steps away. It had some primitive chemical senses: it could identify the aroma of food cooking and pick up the acrid scent of sweat.

"That's important," Kamishiwa had said. "You won't be able to read expressions as well, since your visual acuity is limited. So you're going to have to become aware of things that most people react to without ever being aware that they sense. You have to be able to smell nervous sweat, hear subtle shifts in people's tone."

It took getting used to. Imagine learning to walk again. No, that's too easy. Imagine that you know how to walk, but that all your nerve impulses have been redirected. When you try to move your foot, your fists clench. Imagine having to unlearn all the reflexes that are so deeply ingrained that you don't even know they are there. And then, once you have accomplished that, you have to learn new reflexes.

I learned. I adapted. For the first week, Angelbody stayed in the infirmary room where my flesh-and-blood body lay. The mechanism ran across the ceiling, under my control.

At first, I kept my eyes closed, tuned out awareness of my physical body and Angelbody Out, and focused my attention entirely on the sensations and requirements of Angelbody. But after two weeks, I could open my eyes and maintain consciousness of all three bodies, at various levels of attention.

Bina had incorporated subroutines into the central processing unit for Angelbody In. "You can start Angelbody walking and it'll keep going and alert you if it needs your help," she told me.

By the end of a month, Angelbody In was strolling along the corridors of the station while Angelbody Out was strolling on the hull and I was reading in my room. Parallel processing. The human brain is an amazingly adaptable organ.

My dreams changed, sometime during this period. I had, for the past year and a half, been dreaming of being in my body again. These dreams focused on physical sensations — lying in the sun on an earthside beach, making love, walking through a forest in the rain. With the creation of Angelbody In, I took on new dream forms. Sometimes I was in a human body and sometimes I ran on six legs, scuttling along the beach with the sun on my carapace. Angelbody In was designed to feel the warmth of the sun.

+++++

Warmth of sun on skin,
The wisdom of the body,
Peace of quiet mind.

During my waking hours, I could once again participate in the daily life of the station, rather than simply following it on-line. In Angelbody In, I began attending meetings in the robotics department. Bina included me in a project that she was just beginning — design of a set of robotic probes that would visit, one by one, the 274 known near-Earth asteroids, prospecting for rocks that contained platinum, the only mineral valuable enough to export to Earth, along with nickel and iron for continued manufacturing at the station. The mining technology had been worked out — the station had been built with metal mined from a near-Earth asteroid, nudged into Earth orbit with a gravity assist from the moon. The probes were an extension of that initial project.

The probes were designed as autonomous robots equipped with expert systems that could handle navigation problems and basic prospecting. The probes would be able to interface with telepresence operators when they encountered a situation that required creative judgement. Of course, telepresence operators could not continuously monitor the robots — that would have been excessively costly. At least, that was the popular wisdom in the design team.

I didn't agree with the popular wisdom. "You know," I said in a design meeting. "I could provide constant monitoring for a couple of the probes."

Angelbody In was hanging from the ceiling. Over the past few months

I'd adopted that location as the one where I was least likely to be tripped over.

Bina looked up from the computer screen, where she'd been reviewing design parameters with Chaz and Luce. "Could you handle that along with Angelbody In and Angelbody Out."

"Sure. No problem."

Chaz glanced up at me. Over the past few months, we had gotten to be good friends again. We could even flirt now and then in that strange way that you flirt over the Net — secure in the knowledge that nothing will ever come of this. "That seems like you'd be going in a lot of directions at the same time."

I would have shrugged if I could. One of the drawbacks to Angelbody In was the mechanism's inability to communicate with body language. "Hey, right now Angelbody Out is repairing a transmission antenna. And I'm here talking to you. Parallel processing. I've got neurons to spare."

Bina was still watching me. "You think you could handle two more bodies?"

"I'm sure I could."

"We'll do some tests," she said.

So over the next month we did some testing. Kamishiwa was there when Bina hooked me up to three remotes on the hull, in addition to Angelbody In and Angelbody Out. Relying on the remotes' subroutines, I was running all three simultaneously.

"What does it feel like?" Kamishiwa asked me.

I stared at him, startled by the question. "Well, you've been in your own body and a remote at the same time. What does that feel like?"

"Like being in two places at once," he said. "Like a division and an expansion. Like there's more of me."

I hesitated, thinking of my other bodies. Angelbody was heading toward the cafeteria — I had activated a subroutine that the body was following, though part of me was also monitoring its progress. One of the remotes was adjusting the antenna on a communications satellite, an activity that required a little of my attention, but not all of it. Another was heading toward the next job, a transmission dish that had a loose wire. Angelbody Out was following that remote, recording its activities for my later review. My flesh-and-blood body was there with Kamishiwa, talking about robotic probes. And all of these bodies were connected, connected through electrical signals just like the signals that told Kamishiwa's hand to push his glasses back on his nose, just like the signals that told his eyes to squint in a frown.

"That's not quite it," I said. "It's more like I'm just larger than I was. And part of me is over there and part of me is here."

"Is it confusing?"

"Not really. I got over that."

"Write a poem about it," he said. "Do that, will you?"

+++++

Fireworks exploding —
sparks fly in all directions.
Why not let them go?

So one of the probes was assigned to me and dubbed Angelbody Far. Angelbody In stood with the rest of the design team on the viewing deck and watched Angelbody Far depart the station, flying off into the darkness in the direction of Betulia, one of the Amor asteroids. Angelbody Out stood on the hull, watching the points of light recede. And from Angelbody Far , I looked outward toward the darkness and the specks of light, feeling myself growing larger.

On the anniversary of the birth of my flesh-and-blood body, the day that body turned 24, Angelbody Far reached the third of the asteroids that it was scheduled to sample. During the party in the recreation room, my attention was focused on Angelbody In, who hung from the ceiling while all of folks from Robotics sang *Happy Birthday to You*. It was a good party. Kamishiwa recited some of his latest haiku; some of the engineers started composing dirty limericks, improvising from the first line: "There was a young woman from Earth..." Everyone had a little too much to drink, which got a bit dull for me, since Angelbody In couldn't join them in that.

Toward the end of the party, I shifted my focus from Angelbody In to Angelbody Far, which was sampling the asteroid. I was dimly aware of the noise of the party winding down, people shouting their goodbyes.

It took a moment to adjust — to relax and accommodate the two-minute delay. For me, the sensation was one of slowing down, like swimming in molasses. I'd instigate an action and wait, relaxed and ready, for the mechanism to respond. It took some getting used to.

No visual monitoring for Angelbody Far, just then. Focusing on the chemical senses meant tuning out the visual sensors, which weren't terribly useful once Angelbody Far was on a rock. The probe's expert system had analysed the mix and found iron and nickel with traces of cobalt. Worth investigating further. Platinum, one of the few minerals valuable enough to export earthside, could be associated with that mix.

Following a standard subroutine, Angelbody Far had sent a pulse of sound waves through the rock, listening for the echoes that would provide information about variations in the asteroid's density. Some promising areas of high density. Just before I focused my attention on the probe, it had begun drilling toward one of those areas. Present in the robotic probe, I tasted the dust on the drill bit, my interpretation of the robot's chemical senses. The tang of iron, the salty acid taste of nickel.

"Angel?"

Kamishiwa's voice penetrated my concentration and for a moment I was disoriented, shifting my attention back to my flesh-and-blood body in the infirmary.

"Angel?"

I blinked, a blur of colours. It took a moment for me to make sense of the pattern of brightness and shadow. The metallic flavour of the asteroid faded. Kamishiwa and Bina were in the infirmary. Bina held a piece of birthday cake, wrapped in clear wrap so that the crumbs wouldn't float away.

"Angel," Kamishiwa said. "We thought you might want a taste of birthday cake."

Strange to realise that I hadn't even thought about the taste of the birthday cake, when I was in the recreation room as Angelbody In. I'd forgotten that my flesh-and-blood body could appreciate it. Lately, with so much activity related to my remotes, I didn't pay much attention to the meat. "It hadn't even occurred to me," I said slowly. "I guess that would be good."

"I noticed that you were distracted at the end of the party," Kamishiwa said.

"Angelbody Far is drilling," I said, feeling the tingling of the drill even as I said it. "I was monitoring that."

"Well, would you like a bite of cake?" Bina began unwrapping the cake, preparing to break off a piece for me.

As I looked at the cake, the flavour that came to mind was the rich, sweet taste of platinum. My attention returned to Angelbody Far. "Bina," I said urgently. "Bina, we've just hit a deposit of platinum. Looks like a big one."

+++++

Searching for platinum
Among the rocks in the sky
Joy when I find it.

Bina and I worked out the numbers and Angelbody Far gave the rock a nudge that swung it closer to the moon. The moon's gravity provided an assist that propelled the rock into an Earth orbit that closely matched that of the station. The precious metal was separated from the free nickel-iron using a relatively very simple thermochemical Carbonyl process.

It was a big deposit and a share of the profits were mine, a generous finder's fee. I was suddenly wealthy. Bina and Kamishiwa came to visit me in the infirmary and I talked with Bina about how I could spend the money. "I'd like to build another probe — Angelbody Farther," I said. "Or maybe Angelbody Farthest. I was thinking of one that could head out beyond the asteroid belt."

She frowned at me. "Too far for mining."

"Not for mining," I said. "Just to go. I want to see what's out there."

She still looked sceptical. "You won't be able to maintain contact the way you can with the other remotes. It's too far off. There'll be a long delay."

"Sure. I figure we'll need a more intelligent system, a step beyond the expert system in Angelbody Far. An AI with the capacity to learn. Sort of a partnership arrangement."

Bina was silent. I noticed her glance at Kamishiwa, one of those unspoken communications. Kamishiwa said, "You know, there's another possibility that perhaps you aren't aware of. In a case very similar to yours, one of the Japanese earthside labs has made considerable progress in nerve regeneration. They've successfully repaired spinal damage. It's an expensive proposition, but you've got the money now. You could have your body back."

I looked at him blankly. My body? For a moment, I didn't know what he meant. After a moment, I realised that he meant I could re-inhabit the body on the bed. I frowned and felt the muscles in my face shift and pull.

"Right after the accident, that's what you said you wanted," Kamishiwa continued. "I thought you should know that now you can have it."

Right after the accident, I had regularly read all reports coming from labs doing work on nerve regeneration. But I had stopped paying attention to that years ago.

I looked up into the mirror at the reflection of my body. Most of the time, I ignored the flesh and blood. The machines and the doctor cared for the meat, keeping it healthy, using electrostimulation to maintain muscle tone, feeding the flesh to keep it well-nourished.

My body looked good. It was thinner than I had been at the time of the accident; I had always been a bit stocky and that fat had gone. The muscles were toned and the skin had just a hint of colour from the full spectrum lights.

My body looked good, but I had no feelings in most of it. If I paid attention, I could feel that my neck had a sore patch where the harness that supported my neck had chafed the skin; my cheek itched and I couldn't scratch it. The rest had no feeling. I was aware of its presence in a distant sort of way. But I had little interest in it.

"That's what I wanted then," I said slowly. "But now...I don't know...." I watched Bina. "If the body were functional...." I couldn't call it 'my body.' I had many bodies. "If they repaired my spinal cord and this body were functional, could I keep my connection to Angelbody Far and Angelbody Out and Angelbody In?"

Bina shrugged. "Not in the same way. You wouldn't be able to dedicate as much of your attention to the mechanicals. You'd need it for your own body. But you wouldn't need all these mechanicals anymore. You could have a human body again."

They were both watching me closely. I closed my eyes, trying to remember what it had been like to have a body. I remembered sensations that I had grieved for in the first year after the accident. Sensual pleasures like the touch of a lover's hand on my breast and the rush of orgasm. Common sensations like the comfort of a warm blanket on a cold night or the coolness of grass under my bare feet.

But I remembered pain too: the sharp sting of a cut when the knife slipped as I chopped onions, the dull ache of the healing wound. With pain had come fear — fear of injury, fear of danger to my body. With my new bodies, I didn't feel that fear. My mechanical bodies could be replaced at some cost. They experienced urgent signals, signals of danger and imminent damage, but that wasn't the same as pain.

And when I thought of one body, it seemed so limiting. So confining. One body in just one place.

"What are you thinking?" Kamishiwa asked.

"Thinking of what it would feel like to have a body again," I said. "Just one body."

"What would it feel like?"

"When I was a kid, I had a can that held a snake. Open it up, and this spring-loaded snake came jumping out. It was easy to let the snake out of the can, and hard to squash it back in. Going back into my body feels like being squashed back into the can. Like being packed into a box and sealed away. Like putting the sparks back into the skyrocket." I hesitated. "It's too late for that. I don't need a human body. I don't want to go back."

+++++

Three years later. Night in the infirmary and my human body was drifting off to sleep. Angelbody In hung from the ceiling; Angelbody Out was parked on the hull, temporarily at rest; Angelbody Far was on automatic pilot, heading for another near-Earth asteroid that looked promising. Angelbody Farthest was passing some 50,000 miles from Io, Jupiter's innermost moon.

Angelbody In and Angelbody Out and Angelbody Far all felt like parts of my body. Angelbody Farthest had felt that way at first, but as the probe moved farther and farther from the station, the delay in transmission changed my feelings. At this point, it took half an hour for radio signals to travel to the probe and half an hour for the probe's signals to return to me. The delay in transmission made it impossible for me to feel as linked to Angelbody Farthest as I was to the others. I could control the probe's actions directly — and had done so when the delay was a minute, two minutes, even ten minutes. But now, because of the delay, direct control made no sense.

Bina and I had included in the probe an AI system that was capable of independent action and learning. Over the past two years, the AI and I had been in close communication. The AI had watched my actions and questioned me about them, changing its programming as a result. Rather than directly controlling the probe, I advised the AI. At this distance, communicating with Angelbody Farthest felt like talking with a very close friend who understood me very well.

For the past two years, the AI and I had been working on poetry together. I sent Angelbody Farthest my work and the latest work from Kamishiwa. The AI responded with poetry of its own, created according to rules stored in its expert system and modified by analysis of the poetry I had sent.

Angelbody Farthest sent me a continuous stream of data, on which I could focus if I chose. The same data was collected and stored, so that it could be reviewed later. Everything I received was half an hour old, but it was the most recent information I could receive. Sometimes, there was poetry in the stream of data.

That night, as I drifted toward sleep, I focused on Angelbody Farthest. Through the probe's sensors, I was listening to Jupiter's Red Spot. The storms made music with radio waves, and Angelbody Farthest was listening to the white noise that ebbed and flowed like the sound of waves on the beach or wind in the trees.

"A poem." The words came to me as a whisper in the speakers near my head, a radio-transmitted voice-simulation from the AI. Then the voice whispered a haiku.

Not bad, I thought. In the morning, I'd have to pass that on to Kamishiwa. The AI thought of itself as human. That was good. I thought of the AI as human — an extension of myself, something like a daughter perhaps.

I was almost asleep when the rush and flow of white noise from the

Red Spot was joined by another sound. Hard to describe that sound — I was half asleep when I heard it first. I've listened to the recording since and description is still elusive. A sound with the timbre of organ pipes, the sweetness of a children's choir. It wove itself into the white noise of the Red Spot, borrowing rhythms from that hash of static and weaving them into a strange music.

The view in the visual spectrum showed something strange near Io. In that strange state near sleep, I drifted, watching the anomaly. Something spherical, like a soap bubble or a fish egg; more like something organic than something mechanical. The sphere was the colour of a soap bubble — that is, it was no colour at all. It took all the available light-light from Jupiter, light reflecting from Io, light from the distant sun-and reflected it back in shimmering, iridescent colours that shifted and changed.

Angelbody Farthest changed course to fly closer to the bubble — the AI had my curiosity and tended to investigate anything out of the ordinary. Against the background noise of the Red Spot and the pattern of alien beeps, the verbal stream from the AI whispered the co-ordinates of the bubble and the co-ordinates of the probe. As I watched, the co-ordinates of the bubble changed as it drifted toward the probe.

There was no indication of how the bubble propelled itself. The probe's infrared sensors detected no exhaust, no indication of increased energy expenditure. The ethereal music — the signal from the bubble, I had decided — continued as the bubble grew larger and larger, then filled the probe's visual screen.

Suddenly, the visual screen was filled with coloured light. From Angelbody Farthest's motion sensors, I received signals that made no sense, touching me with vertigo. The music that had borrowed rhythms for the Red Spot swelled, growing louder and sweeter. The probe's temperature sensors registered a comfortable warmth.

A moment later, the signal from Angelbody Farthest vanished. The probe was gone, a departure as sudden as an amputation.

+++++

The bubble was, I believe, an alien ship, visiting our solar system and taking samples. When it went, it took Angelbody Farthest with it — either as a sample of human technology or perhaps as an emissary, a representative of Earth culture. The probe could serve as both.

The last few minutes of the recording were analysed and reviewed by corporate officials, by officials from the US government, by anyone and everyone concerned with threats from beyond our solar system.

For the most part, all of these people concerned themselves with the last few minutes of the recording — the swelling bubble, the strange music that could also be a communication that we had yet to decode. Only Kamishiwa commented on the last poem that Angelbody Farthest had sent:

Escaping the world,
Expanding into darkness,
Becoming human.

"I think perhaps Angelbody Farthest will be a good emissary to the aliens," Kamishiwa said. He had come to the infirmary to talk with me

"I think that's so."

"And how are you feeling?" he asked.

"When I was a little girl, my mother took me to a fireworks display. I remember watching a skyrocket go up, leaving a trail of light behind it. Then it exploded into thousands of sparks that darted off in all directions. That's what it feels like. Exploding like a skyrocket and no one can ever put all the pieces back together again." I smiled.

Like sparks from the fire,
Stars in all directions.
Time for a visit?

The Media Dinosaur Meets the Media Boutique

Greg Bear

Greg Bear is one of the best writers of science fiction in the US. In a thirty-year career, he has written a stream of novels and short stories which have been awarded the major awards in the genre. His books include *Blood Music, Eternity, Eon, The Forge of God, Anvil of Stars,* and *Queen of Angels, Legacy,* and the forthcoming */,* or *Slant,* which explores many of these issues. He also consults for media and software corporations. Stephen McClelland interviewed him in Seattle.

The Media Dinosaur Meets the Media Boutique

Greg Bear

If you want to know the future, you could do much worse than talk to your local SF writer. The impact of science fiction has been amazing. It is the subconscious mind of science. SF writers do what scientists would love to do. And while it may not be reliably predictive, it can certainly inspire. The first practical submarine was built by a man who said he owed it all to Jules Verne's stories.[1]

SF Magazine editor John Campbell anticipated nuclear fission's application as a weapon in 1939 and during World War II was involved in an FBI investigation when the authorities thought atom secrets were being leaked. Modern cultures are almost as afraid of imagination as they are of sex, but a rugged and powerful coterie of individuals and corporations realise their collective futures depend on dreams and serious speculation. They love SF and what it can offer. They may actively seek out possible future scenarios, and on occasion talk to SF writers as entertaining gurus. This is good, but I have real concerns for the shift in money and culture in the media industries. Some of the directions they are taking are not good. Software companies have turned their backs on New York publishing — too antiquated and not very sexy — and are leaping into bed with cinema and multimedia companies, Hollywood-style outfits, in an attempt to both determine and control the future of entertainment. There is a lot of pushing and shoving in the generic multimedia market at the moment, but little actual market research as to what the mass audience wants. Software giants seem ready to accept what West Coast entertainment experts tell them the public needs. Clearly, the market — and indeed the whole culture — is moving away from a text basis. A generally dispirited publishing industry, suffering from a lack of inspiration and in many areas declining revenues and audiences, turns to cinema and TV projects for marketing hooks and show little spirit for promoting on their own, or for playing up and advertising their own glorious accomplishments. Conventional publishing as we know it sadly may well be in decline.

There's a general notion that for most people images present far greater seductivity. That isn't necessarily so, but text-based entertainment simply refuses to do effective and general advertising. Motion pictures and TV clobber them there. Newspapers and TV news shows fill their pages and time with subjects that generate ad space-and so general book awareness is falling by the wayside across the country.

To counter the massive dinosaur structures of the present media companies, we need lots of what I would call boutique creators, on the lines of text authors today. A text author writes a book on a very low budget. Now, practically anyone with talent and some small start-up money, even aspiring teenagers, could in a few years produce quality film or media products in a garage, with relatively modest facilities. There is no doubt that this will happen but it might take 10 or 15 years before this young, new bicoastal, international culture starts to roar. It will be similar to present day music industry (the healthiest sector of the current media), where it's possible for an unknown group to cut a demonstration track for a few thousand dollars and get launched.

However, what will allow entertainment product creativity and creation to be transformed will be the breakdown of current distribution channels and mechanisms. Current channels, both east and west coast (and in particular Hollywood-type distribution) are just too fossilised. They are fossilised in the way they conceive the marketplace. These attitudes have distinctly undesirable fall-out: because movie and TV product costs to much, they show a distinct preference for safe bets, and putting the emphasis on sure things and safe bets means a reduction in the numbers of individual products, as well as entry-level creators and overall product variety.

The consequent restriction of choice in the media affects everything in the sector, even publishing. Meanwhile, with so many distractions from multimedia and television, there's less time for our younger generations to read, and why should they want to do something as unpromoted and ignored as read books in the first place? What replaces reading becomes more and more standardised and optimised and blanded out, and therein begins a vicious circle.

The situation is unsustainable. There are big changes on the way here too. Hollywood studios and the associated media may be powerful; they may be currently well capitalised but they have their limitations. They're great at what they do, but they do not react quickly. And if the new media of tomorrow there are 500 channels available, these agencies will really be only to fill perhaps five or ten, and the audiences will have time for maybe twenty. What will become of the other 480 or 490? They'll be filled with endless reruns or spin-offs or other safe and already established content. Surely this is the chance the boutique creators have been waiting for. They will be able to supply material here, over the distribution system with the Internet as its backbone, while the big players respond with more cynical recycling strategies. Look for a limiting of information choice from the big boys, and exploitation in areas such as 'Character Estate.' There are already television shows in the works that will resurrect dead movie stars, digitally recreating realistic imagery from past famous and popular film characters for delivery direct to present media. It will be a sort of cannibalism. Perhaps they'll even be available as holograms for your house party!

But this endless recycling won't satisfy in the longer term — it has to break down. As Gen X and later groups age, they will demand something far more interesting and challenging. If I wanted to invest in entertainment now, I would not pump my money into TV and films at this point: the companies that make them are rapidly becoming slow and inflexible media dinosaurs. Their future looks similar to that of text publishers in New York. What will change the balance of the equation? The Internet of course. It will offer entirely new and independent means of distribution of products from these boutique creators. Big money is being spent by service providers laying down fibre and cable for all of this information. It's hard to ignore the revenue stream when you get a dime every time something is carried. Moreover, service providers should not need or desire to know what is being carried: that is someone else's business. Let the big boys lay the track, and tell the dinosaurs to step aside! It's time for a new generation of small, fast mammals to take over.

Think Tank

Stephen McClelland

Stephen McClelland is Editor-in-Chief of Telecommunications® International magazine, and is based in London. The story that follows is proof that anyone – even an industry commentator – can be stimulated to try to think creatively, if they are in the company of the sort of talent that appears elsewhere in this volume. Readers hopefully will forgive this editorial indulgence. The story centres around one night in a future Cambridge. It's about a search for a new communications paradigm for the future, by way perhaps of a personal exploration of the innovation that gives us the present. Residents of Cambridge will also forgive this fictional representation of their beautiful city.

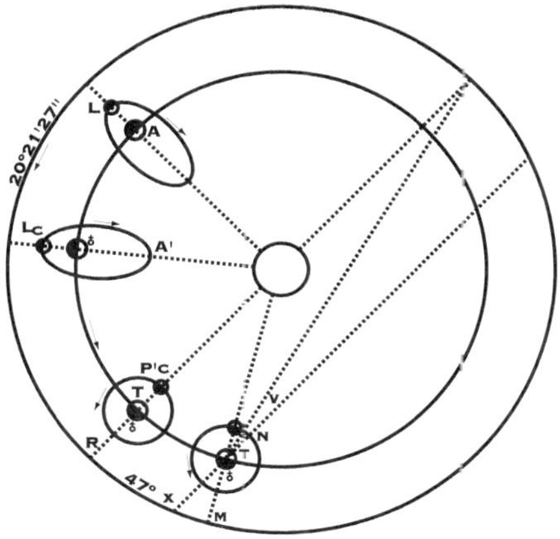

Think Tank

Stephen McClelland

2026. September 9th.

6.00pm. It was a Tuesday night in Cambridge, two years to the day since I had invented the No. 1 mixed drink in the world.

I hate this job. It is a bad day to be in a think tank. A bad day to have a deadline.

My name is Mark Davidson, and I am responsible for this. The client meeting is in three hours and I don't have anything to tell them. Nothing. We are paid for ideas and I don't have any. I sit here in solitary desperation; across the TCI office workspace, I am getting the worried gazes from co-workers, and Atsuko five feet away is giving me the silent staring routine. She knows I'm desperate, may be getting to panic level. I'm completely unprepared and it's beginning to show. The usual signs are building up, the sweating, the headaches, the inexplicable fatigue have already started. I can't cry off, walk away or delay on this one. It's too big. The client wants ideas, and they came to us for them. We are supposed to be the experts in the business.

6.03pm. My only positive thought at the moment? I am toying with going out for yet another walk around Cambridge, the third today. I will have to do something. I am going quietly crazy.

"The Global Com videocon is in three hours," Atsuko drones flatly, and unnecessarily.

"Yes, I know" I reply, " I am going out for a walk."

"What are we going to tell them?" she persists.

"I will have a presentation prepared," I answer evenly.

For perhaps the first time in my professional life, I'm worried. I even have an insistent nagging feeling of being past it, over the hill, beyond my better days. A fraud. I always thought of the creativity business as a bit of a game, but then I was usually on the winning side, or at least the side that was seen to win. Enough home runs to keep everyone happy, particularly my employer — TCI, or more formally, TeleCollected Intelligence. TCI is the world's biggest think tank, but it has to bet the store with even bigger clients these days. Big clients need big ideas, world-changing, gut-sizzling ideas, the last competitive frontier of the Information Society in a post-industrial age.

"They need something very big," Atsuko again, unconvinced.

This part was true, but I ignored her. I had been up against it for weeks, but most of the pressure today had come from a jump in Global Com's stock price, as the news that we were about to provide them with a new set of strategies had been leaked. Not by me, that's for sure. Without anything substantive, both TCI and Global Com were set to take a major hit. There would be inevitable and serious repercussions. Atsuko opened her mouth to say something else, but closed it when she saw my look. Didn't the woman ever stop?

True, I had had my share of the big ones. I had ridden the wave along with TCI's growth and some of its best ideas had, in fact, been mine. Remember the raspberry flavoured shochu for the Japanese market, that had knocked the big C-C off its perch in both North America and Eurasia within the month? That had been mine — at least originally. A follow up idea based on Argentinian maytay had become almost as big, but far more briefly. Surprised? Well, I didn't exactly get the recognition I deserved, but it was certainly mine. I'm surprised, actually. I wandered in, and blundered in, and got something successful. Perversely, it was something I was never trained for, but that's showbiz, or at least the creativity biz. My speciality was communications-related products, although after the *shochu* launch, most people in the company still thought of me as a consumer drink specialist.

6.04pm. A simple attempt to re-launch a flagging career was turning into a nightmare.

You can't survive on past successes forever, at least I certainly couldn't. Corporate memories are fragile. But the communications specialism is the reason I am running Global Com, currently a blank sheet of paper. Bizarrely, Global Com's problem is relatively obvious, if intractable: a communications company, with too many competitors, most leaner and hungrier. To win, it had not to compete but to change the rules of the entire game. They need a new paradigm, if we could give them one. The big idea. To go global, but to live for days or even hours before the competition catches up. Ideas are short-lived in a global marketplace, unsuccessful careers, likewise.

6.05pm. Look round office for inspiration. Rock back on chair. Purse lips. Stare at ceiling. Stare at walls (part of the ceiling, in fact, given we were in the rooftop spaces of one of Trinity Street's old buildings. (TCI believes 'non-orthogonal space' enhances creativity).

Trying hard to focus past a still-rigid and evidently suspicious Atsuko, I mentally listed the artefacts designed (by the company) to statistically enhance creative inspiration. My intellectual tools. Intelligent desk: one. Wall covering: yellow, one. Paintings: expensive, two: Mondrian, Klee. Clever executive toys: none. Clever messages: two. Colleagues: three, silent, engaged in own activity, or possibly busy work, apart from Atsuko, of course, who could maintain an unblinking stare at me for hours on end. I wondered what she might be telling the management about me. There wasn't much to tell, but it was reasonable to assume that a company that spied on the rest of the planet might do the same to its own staff.

Depressed by the thought, I turned and looked out of real windows. I looked out, over a variety of collegiate rooftops. Stacked together, sharply flashing the dying sunlight in wet grey slate, the scene looked improbable: like the set of a Hitchcock thriller set in Paris. I expected some chase risking life and limb to take place over them one day.

I flicked my gaze back to the office; I had never really gotten use to a quiet place, where people tended to speak in barely audible whispers like the users of some ancient and venerable library. Whispering was drowned in TCI's piped baroque musak; TCI had good reason to think that baroque musak enhanced creativity. It generally did.

I was surrounded by the most sophisticated tools known to the creativity business. Computers, communications, databases, TV feeds, artworks, music. In the past six weeks, I had tried everything, used every technique we had to work a miracle. Together we probed, and skimmed our knowledge of global cultures looking for something valuable. The combing as always had been relentless: not just recorded inventions, images, commentaries, soundbites, nearly ten thousand broadcast channels, Internet web pages for a billion people, all the literary scenarios ever produced, displays, stickers, operettas, rock music, ad hoardings, poems, beer mats, pub signs, slang, even jokes (they often indicate a switch in the mood of popular culture). We even poked through the global garbage (not an original concept, admittedly, but it's more thorough than most).

If an electronically-recorded change in planetary culture, however small, was out there we would find it. We predicted changes of fashion and taste, anticipated nostalgia, and duly invented new corporate strategies to suit. Just like clockwork. Retro, modesto, post-punk, ascendancy, you name it, timed for every generation, and usually borne out by demographic predictability. (By the way, did you know post-punk will again hit south Eurasian culture in a fourth wave sometime during the summer of 2028? It's a tip worth noting — if take your money out of utilities and put it into plastics and titanium processors by the end of March).

6.16pm. Our sifting is relentless. The cultural information of an entire planet. Simply juggled, jiggled, panned, skewered, tapped, taped, distilled, recycled, refurbished and released... back onto the market as new forms. Call it cultural regeneration.

"TCI Corporate will need a report at the same time," Atsuko again, closing off any delaying tactics I might conceive. Hers was a distant voice, I was lost in thought. If I had bothered to think about it, I might have wondered why the management were giving me a lot of latitude on this one.

My reverie is, however, broken by a break in the classical music to permit a few bars of modesto-rock to air. Incongruous. At least it kept people awake. I briefly envisaged Global Com associated with a rock group. Music was a powerful, multilingual medium, a compelling one. The world's twenty mega-rock stars — with combined earnings of over 80 billion dollars this year alone were direct but barely traceable derivatives of much earlier models. But this theme had been overworked. Reluctantly, I dismissed the idea.

6.30pm. Finally give up on office life. Reflect on work pressures. Take steps towards door avoiding Atsuko. Silently, she watches me go. Am I getting paranoid about her contact with the management? Paranoia was a consequence of my relative lack of communication with anybody, I reflected.

"I'm going for a walk," I say again pointedly to Atsuko as I sweep past in a tone that didn't brook argument, "I'll be back later."

6.35pm. Leave office. Stare hard at Global Com interactive ad 'The Wireless ID Company' in elevator. Not for much longer perhaps. I sighed again, nearly soundlessly. I looked back at the office reception as I left. Think tank. Hothouse. Elegant and gilded pressure cooker.

Not that there would be any objection to my movements. TCI consultants, true knowledge professionals, could effectively come and go as they pleased: they only had to deliver, and everyone knew what their exact contribution was supposed to be. Today's inescapable demands reminded me of the spy character George Segal played in *The Quiller Memorandum*, left by his captors to roam Berlin for one night until dawn, entirely free to walk the streets, but impossibly tethered by their demands.

On the way down, I wondered if it was time to leave, strike out on my own. It was a thought that had occurred to me with increasing regularity recently. Perhaps, even risk an investment in post-punk nostalgia myself. The near certainty of imminent failure in early middle age, leaden feelings of fear and insecurity were walking me towards any exit before I was even pushed. Perhaps it was a commentary ultimately on an absence of life outside my work and a lack of companionship around me, a symptom of a deeper malaise. After all, I had barely exchanged twelve words with anyone all day, and most of those were on the defensive.

Still, the idea of a new venture had a compelling basis, although I could never hope to get TCI-level clients. They had sewn much of the field up, and were already the stuff of mythology, right from the early days in the archetypal Silicon Valley garage. TCI specialised in combing the world's communicated output for the best ideas and fashions for the Next Big One and its foresight took it from the garage to a 600 person-strong think tank. It anticipated global lifestyles with uncanny accuracy, and always billed a mind boggling per capita revenue. At this level, in the refined, high-octane world of the think tank, no idea would ever be thought too extreme, as long as it worked. There are no inhibitions, no blocks, few checkpoints. Lots of blind alleys. But no road maps.

6.37pm. Street level in Cambridge: Modern city-state. Ancient University town. Still no inspiration.

In other circumstances, it would have been a very pleasant, if wet, Autumn evening and relatively quiet before the start of the undergraduate term. Several good-humoured groups were drifting down to the Market Square to visit the County Fair. I stepped on to the street level, and felt the cool evening, at a quiet season and best Cambridge had to offer. The air had settled, and the silence magnified my steps. A clear, unadulterated sunset had taken place, silhouetting the college skyline, the darkening blue sky, now clear, adding emphasis.

Cambridge has an advantage of sorts over Oxford given a concentration of colleges and hence intellectual life into the centre of the city. Many of the 33 collegiate institutions — although founded quite independently over a thousand year period — are effectively parked together between Trinity Street and bordering the river. Trinity College, and Trinity Great Gate. Trinity — probably Cambridge's richest and best endowed college — sparkled in the dying evening light. In the 21st Century, colleges had once again enjoyed some financial as well as intellectual power. Trinity fellows still remember the days when it was one of the dominant land owners in the entire country, excluding the Church, and the Monarchy, and various state trusts of course. Once you could walk from Cambridge to London and not leave Trinity College land. Trinity's heritage some six hundred years in the making, still dominates: faintly disdainful of temporary fashion or innovation. I think heritage is deceptive: there always has been and will be change. Any sense of permanence, even a historical one, is deceptive.

6.47pm. Wonder around, moodily.

In the nearly deserted street, I see them before they, me. With a suitable nod of acknowledgement, I take care to swing around in the narrow medieval alley, two battle-dressed and rather intimidating members of the Cambridge Constabulary. They seemed to be expecting trouble. If they were interested, my identity would immediately present on their head up displays, another consequence of the wireless ID card I was carrying, and their own wireless interrogators. Technically it was an offence if they were not able to swipe you, or if you were trying to conceal your identity.

Verbal interaction because of Wireless ID in general was fortunately much minimised with the Constabulary. Given the current police relationship with the general population, this could only be a good thing, as the force was now privatised, and a wholly owned subsidiary of NYPD. The pairing was hardly the expected match of civic cultures — but our competitors, Virtual Ideologies, had assured the general public all would be well. Our third major competitor, Cognoscens, had also supported it. Personally, I felt aligned with the general gut feel — it was a bad idea. Nevertheless, in one or two areas the Constabulary had won a grudging amount of respect. They were tough on auto traffic — there was none in the City State of Cambridge apart from their own vehicles, nor was any needed. And they were conspicuously tough, even ruthless on the hard drug trade.

But our competitors on the other hand usually had several agendas, most of them usually well hidden. Nor were they above being global spin doctors, feeding political memes — with ingenuity, admittedly — to Internets worldwide. Of course, anything could become a business. The memes themselves required constant inoculation by people like TCI's network inoculation division. But the impression remained that in the age of the network, truth itself was a networkable, privatisable and ultimately marketable commodity.

So was privacy, it seemed.

Our competitors kept tabs on email and cellphone conversations too, upwards of a billion conversations per week, and quite illegally, if you believed the rumours. The first signs of a popular *profitable* mood shift often might be picked up in a couple of isolated conversations half a world apart. We were against it on ethical grounds, although I believe people tracked my raspberry *shochu* (a charming but deceptively potent mix of sake, lemon and raspberry liquor) from launch; complimentary pickups about it within a week in Brazil and Korea encouraged further investment and made some people a lot of money.

6.51pm. The major coffee shops of Trinity Street awaited. Perhaps I would catch some inspiration there.

Coffee shops had changed even in my working lifetime, as much from fashion as from lawsuits by people inexplicably careless with their own hot coffee. Many had become extraordinarily formalised art forms in themselves. Now, many coffee shops and all restaurants required an entry fee for your food in advance *plus* an insurance premium (collected automatically via your wireless ID card). With no ill effects three days from consumption the same system also ensured a rebate. Failing that it was signing two pages of disclaimer drinking, hardly guaranteed to win customer confidence.

My coffee shop walks — well practised — probably unconsciously copied another Cambridge phenomenon — a compelling undergraduate need to drink and run competitively, usually at the same time. It's most notorious in King Street and among medical students — future guardians of our collective health. In middle age, I opted for coffee shops, less damaging and more entertaining than pubs, and still with a sense of the communal. TCI had its own of course, rather oddly called 'The Water Cooler' in homage to well-known consultancy folklore and the supposed wellspring of creative thought in business in the past.

I mused about Global Com and the insurance business, but didn't turn up anything particularly novel or inspiring. Most insurance niches had probably been filled anyway, and the communications business was in general doing well from the resultant network traffic: the average individual going shopping on an average day automatically triggered twenty or thirty wireless insurance (and other) agreements within minutes of leaving home. Tweaking collective insecurities in a risky world was good for a lot of global business.

Trust is now an electronic commodity.

The coffee shop I chose was Brazilian RetroMetro, in the warren of ancient cellars nearly two levels beneath Trinity Street. Like all coffee houses in central Cambridge it provides heavy VR atmospherics. Entertainment as experience is a persistently popular formula, and the more unusual the better. Something of a cross between the truly bohemian and the ersatz Rio imagery, RetroMetro always provides a talking point. Its owner/proprietor, Jaffa, was shrewd enough to keep the atmosphere bubbling with the right ambience or rather ambivalence I often termed it. Around the clock opening with subtle changes of taste kept a huge variety of customers quietly happy. There were no insurance agreements operating here.

Jaffa's VR work was superb, if eccentric: if in the outer chamber he had wanted to recreate a Rio nightclub from the 1930s, the inner sanctum was dead set on planetary ecology, and best provided it by the high quality floor to ceiling images he had piped through. They came straight from Amazonia often in real time onto polymeric display layering which seamlessly covered the curving cellar walls right around and above you. The temperature and humidity were both kept elevated here to give you the full experience, as was the smell, so if you came in from the street in the average Cambridge winter, you could be in for a shock. If you went for the VR glasses, with multimedia wireless beamed straight from concealed projectors, the effect was unimaginably stunning, particularly because the simulation and projection area were usually highly localised. The ultimate step was the containerised VR wet suits, rubberised pods, but for the truly uninhibited alone. In the coffee bar itself, the effect was persuasive enough, similar to a planetarium, except you were in a clearing in a dark rain forest.

If you know the right psychological tricks, you can get away with murder in VR, even with otherwise low quality stuff, and this was much above that. I didn't have to order the coffee — it was my regular brew delivered piping hot to the low table. There were several people in the chamber, but they were largely shielded from me and I was alone in my place. Across from me, Jaffa smiled, his grin accentuated in the candlelight in one corner of the chamber. The heavy sweet odour — possibly simulating a decay programme — of the forest hung around the place like a fog. It was in near total darkness, enhancing the VR. By the time my eyes began to adjust, the walls were becoming tinged with bluish milky light as background, faintly acknowledging a new Brazilian dawn somewhere in the Mato Grosso. In a morning mist simulation, misty tree tops gradually lightened. The unmistakable call of distant but invisible animals greeted the day. Few people spoke.

7.15pm. I'm sipping constantly from the short stumpy pot container; the coffee thick, hot and heavy, slightly more bitter than usual. In spite of the coffee, my lips are dry and breathing is heavy. Escape is never possible is it? Most of all from your self-esteem.

But I'm relaxing, and I'll be left alone by everybody. I'm not sure I want that or not. Perhaps the mood is catching, the sense of failure contagious.

7.25pm. Still no inspiration.

I was surrounded by the evidence of very smart people existing through the ages in the streets somewhere above my head. Within one mile of where I sat, Rutherford had split the atom, JJ Thomson had discovered the electron, Watson and Crick had scuttled from pub to pub telling everyone they had elucidated DNA. Babbage and Turing a century apart had thought about very different computer designs, Ozark had evolved principles of social psychology and intercultural habit transference in a mass media age (work which had directly led to the creation of TCI). Albert Einstein had lectured on a visiting tour many decades ago, padding around in his favourite carpet slippers. Isaac Newton had captured the secrets of the known universe, but still recorded in minute detail his weekly shopping in a notebook, a prosaic item still held in Trinity Library. Byron had kept a live bear in one of the Trinity towers. All were part of an intellectual culture. A supremely, dismissively, individualist one.

I wondered what my memorial — if any — was going to be. The famous blue plaque could one day read 'To the Unknown Soft Drink King.' You may argue I'm appropriating clothes that don't belong, yet as far as I'm concerned all innovation is worth admiration. Even ours. There's too much intellectual snobbery around as it is about this. Innovation underpins civilisation, I'm convinced. Mine are popular, but impermanent. They will only last for a matter of hours even if successful. But we innovators are all strangely separated and separated from the rest of the human race, hygienically boxed up in ivory towers away from real life.

7.30pm. More random word associations?

This morning I fruitlessly trotted through random word and image associations...a favourite toy of think tanks and brainstormers everywhere. Without joy, unless you count 'orange' and 'pterodactyl' as a significant relationship. Proving once again that trying to engineer creativity is generally speaking a fruitless, if occasionally, comic objective. Still, myths arise. Outcomes invariably outshine processes — and failures. But behind the scenes, creativity quietly has all the discontinuities of being human. It undergoes hops, erratic jumps, false starts, fruitless digressions, pointless circles. It is rarely logical.

Still, in think tanks like ours, no inhibitions were permitted. The ridiculous was permitted at times. In a effort to stimulate creativity flow, for example, we once spent a week at TCI Cambridge absorbing nothing but cinnamon tastes and flavours — would you believe, for breakfast, lunch and dinner. Plus coffee, tea and soft drinks. The result? Nothing, except a general feeling that it was an eccentric piece of control by the management, and a lifetime aversion to cinnamon for me. A failure, but it would not stop a hundred other initiatives like it, all in search of the multi-billion dollar idea.

7.32pm. Think weird.

Creativity definitely has a weird side. Even TCI eccentricities pale into insignificance set against historical figures. George Kneller's book on creativity records, Schiller's need of the stimulation of a desk full of rotten apples. Proust, ditto, but in a cork-lined room. For Dr Johnson it was a cat, orange peel, and lots of tea. Kant? Possibly the most self obsessed of all. He would focus on a tower he could see from his window — he often worked from bed — and when the tower was eventually obscured by the growth of trees, the city fathers immediately felt compelled to cut them down and preserve the great man's intellect.

7.34pm. Unless I was prepared to sign myself into a mental institution, I didn't see how this line of thought could help.

I tried turning the problem on its head. Was it necessary for Global Com to market communications at all? Perhaps Global Com should sell no-communication spaces, a guaranteed lack of disturbance for the world's overworked and over communicated masses? It was an attractive idea, but unlikely to really appeal to the world's biggest communications service provider. Wireless ID developments, then?

7.36pm. No, perhaps wireless ID had been extended enough, at least for the time being.

7.39pm. I paid (unconsciously by wireless transaction) and re-emerged on Trinity Street. A walk to the somewhat more restful and relaxed Japanese tea and bath house, Ocha No Mizu, near Christ's College.

I had a choice of routes: via Caius College (famous alumni: John Venn and William Harvey, of diagram and blood circulation fame respectively), then King's (Alan Turing, Rupert Brooke, EM Forster and John Harrington — inventor of the water closet), or via Sidney Sussex and Jesus (Oliver Cromwell, Laurence Sterne and Humphrey Davy, respectively). A pragmatic romantic rather than revolutionary, I chose the Caius direction.

The cool dampness was unsurprising. University wisdom confirmed all of Cambridge sat below twenty meters in elevation, with no higher ground between us and the Urals. East Anglia was therefore potentially Siberian. Theoretically, a Cambridge winter should be stimulating. An unpublished TCI report speculated that depressing cold should be conducive to creativity, and was rumoured in office gossip to have the company seriously considering opening its next offices in Murmansk or Spitsbergen or Tierra del Fuego. Temperate climates — unlike tropical ones — did seem more proactive post-Renaissance terms. Location wise, almost anything was possible, however, with telework. But we found out pretty early at TCI you need some sort of human contact. More speculatively, this might be with people you couldn't stand — but given Atsuko, I was prepared to argue this. A further TCI study (unpublished) rated teams of diverse individuals experiencing friction more effective than harmonious groups, with otherwise complementary skill sets and personalities. Rough translation: teams of rude, discourteous people got things done. And that conclusion didn't even include our sales team.

Ocha no Mizu was a warm beacon of hope in an unfriendly world.

It ran a sort of cut down tea ceremony, probably the best one in Cambridge, on the third floor of a building near Christ's College. Soothing atmosphere, low tables, water (for the tea) imported directly from Japan. A sense of permanence unusual in contemporary Japanese culture. At least working with the Japanese market, one got the message on shelf lives in social innovation. We had tracked the life cycle of the short-lived Japanese rock phenomenon *Goruden Suweito* (Golden Sweat) at all of 21 days. Golden Sweat's digital output was in the millions of terabytes of music, roughly equivalent to every man, woman and child in Japan listening about ninety times to each of the only two tracks produced. Now gone without trace, they still had a Net existence (we measured a popularity half life for this phenomenon at just over 42 *hours*, post peak) During active popularity cycle, the media distributor (advised by TCI of course) had collected some 5.6 billion dollars in fees and royalties, mainly on a pay-per-experience basis. TCI had done pretty well too.

7.55 pm. I forego bath. Tea arrives, ceremony in progress. Me? I'm getting resigned to the prospect of total, disastrous failure.

Constructive thought was being replaced by wild ideas about my own future, when a voice behind intruded:

"Mind if we join you?"

It was a superfluous enquiry: the owner of the voice began to sit down opposite me. He was a large framed man, brown haired but with a pink face, with small rather affected gold rimmed spectacles, and in obvious difficulties when it came to sitting at a Japanese table. His squatting awkwardness had all the grace of a hippopotamus balanced on its hind legs. By the time he had actually seated himself, he was nearly short of breath. He was not alone. A helmeted member — Officer Class, by the look of him, of the Cambridge Constabulary was with him. Pink Face introduced himself with the glowing image of an electronic visiting card sweeping across the table to me; the cop was silent but watchful.

"Mark Davidson. TCI." he said, peering forward, flopping a hot damp oshibori around his face.

"What about it?" I replied, irritated. Don't ever disturb me at tea.

"I'm Ben Latimer. Virtual Ideologies."

Oh. I realised belatedly that Virtual Ideologies probably had a direct and illegal feed from the Constabulary on my movements via Wireless ID. The way VI people disguised themselves, Latimer probably wasn't even his real name.

"I see."

I noticed the waitress in a silent hover behind Latimer. "O-negai shimasu. Ocha ga..." The waitress nodded immediately and swivelled around to the doorway. As with all Japanese language, it was almost rude to complete a spoken sentence grammatically. I sometimes wondered why the culture remains resilient, functional and successful yet possesses a language elliptical beyond belief.

Pause for effect for both sides. Latimer started up again.

The superficial warmth vanished. "Let me come straight to the point. We're interested in your ideas for Global Com."

Well that was direct. VI clearly had a high bandwidth grapevine. I said nothing. I picked up the hashi chopsticks and made a elaborate job of splitting them. A bit over-elaborate, actually.

Another pause.

"Yes, very interested," but this time the voice came from the cop, who hadn't introduced himself. The Constabulary and Virtual Ideologies. How cosy.

"We'd like to be involved," intoned Latimer, leaning forward slightly as he picked up his own hashi. I thought he was going to use them as toothpicks. These people had clearly been watching B-movies. It was the sort of thing they would do at VI. 1930s B-movie analysis to find hidden meanings. The VI staff were probably thoroughly trained for the part: 'Impress the client. Support the Boss. Intimidate the Competition. Be a gangster.' There were probably VI practice sessions at work to do this complete with authentic mannerisms as well. Not so much Wagnerian but Cagnerian as it were. Or perhaps Bogartian, even Robinsonian, if you will. Actually this impressive restaurant encounter seemed hilariously to be straight out of *The Godfather*.

"You seem to have .... a creative block at the moment," said Latimer slowly, his eyes focused in the middle distance somewhere above my head, as if to no one in particular. His eyes sharply flicked back to stare at my reaction. Quite deliberately.

My blood froze. How did they know? TCI was surveillance-screened.

I felt undressed, exposed, paranoid. I carried on mopping with the oshibori, but caught the eye of the waitress.

"No comment at any time on anything," I said.

"We'd like to help," Latimer intoned again, rocking slightly back and forward. It wasn't an offer.

I held up my cup for a refill of green tea, but said. "Sumimasen. Ano hito wa akunin desuga...Musukashii desu. Go-chuii kudasai." I relied on the fact I was a good customer here but didn't need to go into details.

"I didn't think I would have to repeat myself with a smart guy like you, Davidson. We want that contract and if you can't do it, we will. From what we hear you won't be around at TCI much longer."

"Save the gentle persuasion for someone else," I replied evenly.

There was a gentle pause, broken only by the appearance of Takahashi, the very large Japanese chef immediately behind Latimer. Takahashi was wordless, but Latimer and the copy exchanged glances. The message being communicated — given that Takahashi was about as wide as he was tall and made an unmissable feature in a brilliant white and blue evening kimono — was obvious. It was fortunate that Takahashi did not have a reputation to lose with the Constabulary; many suspected he was backed by yakuza anyway.

Latimer took the hint. "Tomorrow, Davidson, we will have the contract," stated Latimer baldly. "And you won't have a job to go to." He stood up, with almost as little grace as he had sat down. "Just remember that."

They made for the door, still eyeing Takahashi as they went. The Constabulary was as silent as he had been before. Clearly his visit represented unofficial business, after all. Or perhaps it was just part-time.

8.00pm. Melodrama apart, what they had said was true. I obviously didn't have much future in this business either way.

I couldn't exactly stay all evening in the tea house.

As soon as they had left, I made for the kitchen exit, with a nod of thanks to Takahashi.

I had to get well away from the likes of Latimer and the Constabulary, but confuse any wireless ID tracking. They would be waiting downstairs, anyway, or someone sent by them would. The safest place was undoubtedly either in an underground coffee shop, perhaps the private territory of one of the colleges. Better still back at the TCI building, Faraday-shielded and thought to be EM impervious, and proof against external industrial espionage.

8.05pm. This was turning into a hell of an evening. At this rate, if I lost only my job, I would be lucky.

It was quite clear that there was monkey business around Global Com. I had never seen such tactics employed before. But then again, I was proving naïve in the way this industry really worked. The worst thing was: I felt I'd collapsed at the first sign of intimidation. Yet I knew they were merely toying with me. Latimer knew they would be getting the contract, rescuing the stock price for Global Com, saving the day. I wondered how. If I appeared on the street, I could easily be kept out of circulation, and incommunicado for the night.

The way out of Ocha no Mizu was rather less elegant that the front, and given that we were on an upper story, it was inevitable that I would have to do some scrambling. The tea house's back exit lead directly onto a narrow, railed walkway and fire-escape. I thought about chucking the wireless ID, but I would need it to get back to TCI. So it stayed. Outside, it was fully dark, and the only external light appeared to have broken, or being switched off. Somewhere below another passage would lead around to the front and the shopping centre of St Andrew's Street. This was obviously not a suitable route, but hopefully anyone looking up from ground level would find their view obscured by a mass of tea boxes that stood around the doorway and onto the fire escape. A cautious step up and down the walkway revealed no other exit. But to the right, the bulk of Christ's College loomed. Further back, several college gardens.

I could see that the restaurant building was nearly contiguous with the side of the college's Gate Tower. The levels were different, with the top edge of the Tower running at least three meters above my head and off left parallel with the street. Gingerly, I began stacking the boxes together, hoping they would bear my weight. They appeared more flimsy than they actually were: the sort of boxes that street people in Japan used every day and night on the Tokyo underground to make homes and furniture for themselves. Three stacked boxes together came past the level I wanted. Slowly, balancing weight from one foot to the other, I began the climb up. If I fell at this point, I would be lucky to hit the walkway cleanly, more likely concussion on the rail, or a fall to the ground below. The stack rocked but I continued. By the time I planted both feet on opposite corners of the second box, I could see the top of the Gate Tower. It was further than I thought. I shivered at the thought of jumping the gap, but there was no alternative. Night-climbing college buildings is hardly unknown in Cambridge, but after a brief erratic burst in the sixties and seventies, it was not a frequent past-time, and more than a little dangerous.

I fixed my thoughts on the group that had reassembled a compact car on the roof of King's College Chapel many years ago (was it a Vietnam War protest?), and jumped.

8.10pm. Gate Tower.

The walkway was about 50cm wide, but ran behind the battlement facade built from Ketton Stone that Christ's had thoughtfully been remodelled in. I was hidden from view even from watchful eyes in the street below, but I could hear the sounds of Fairground activity in the Market Square. On the college side, the pitched roof of the Gate Tower rose to my left, partly hiding me, and there was little lighting in the court below, mainly used for day-time administration with many offices and some Fellows' Rooms. I was grateful for the extended layout of the college architecture.

I inched quickly along it, suspecting inadequate fixture, with parts more than five hundred years old, trying not to alert the porters who would be certainly in the archway offices underneath me, out of sight. The stone was slippery, but well-found, and within five minutes I had reached the Hobson Street side of the college, and... a ladder fixed to the wall. I clambered down without further incident. Across the way, a concealed passageway to the College Fellows' and Master's Lodge entrance.

Further on, a quiet street exit.

All encountered without notice. Cambridge colleges were quiet tonight.

8.15pm. Hobson's Street.

I paused to look round. There was nothing suspicious below. I thought, oddly, of Hobson, an eccentric Cambridge resident of long ago. He hired out horses giving people what he wanted regardless of what they asked for. Hobson's Choice has passed into the English language.

I should take a job as a guide to Cambridge University as my next profession. I've seen it from more angles tonight than ever before.

An aerial pedestrian walkway conveniently connects Sidney Sussex and Christ's Colleges. Down into Sidney Sussex. Through two small courts. Acknowledged by a porter. Into the Fellows' Garden, and out through a doorway in the far wall of the garden.

Out into Jesus Lane, and finally across a busy Bridge Street.

Nearly home. Through Whewell's Court, a two-and-a-half court unprepossessing and largely hidden Victorian extension for Trinity. On very familiar ground.

8.21pm. Trinity Street.

Something's wrong.

The front of the TCI building was generating too much activity. A group of cart vehicles. People. Constabulary. I stepped back into the shadows of the Whewell's Court archway, and looked out. Across Trinity Street next to Trinity Great Gate, a DEA motorcade. TCI staff, sullenly, some evidently intimidated, herded into a jeepcart.

A belated realisation. They're busting the office for drugs.

It was a ridiculous notion. TCI was problem free with infringement mandating instant termination. The building even had sensors, for goodness sake.

I looked out again. Standing near the Porter's Lodge in the Gate House. Latimer, looking up surveying the scene.

It was a frame-up. Following the encounter in Ocha No Mizu, they decided to make sure any work in progress would be disrupted this evening.

Except for Atsuko. Totally composed, she was standing next to Latimer.

Still in the shadows, I stood still for some minutes, disorientated, unsure of what to do. I felt a mess. I was still breathing heavily from the exertions getting to Trinity Street. I was sweating too, jacket and trousers both scuffed from the jump from the restaurant walkway. I considered options. It would be meaningless joining the group, if anything I should seek some sort of refuge until this blows over. There would be recriminations tomorrow of course, but no one could ever prove that VI had instigated the raid. TCI would be needing its own network inoculation services in the next few hours.

8.27pm. The need to backtrack. And get lost somewhere. I ditched the wireless ID card.

The back entrance to Whewell's Court was still open and it was easy to drift with several groups of people back down to in the direction I had just come from, towards the city centre. They were all heading for the same point: the Fair in the Market Square. I trailed, without any thought of strategy.

8.31pm. A Victorian-style steam driven fairground temporarily erected in the Market Square looks almost normal to me this evening, after the events that have transpired.

It's instructive that something not dependent on VR or simulation technologies at all can get such favour, but the crowds must number five thousand or so. I wander around it, at first lost in thought, oblivious to everything, but gradually am absorbed by the activity, the reality. Lights, action, a feeling of space, of people enjoying themselves. Of community. The barrel organ theatrics heightened by a wash of white dry ice clouds issuing from centre of the Square. Mist clouds hugging the ground. People, ghost-like, cut off above the knees by the swirl of white fog, splashed by pink and blue light from floodlights. Carousels from another age, rotating. Children laughing. High spirits. Happiness.

The scream came from directly behind me.

I turned around. A scene frozen in time: a child, a small body turning over and over in the mist as the carousel turntable unseen beneath the ice clouds continued to rotate. A woman in shock bending forward. Wide-eyed. Disbelieving. Screaming. People running.

Real-time. I run forward. The body, whirled towards me, like a bag of clothes in a washing machine. Over and over. Something red and liquid splatters my hand. I tug the bundle, hold it, pull it to me. Something on the turntable hits my leg, I reel, but keep the bundle aloft.

I was still gripping the bundle, when the mother reached us. The child. A baby, less than two years old, opened her eyes and grinned.

A paramedic came running over, summoned by the noise. A group of people surrounded child and mother, their faces bafflingly protective. Constabulary jeepcarts pulled up. People behind me made approving noises, one slapped me on the shoulder in congratulations.

The pain in my leg was becoming dull agony. I looked at the redness in my hand. Not blood. Paint.

The baby oblivious of the attention held out a face paint tube to the mother. Still crying inconsolably, she gave gasps of laughter, of relief. She took the tube applicator and began to crayon whiskers on the baby's face, pausing to cry.

The paramedic looked up. No serious injury.

The child patiently waited as the face painting was complete, and grinned proudly.

But I watched, and without warning, had answers to a few more questions, driven underground in the past two minutes.

People mattered more than things. The baby was the first human being I had touched, had held, had cared about, today.

Perhaps the only knowledge worth having.

I stood for minutes, thinking.

Something else was apparent. I unconsciously reached for the voice module on the wireless ID, and realised it was on the ground in Trinity Street.

It would have to be a more traditional means. I leant across to a member of the crowd. "May I borrow your phone?"

The woman smiled approvingly. She rummaged vigorously in a handbag, and pulled out a pen-phone. I dialled a number, and had a scrambling signal re-routed. It took two minutes to have the system segments on line, auto-dictation, high quality translation, simulated office acoustic, privacy interlock. Far away the analysis started.

8.58pm. "Proposal as follows. New paradigm for Global Com is Global Intimacy. Slash. Global Community. New totality paradigm of communications. Suggest study of planetary mood changes over time. Mood mix suggested. Study of passion and commitment at global events suggested.

Other Items to be evaluated follow. Neck band communicator. Technology available. Band reconfiguring development required. Polymeric and cosmetic attachment to skin, electrical properties and possible communications applications of communicators directly applied to skin. Target intelligent and communicating hand cream. Possible face paint communicator application. Glove communicator, as fashion accessory. Accessory modules supplied as ring jewellery slipped onto fingers for wireless contact between glove and ring. Visual display in flexible polymer of glove. Input pad mounted in glove or in flexible skin polymer.

Next phase: corporate recognition of communications business as too insistent, too demanding on personal time. Suggest wide-scale language protocol development, suitable for individual cultures. Suggest ritualising personal communications into early Victorian or Regency style. Neglect voice activated communications, at expense of glove dialling, right hand fingers swipe over left hand palm for contact. Protocols based on hand signals.

Global Com advised to seek major alliances with fashion houses. Analyse future business as fashion accessory. Analysis will follow.

I didn't care who was listening. I had the vision clear in front of me. It was obvious, really.

Organic Cyberspace and Geo-Consciousness

Alexander Besher

Alexander Besher is the acclaimed author of *Rim*, a novel featuring a virtual Japan and the convergence of virtual and spiritual realities. He is eminently qualified to comment: he was born in China, of Russian parents, but lived in Japan. Formerly a magazine columnist and sometime consultant on Pacific Rim affairs, he is now a full time author, and has completed a second novel, *Mir*. Stephen McClelland interviewed him in San Francisco.

Organic Cyberspace and Geo-Consciousness

Alexander Besher

I don't actually see myself as a writer of science fiction, but if I can bring anything new at all to the literary and ideas field, it is that we need an integration of technology and spirituality. So my perspectives on the future relate to a sort of 'post cyberspace' or 'organic cyberspace'. As complex as it may sound, my cyberspace is arrived at on an evolutionary path in which cyberspace takes in the spirit, and the spirit accommodates cyberspace.

I should say at this point that this view probably can be attacked by many people; maybe by those who subscribe to Jungian or transpersonal philosophies on the one hand and the supporters of cyberpunk communities on the other. But in my view, Jungian views would say that technology of every sort — including networking developments — as a fundamentally dehumanising and alien thing in itself. Cyberpunks seem to believe that it is effective but subscribe to a sort of individualistic nihilism. I share neither of these views.

I don't share the fears of the technophobes either. They often point to the prospect of a hierarchical control culture, leaving people at the bottom disenfranchised because they have no access to the system. Things could be much more positive than that. The changes sweeping now through will mean rather that access to wisdom will ultimately be so universal that you will not necessarily be disenfranchised if you belong to the real world, or 'exist' in the wired world.

This leads to a number of interesting thoughts. If you look at the history of human consciousness study, for example, time and again there are references to collective visualisation. For early tribes, there is some evidence to believe that this may have taken the form of palpable dreaming for example. It is a key characteristic in human consciousness, and one in which I am very interested. The combination of cyberspace and this sort of collective unconsciousness imagery suggests to be that we are seeing organic cyberspace as a democratised universe in some sense, internally and externally.

These things are mutually interactive, and the issues have parallels in human experience in history. For example, the Silk Road which supplied Asia in ancient times with commercial traffic and trade was naturally also the perfect vehicle for taking along texts and philosophies which came along as actually some sort of unintended 'free ride'. We could perhaps talk in an equivalent way we can talk about the 'Silicon Road' which will also be able to convey philosophies.

I would say therefore we are heading towards some sort of geo-consciousness (as an network evolution perhaps). It would seem one of the next logical stages: after all we have already passed through conceptualisations of geo-politics and geo-economy. My concept of organic cyberspace will be something that is essentially in tune with the natural dynamic of the world. Seen in this light perhaps, the Internet probably did come at the 'right time' in the historical development of the human race.

What will be the characteristics of this? One will be the need for increased mental and emotional flexibility at all levels. You can't begin a new world with a rigid mindset so you need to be flexible. You have to look at symbolisation and metaphor too. We are after all living currently in a world of symbols and metaphors. It is all rather abstract in spite of what we may believe. The next steps, philosophically speaking, are to dispose of the remaining metaphors. Once you let go of the metaphor stage you can see that these things were merely tools in the first place.

True, there are the twin aspects of globalisation and fragmentation making an appearance in this culture. Each has a good and bad side. But we will run aground if we depend too much on labelling issues and people. I have a distrust of labels in general; labels may be useful but they can also have a toxic side. True, there are also downsides perhaps emanating from the media industry: I often think these days that we have actually moved from 'information anxiety' — where we thought everyone had too much information to contend with, to 'entertainment anxiety' where everyone has too much choice and variety in entertainment.

In the future, we will have to see much more genuinely enlightened corporate attitudes for a start. Our established cultures and attitudes mean that at the moment vast global 'mind games' are still being played where people are being fooled into believing things are as we thought they were in the past.

In the Flesh

Brian Stableford

Brian Stableford is one of the most prolific SF writers in the English speaking world, as anyone reading the foremost reference to the world of SF, *The Encyclopaedia of Science Fiction* by John Clute and Peter Nicholls will testify. In a thirty year career of writing he has covered most of the SF genre with highly acclaimed work in fields as diverse as fantasy, space fiction, gaming plots and futurology, SF history and criticism, as well as pursuing an academic career as a sociologist until 1988 when he became a full-time writer. In this story, he shows vividly how quality of life is what you make it — and communications can make a real difference.

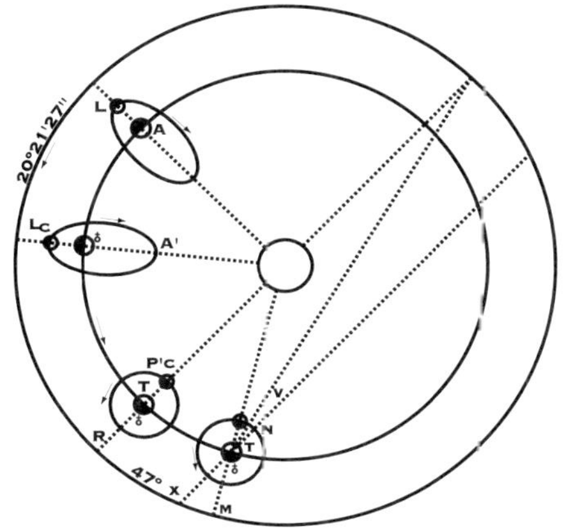

In the Flesh

Brian Stableford

Martha was in the middle of icing Jennifer's birthday cake when the doorbell rang. She wasn't making a very good job of it, but until the doorbell rang it hardly seemed to matter. Once the doorbell had rung, of course, interrupting her in mid-squeeze, the fact that it was a bit of a mess suddenly became the fault of whoever it was at the door and an occasion for resentment. She cursed under her breath as she moved into the hall, wiping icing off her fingers with the hem of her apron.

When she opened the door and saw it was a boy in his early teens the curse rose to her lips again — but it died when realised that the boy was wearing dark glasses.

It was a sunny day, in spite of being Friday the thirteenth. There was no reason why a boy his age shouldn't be wearing dark glasses — but the fact remained that he was *wearing dark glasses*.

He was also carrying a small parcel, about five inches square and two deep. The wrapping-paper enclosing the box was glossy, the colour of red wine. It wasn't wrapped in pink ribbon, tied with a bow, just sealed with sellotape — but it still looked suspiciously like a *present*.

"Yes?" she said, trying hard to sound natural, if not actually pleasant.

"Mrs Mortimore?"

"Yes." Martha was still trying to sound neutral, but even she could hear a note of anxiety in her second *yes.* She told herself that there was nothing to be scared of — but she had told herself that far too often for the telling to have any effect, even though it had nearly always been true.

The boy shifted slightly; he was embarrassed too. *So he should be,* Martha thought. *If being a fourteen-year-old boy isn't enough to cast you into a Hell of permanent embarrassment, what is?* She tried not to look at the dark glasses but she couldn't help it.

"I don't know if Jennifer's mentioned me," the boy said, in the slightly fluty tone of a child who might have been slow to learn to talk. "My name's Carl Ulick."

Martha didn't have to ask him to spell it. Jennifer hadn't 'mentioned' him. Jennifer hadn't 'mentioned' anyone at all. Jennifer found it absurdly easy to keep secrets.

"I'm afraid not," she told the boy.

Because she knew that wasn't what he wanted to hear she had no difficulty in keeping her voice straight, but she couldn't help feeling that she was a bit of a bitch for being able find satisfaction in the imparting of bad news. She knew that she couldn't keep the conversational initiative for long, though — that ominous package he was carrying, all done up in fancy wine-coloured wrapping, gave him the advantage. He lifted it up slightly to draw her attention to it, although the wasn't any need.

"I've bought her a present," he said. His fluty tone made the words trip lightly from his tongue, as if he might have been anybody bringing a gift to anyone.

"A present," Martha parried, hopefully.

"A birthday present. Today *is* her birthday isn't it? She's sixteen, I believe." The tone was more anxious now, and Martha knew exactly why. Carl Ulick couldn't be *absolutely* sure that it *was* Jennifer's birthday. He couldn't be absolutely sure that she was sixteen. He probably hadn't even been absolutely sure that her name was Jennifer until Martha had let the name pass unchallenged.

On the Net, Martha knew, people lied. They lied about everything. On the Net you could change your name, your sex, your age, your sate of mind and your state of *being.* Carl Ulick might have been tap-tap-tapping at Jennifer for years, with Jennifer blink-blink-blinking back as fast as she could flutter her eyelashes, but for all Carl Ulick *really* knew, Jennifer might be an incontinent old man with emphysema and a sick sense of humour. Didn't they have a saying nowadays? *The truth is in the flesh.* Oh yes — the truth was in the flesh all right. The truth of Jennifer was flesh through and through. *Frail* flesh.

As it happened, though, it really was Jennifer's birthday and she really was sixteen. This was the thirteenth of the month, and it was Friday. Poor Geoff would be stuck on the M4 somewhere near the junction with the M25. Come 4 o'clock on a Friday all the trouble in the world was focused on the junction where the airport traffic met up with the commuters streaming out of London, and this was the thirteenth: Disaster Day. Poor Geoff, late for his daughter's birthday. If no one else complained about the higgledy-piggledy icing he would. He had no idea — no idea at all.

"Mrs Mortimore?"

The troubled gaze of whatever was behind the dark glasses was boring into her. For all she knew, Carl Ulick has eyes like Superman's, able to see right through her apron and her blouse, her bra and her breasts, all the way to her beating heart. *It has to be gold*, she thought, *with all the vitriol flowing through it.* But she was being unfair to herself.

"I'm sorry," she said, rallying. "That's very kind of you Carl. I'll give it to her." She stuck out her hand with all the parental authority she could muster, even though she knew full well that he wasn't going to hand it over.

"I'd like to give it to her myself, if I may," said the boy, disguising his adamantine stubbornness with all the politeness a boy his age could muster. "I've come quite a way, you see."

Martha had always known that the greatest advantage of the Net was its vast range. On the Net, you could talk to people in Timbuktu and Tokyo as easily as people in the next street. In the Global Village, everyone was a neighbour — which meant that no one you knew was likely to pop round for a cup of sugar. The downside was that if anyone ever did take the trouble to call, they'd expect the kind of welcome that befitted someone who'd come 'quite a way'.

How much, Martha wondered, *has she told this boy? Which lies need protecting? Am I supposed to let him in, just like that? How am I supposed to know, when she hasn't taken the trouble to tell me?* "Really," she said, without moving aside to let the boy in the house. "Where from exactly?"

"Oxford," he replied.

In Global Village terms, Oxford was practically next door. *Why couldn't the silly little slut make friends in Adelaide or Vancouver?* Martha thought — but she immediately felt ashamed of having called her daughter a slut, and then felt more deeply ashamed as she realised that it might have been a Freudian slip. People had sex on the Net, or so it was said. They tap-tap-tapped and blink-blink-blinked all kinds of dirty stuff to one another, working themselves up to....

"Well, that's very thoughtful of you," Martha said, severing her own train of thought with calculated brutality, "but you really should have phoned first. Jennifer's asleep, I'm afraid, and she really isn't able to receive visitors even when she's...."

"She told me not to," Carl Ulick said, wincing slightly as he realised that impatience had made *him* interrupt. "Phone, that is. I would have....only she told me not to. She *invited* me. I was hoping...."

"That she'd told us," Martha finished for him, feeling that her golden heart might be slowing in its paces — but the obligation to continue the scrupulously polite conversation still remained.

"Well, she didn't," Martha continued. "I think she knew well enough that we wouldn't — *couldn't* — have allowed it. We have to be very careful, you see. Everyone agrees that it's better for her to be at home than permanently in hospital, but we do have to be *very* careful. She had no right to ask you to come." It sounded feeble even to her, in spite of the fact that it was true. Unfortunately, the gaze of whatever was behind those dark glasses was still boring into her like an electric drill.

"I understand how you feel," the boy lied. "You don't have to worry, Mrs Mortimore — I really am a friend. I know all about Jennifer's condition. I'm not going to be surprised, or horrified. I've been helping her, you see — ever since she got the eyes. It was easier for me. I got mine when I was three, and the visual cortex had plenty of time to adapt to the interface. I didn't even have to *learn*, not really...but they put me through the programme anyway. Jennifer has a much more advanced model, of course. I almost wish I could trade mine in, but the adaptation's set now. I really have been able to help her, to talk her through. I know she can do even better than she has, Mrs Mortimore. I know how much the human brain can do, under the pressure of necessity."

The torrent of words left Martha numb. She hadn't even attempted to follow the meaning of the sentences, although she had heard every word. She had been too busy thinking: *I have to let him in. I can't say no. I have to let him in.* She told herself again, truthfully, that there was nothing to be afraid of, but she still couldn't quite accommodate the fact.

"You'd better come in," she said, colourlessly. She let him past and closed the door behind him. He waited politely until she ushered him into the living-room. He sat down on the sofa, in response to another gestured invitation. There was nothing wrong with his common-or-garden eyesight, whatever else his shades were hiding.

"Would you like a cup of tea?" Martha asked.

He wanted to refuse, and nearly did, but he obviously came to the conclusion that it was best to play it by the book in the hope of smoothing things over. He wanted everything to go *well.* He wanted everyone to be happy. He wanted the moon on a stick, and he probably had the means of getting it, even though Jennifer had a *much more advanced model.*

"Please," he said.

"I'm afraid you'll have to wait until my husband gets home," Martha said, seizing the only initiative that remained to be seized. "When he comes...well, perhaps...." She left it at that. Carl Ulick nodded politely, as befitted a boy who'd just sat down on someone else's sofa in someone else's living room and accepted a cup of tea.

Martha left him there, and hurried to the kitchen.

As soon as she'd plugged the kettle in Martha whipped the phone from it's cradle and stabbed out the number of Geoff's mobile. He answered immediately — which was ominous itself. Martha listened for the sound the engine made when the Helvetia was booming along in fast-moving traffic, like a squadron of bumble bees at the bottom of a well, but she couldn't hear it.

"Where are you?" she demanded, without preamble.

"Stuck just west of junction eight. Accident. Bastard must have turned sideways or something — only one lane left. Yellowjackets in sight, but they're filtering half a dozen at a...."

Martha wasn't interested in technicalities. "How long?"

"I'll still be early," he protested. "I left at three, as promised. Not my fault if..."

"There's someone *here*," she told him, trying to keep her voice down in case Carl Ulick could hear her over the hiss of the kettle.

"What kind of *someone*?" Geoff made no attempt to hide his exasperation.

"A boy. He says Jenny *invited* him. He's brought her a *birthday present.*"

There was a pause. Geoff always made a point of pausing when someone told him something he didn't want to know, to give the impression that he was deep in thought. It was a habit he'd picked up at the office.

The kettle switched itself off. Martha wondered whether to get the teapot out of the cupboard under the sink, but decided not to bother. It was only a boy, after all. She did fetch cups down, though, putting aside the mug she usually used for herself. She flipped a tea bag into each cup and poured water on.

"Okay," said Geoff. "You tell him Jenny's asleep. You take the present off him and tell him that we'll give it to her when she wakes up. Thank him kindly, give him a cup of tea and a chocolate digestive and tell him we're sorry."

Martha reached back up to the cupboard to get the chocolate digestives.

"I've done all that," she said, witheringly. "He isn't going to go. He's wearing *dark glasses*. She realised as she said it that it sounded ridiculous, as if dark glasses were the mark of a race apart — a race which couldn't be subjected to the pressures of everyday etiquette. Except, of course, that it wasn't as ridiculous as it sounded, because people who wore dark glasses for the reason Carl Ulick was wearing dark glasses really were a race apart, and because her own daughter was a member of that race apart, and because that really did mean that the pressure of everyday etiquette wasn't adequate to get the boy out of the house and away before Geoff got home.

Martha took advantage of deep-thought-pause number two to agitate the water in the cups and press the tea bags against the sides to make them yield up their treasure.

"She invited him, you say?" Geoff asked. It wasn't so much a comment, more a punctuation mark to signal that he was still thinking hard.

"So he says," Martha agreed, unable to stop herself from adding: "She would, wouldn't she? Not tell us, I mean."

"It's okay," Geoff said. "Maybe. No need for....well, what I mean is, maybe we should just accept it as *normal*. I mean, it *is* her birthday and she *is* sixteen, and...well, hell, just wait till I get there, okay. Don't do anything. Just hang on. It's no big deal."

Martha hoped that he could perform better than that in the office. If he couldn't people must fall about laughing every time he launched himself into one of his pregnant pauses. On the other hand, if he could perform better than that in the office he wouldn't still be in the office. Anyone who was anyone these days used a home-based work station. The only people who still set out every weekday morning to run the gauntlet of the M4 were salesmen, delivery boys and people too stupid to get fully to grips with the new technology.

It's alright for people like Carl Ulick, she thought. *Born blind and probably born deaf too, he's still a child of the twenty-first century. He grew up with it all, when it wasn't just his visual cortex that was nice and pliable, ready to adapt. I was born in 1980 and never laid a finger on a keyboard until I was in Miss James's class, by which time I was a fully fledged technophobe. Geoff's five years older than me, and never got closer to IT than his playstation. We're dinosaurs. Jenny's may be the last generation to suffer what she's suffering, but we're the last generation to suffer what we're suffering. All wrecks together.*

"Thanks a bunch," she said aloud, as Geoff bid her goodbye without giving her time to formulate a proper reply, pretending that he had to put the mobile down and get stuck into some serious driving. She knew that the phrase had been out of data since she was a child, but it still stuck in her mind, still likely to come through in her private thoughts because her brain simply wasn't adaptable enough to discard it.

Martha hung up the receiver and fished the tea bags out of the cups. She put the saucers on the tray with the milk jug and the sugar bowl, then placed the cups carefully upon the saucers. Then, fully armed for the fray, she set off for the living- room, wishing she had married someone with more sense and better genes — and regretting, even more, that she hadn't been born with more sense and better genes herself.

✢✢✢✢✢

"I was just icing Jennifer's birthday cake when you rang the doorbell," Martha told Carl Ulick, making the point that Jennifer did have birthdays, ad parents who cared about them — parent who *made an effort*, in spite of the fact that they hadn't actually bought her a present this year. There was no way of knowing what Jennifer might have told the boy, but he could see for himself how things were, how neat and normal the house was, how decently aproned and ever dutiful Martha was.

"Don't let me keep you," the boy said. "I'll be okay."

Martha wanted to take advantage of the invitation to retreat but she didn't dare. If she'd gone back into the kitchen she'd have been safe from conversation, but not from embarrassment. The problem was that he *would* be okay, that in a sense he wouldn't even *be* here. His body would be sitting patiently on the sofa but his eyes would be looking out upon some other world entirely — a world that was exclusive to him and his kind: the empire of the blind. He had been helping Jennifer to find her way within it, to make the journey that was far more difficult for her because her visual cortex had become set in its ways while she could still see out of her own eyes.

"That's all right," she said. "It won't take a minute, once Geoff's home. He's stuck on the motorway. An accident."

"I'm sorry," he said, probably referring to the accident rather than Geoff being stuck.

"The roads don't get any better," she said. "Ever since I was your age they've been saying that the day of the commuter is dead, but it doesn't seen to make a jot of difference how many people work from home. It's partly the airport, of course. We signed a petition against the sixth terminal, but no one ever takes any notice of petitions." The more she talked the easier it became. Now that she was sitting down, sipping tea, she felt much more at home, almost in control of herself, if not the situation.

"May I take these off?" the boy asked, as if he'd read her thoughts and knew exactly how to throw a spanner in the works. He meant the glasses, of course.

She barely hesitated. "Of course," she said. After all, she saw Jennifer's eyes every day. Jennifer never wore dark glasses.

The boy removed the shades, folded them up and tucked them away in the breast pocket of his jacket. It was good jacket — must have cost at least four hundred, with a quality label.

Carl Ulick's eyes were blue. It was a discreet blue, though, not the kind of Day-Glo blue that the kind of people who used contact lenses as fashion accessories went in for. It was easy enough to see, if you looked hard, that the eyes were false, but they weren't *obtrusively* false. All the miraculously-compacted electronic bits were tucked away inside. Martha didn't have a clue what any of that stuff actually looked like, or how any of it worked; she still had to think in terms of miniature computers and miniature radio stations, as if Jennifer's eyes were lumber rooms packed tight with tiny screens and keyboards with tiny cinema projectors to project the virtual displays on the retina.

"How long have you known Jennifer?" Martha asked, trying to make it seem like the perfectly natural question that it was.

"Three years," he told her. "She posted a notice asking for advice — about training the cortex, that is. She needed moral support. I couldn't tell her anything the doctors hadn't, but it makes a difference if it's coming from the *inside.* The doctors know the theory, but they don't know how it feels. Only people who actually use their eyes really know what's involved in learning to see."

Martha felt a stab of guilt when he said that. *Of course* Jennifer couldn't get adequate moral support from her parents. *Of course* she had to go to the Net in search of fellow citizens of the New Self. *Of course* she never told her parents who she was talking to, or what about, or to what effect. Why waste time blink-blink-blinking at your parents when you could be talking to somebody *real*? Why bother to tell them you've invited some smart kid to your birthday party to see that the stupid icing on your futile cake is all over the bloody place?

"I suppose the time will come when we'll rip out the eyes of new-born babies as a matter of routine," Martha said, deliberately treading on dangerous ground. "Why leave them with a handicap when it's so easy to train their visual cortex to use supersight? In a hundred years time, people like me will be freaks. And it won't just be eyes, will it? By then, it will be whole bodies. Maybe they'll just take out the babies' brains and put them into different flesh, better in every imaginable way than the stuff mere genes provide. On the other hand, maybe they'll be superintelligent brains made out of silicon chips, so that we won't need the babies at all."

The trouble with dangerous ground, she thought, as she lowered her eyes to avoid his accusative stare, *is that it's always downhill every step of the way.*

"I don't think that's the right way to think about it," Carl Ulick opined, his fluty voice as mild as milk. "In my case, it really was a case of *replacement.* My eyes and ears didn't work, so the doctors took them out and gave me ones that did — ones that had extra abilities. When they're dealing with people whose eyes *do* work, they don't think in terms of replacement. They think in terms of *augmentation.*"

Martha didn't want an argument, especially today. It was Friday the thirteenth, after all. Jennifer was sixteen. Sweet sixteen and never been kissed, except perhaps in virtual reality. In virtual reality, she might have done *anything* — except, of course, that her visual cortex was still having trouble with adaptation. She could look out into cyberspace, live within the Net far more comfortably and far more fully than she'd ever be able to live in the world of her parents, but she was still half-blind there because her brain was too set in its ways. Even in the empire of the blind, she was still a cripple of sorts — and this was the guide dog who had come to her aid: the sighted man who was a king in the country of the exiles, the country beyond the borders of reality. Maybe Jennifer hadn't had sex even on the Net. Maybe she was still a stranger, and afraid, in the land she never made.

I ought to know! Martha thought. *She ought to tell me. I'm her mother, after all. I don't even know if she hates me for not having better genes, or the benefit of genetic counselling, or for having eyes that see after their own stupid fashion.*

"I'm sure they do," she said, in answer to Carl Ulick's little homily. "And I'm sure you're right about the proper way to think about it. I'm really very glad that Jennifer has been able to use her eyes, and that there are people out there who can help her. It's just....so difficult to understand. She doesn't talk to us much, you see. Now that she's found a world where she can function so much better, she doesn't like to come back to ours. But she's still in ours, day in and day out." *The truth is in the flesh,* she added, silently.

"It must be very difficult for you," the boy conceded, graciously. "it was difficult for my parents, at first. I anchored them down for a long time, and when I wasn't a burden any more...well, as you say, it's as if I stepped into a world of my own, where they couldn't follow. I couldn't explain it to them — how it felt to be permanently tuned into the Net, with access to every printed page and every visual image stored there. I did try, but it wasn't so hard for me. Once the implants in my ears were working it was easy to learn to talk and I was so glad of it I babbled all the time about anything and everything. It's not so easy for Jennifer. For her, it's far easier to talk to me, or anyone else wired into the Net, than it is to talk to you. You mustn't think that it's because she doesn't want to. I'm sure she loves you very much, and I'm sure she's very grateful for everything you do for her."

"I know that," Martha assured him, dishonestly. "How much, exactly, do you *know* about Jennifer's condition?"

"I don't know much about medical science or molecular genetics," Carl Ulick told her, although she couldn't tell whether he was missing the point on purpose. "The technical terminology's beyond me. All I know, really, is that her motor nerves don't work and that the condition is still deteriorating. I gather that she's almost entirely paralysed. She told me that she needed the new eyes even if she never learned to see properly, because her eyelids were the only part of herself she still had enough control over to use — instead of fingers, that is. Sorry, I didn't put that very well — what I mean is...."

"It's alright," Martha told him, brusquely. "I know exactly what you mean." After a moment's hesitation, while she wondered why she didn't feel relieved that she didn't have to protect any lies that Jennifer had told, she continued: "She used to be able to use her fingers, you know — just a bit, for a while. Then, after they gave up on speech therapy, they fitted a keypad gizmo to her mouth so that she could pick out the letters with her tongue — but the disease is degenerative, you see. It just gets worse and worse."

"I know," the boy said. "She told me. I can't follow all the jargon, but she can."

Martha felt tears welling up then. For some reason, the thought that Jennifer understood what was happening to her — that the fancy eyes which had allowed her to look directly into the information-world of the Net had allowed her to read and inwardly digest every single research paper ever written about her condition — always seemed to add that extra turn of the screw to the tragedy itself.

Taking a defensive sip of tea, Martha tried to blink the tears away. She was determined not to make a show of herself by reaching up to dab at her eyes while the boy was watching her. "Why did you come here," she whispered. Her confusion made it impossible for her to hold the question back any longer.

Carl Ulick paused, but it wasn't one of Geoff's theatrical pauses. The boy really was thinking. Eventually he said: "I'm sorry if I've upset you, but it was Jennifer I came to see. I just wanted to give her a birthday present — and she wanted me to come. If you'd just let me see her for a few minutes....it really will be alright."

He's right, of course, Martha thought, still fighting back the tears. *I'm the one who's being stupid. I'm the one who's being blind. I'm the one who doesn't understand. Of course she's told him everything. Of course she wanted him to come. Of course she wouldn't think it was worth her while to try explaining it to us, blinking and blinking and blinking and knowing all the while that she wasn't getting through....*

Outside, in the road, she heard a car door bang. All the banging car doors sounded alike, but she knew that this particular bang was Geoff's. He'd been within sight of the men in yellow jackets, after all, and on the other side of the accident the road must have been beautifully clear. He'd probably had the accelerator flat to the boards ever since, and now he was here to complicate matters — after they'd only just been simplified.

She heard the sound of a key in the front door, and then she heard the door open and close. It didn't bang; no matter what kind of noise he made in the street Geoff always came into the house on tiptoe, out of respect for his daughter's condition.

"That's my husband," she said, wishing that she didn't sound — or look — so utterly foolish.

✢✢✢✢✢

"It's very kind of you to come all this way," Geoff said to Carl Ulick, "but I really don't think that Jennifer should have asked you without telling us."

"I'm sorry about that," the boy replied, doggedly, "but she is expecting me, and I can't see that there's a problem. I just want to give her a present."

Martha waited by the door. She knew that she ought to go into the kitchen and finish icing the birthday cake, but she also knew that she might be needed here. She now regretted the instinct that had sent her scurrying to the phone, anxious to turn the problem over to Geoff so that he could sort it out. It was an instinct that was utterly reliable where dripping taps and defective light-switches were concerned, but now that she thought back on all the Jennifer problems she had automatically turned over to Geoff she wasn't so sure that he had ever been the best person to handle them.

"The thing is," Geoff said, depositing his briefcase in the gap between the TV and the rubber-plant, exactly as he always did, "that I'm not sure you understand the situation here. Jennifer's a very sick girl. She doesn't have visitors, apart from doctors. I suppose she can communicate with you — and other people like you — fairly readily, in spite of the problems she's had adapting to her new eyes, but she isn't nearly so good at coping with face-to-face communication. I don't think you understand the kind of pressure you'd be putting her under by coming here *in person* to see her *in the flesh*. I can understand why she might have thought that that it was a nice idea, but I'm certain she hasn't *thought it through*. It's very kind of you, as I said, and we'll be only too glad to pass your present on to Jennifer, but we have to be *very* careful. I really don't think...."

Martha could see that Carl Ulick was becoming slightly annoyed. She was becoming rather annoyed herself — and that was unusual, because Geoff's speeches usually washed over her like steady rain, gradually wearing her down without ever raising the slightest hint of anger or resistance. She was afraid that the boy might say something that would make things worse, so she stepped in before he could.

"Would it really do any harm, Geoff?" she said. "Maybe if he just *looked in....*"

Geoff turned on her in frank astonishment, raising his eyebrows as if to say: *Is this what I rushed home for? Did I come hell for leather in answer to your hysterical call, only to find that you've gone over to the enemy?*

"I think it *might* do some harm," Geoff said, as if anyone but a complete idiot would have been able to understand his concern and support his stance. "I don't think this young man understands...."

"Actually, Mr Mortimore," said Carl Ulick, doing exactly what Martha had been afraid he'd do, "I think it might be you who doesn't understand."

Geoff's pause was the mother of all pauses. For the first time in her life, Martha understood what people meant when they said that there were times when you could hear a pin drop. She felt that she could have watched the pin fall, in slow motion close-up, even though she only had the eyes that nature had given her.

Like all Geoff's pauses, though, this one only led to an anti-climax. There was nowhere else it could lead, in a household as civilised as this one. "Indeed," he said, in a tone so falsely polite that you could have cut it with a paring knife. "In that case, perhaps you'd like to explain it to me."

Martha realised that Geoff thought he could deal with Carl Ulick as he might have dealt with any common-or-garden fourteen-year-old boy. He thought that his acid request for an explanation would only bring forth bluster and confusion. He thought that he had the upper hand within the ordered sanctum of his own home. Martha already knew that he was wrong on every count, and couldn't tear herself away even though she knew full well that he presence would make his humiliation worse.

"You said that Jennifer's a very sick girl," the boy said, by way of preamble.

"She is," Geoff confirmed, feeling that he was on safe ground. "Very sick indeed."

"In fact," Carl Ulick said, "you think she's dying."

Martha winced. Even Geoff winced. Neither of them wanted to make the obvious reply.

"Well, she isn't," the boy told them, with all apparent sincerity. "She used to be. She told me once that she used to think that there was nothing to life *except* dying, and that she was just saving time. Now she knows that she's *living*."

Martha could see that the boy was taking care not to go for the jugular. He was taking care not to say aloud what Jennifer must *actually* have said — that she was the only one in the house who had turned the corner, had given up dying and taken to living. But Jennifer had never said that to Martha. She had never said *anything* to Martha about *any* of this. She had turned for help to someone who had ears to hear and eyes to see — someone lucky enough to be born deaf and blind; someone lucky enough to take full advantage of the wonders of modern technology.

"I'm glad...." Geoff began — but Carl Ulick hadn't finished. His pauses were honest pauses.

"Jennifer knows that she's in a race," the boy said, "but she honestly thinks she has a fair chance of winning it. She's keeping a close eye on every team involved in relevant research. She thinks that they'll find a way to control the regeneration of neural tissue accurately enough to begin stitching her back together again — her phrase, not mine — before the degeneration kills her. She thinks they'll be able to hold her together long enough and well enough for what she calls *serious cyborgisation*. I think she's right. She can't see half the things I can see, because her visual cortex can't produce the illusion of deep immersion in virtual reality, but she can *read* and she can *hear*. I wish there were better ways to describe it, but there aren't. I suppose the only way you can imagine what she's experiencing is to think of her new eyes as little videophones planted in her skull — glorified versions of the mobile in your car — but the sight they offer is so much *richer* than that....*she's not dying, Mr Mortimore*. She was, but she isn't any more. I wish she could have explained that to you herself, but I can understand how difficult it is for her."

This time, Geoff didn't bother to pause. "Is that why she told you to come?" he wanted to know. "To *lecture* us?"

Of course it is, you bloody idiot, Martha thought. *And how else could she do it, when it's so hard for her to speak to us, and so much harder for us to listen?*

"Of course not," Carl Ulick said, as generously as he could. "I wanted to come, and she said I could. I wanted to give her a birthday present." He was still clutching the square package sealed in wine-coloured wrapping. *I bet it's a good present,* Martha thought. *I bet he knows what you ought to give a girl who has everything — everything, at least, that he could think of.*

"She should have told us," Geoff insisted, doggedly. "This isn't *right.*" But he knew he'd lost the battle, and the war. He didn't have any answer to the boy's charges.

"It's just a present, Geoff," Martha said, as soothingly as she could — and she'd had a *lot* of practice. "It can't do any harm to let him give it to Jenny himself. She'd never forgive us if we didn't." *And she'd be right,* she added, silently. *What can I have been thinking of, to be so scared?*

Geoff wilted. He could have shot Martha a venomous glance, but he didn't. He just wilted. Those blue, unshaded eyes had knocked the stuffing out of him — as if, like Superman's eyes, they had looked right into his heart and shrivelled it with heat. "Alright," he whispered. "If that's what you want."

He was talking to Martha, trying to shift the blame — but it was the boy who said: "It is."

"If you can hang on for two minutes," Martha said, "I'll finish icing the cake. We can all go up together." She wasn't ashamed of the cake any more. She knew that Carl Ulick wasn't going to look down on her because she couldn't ice a decent curve. She knew too, that he wasn't going to flinch when he saw Jennifer in the flesh.

✢✢✢✢✢

While they went up the stairs Martha wondered what was in the box. In times past she and Geoff had all kinds of options when Jennifer's birthday came round. They had bought her pictures to decorate the walls of her room, music to play on her stereo, textpaks to slot into her king-sized bookplate. Ever since she'd had her new eyes fitted, though, she'd been tuned into the Net.

Now, Jennifer could summon any piece of music she wanted, and she could replace the walls of her room with any of a million virtual rooms — and even if she couldn't see them very well, that was far, far better than the prison-cell in which she'd lived for more than twelve years.

Now the king-sized bookplate always faced away from the bed, displaying nothing but the things Jennifer said, when she took the trouble to use her blinking eyes to say anything at all.

Geoff had to open the door of Jennifer's room because Martha was holding the cake in both hands. She'd put a single lighted candle on it in the hope of making amends for the lousy icing. She intended to invite Carl Ulick to blow it out.

Jennifer wasn't asleep. She couldn't actually *look around* when the door opened, but her eyes shifted in their sockets. Like Carl Ulick's, Jennifer's eyes were blue, but they were a brighter blue than his. Her hair was bright too, and the time Martha had put into grooming it earlier that afternoon hadn't gone to waste. Jennifer wasn't pretty, and the wasting of her nerves had taken all the life out of her flat cheeks and slack mouth, but she did have nice hair.

Geoff should have introduced the visitor but he didn't. He just stood aside, unwilling or unable to rouse himself from his sulk. It wasn't that he was ashamed of the way his daughter was — he just couldn't avoid being infected, in spirit if not in body, by the fact of her slow decline. What the boy had told him hadn't made any difference; when he looked at Jennifer now he still saw a hopeless case. He didn't *dare* to hope.

Do I? Martha asked herself.

The lack of introduction didn't matter.

"Hello Jennifer," Carl Ulick said, shuffling nervously towards the bedside. "I'm Carl. I'm sorry I'm a little late."

HELLO CARL. GOOD TO SEE YOU AT LAST. The words appeared on the out-turned bookplate with marvellous alacrity, red letters against a black background. Martha realised that Jennifer must have set up in advance, ready to flash at the least twitch of her eyelid.

"Your mother's bought your cake," Carl told her, dutifully, "and I've bought you a present."

But the cake's useless, Martha thought. *Now that you can only take liquids, cake's just as useless as all the other things we used to give you. We can think of you while we eat it, but all you can do is look at it and weigh its worth as a measure of our love.* She knew that she was being stupidly maudlin, but she couldn't help it. She blinked away the threat of a tear and concentrated hard on Carl Ulick's slender fingers as they tore the sellotape away, peeled back the burgundy wrapping-paper and lifted the lid of the white plastic box within.

Jennifer was watching too. For the moment, her eyes were turned away from the wide world of the Net, bringing the *ordinary* world into focus — the world where her poor half-blind parents were condemned to spend their relentlessly ordinary lives.

The thing that lay in the five-inch box was less than four inches across. It was round and lenticular, like an oversized magnifying glass. Martha could see that it wasn't glass, though — it had a texture like jelly, or one of those silicone implants they used to implant in women's breasts in the days before cosmetic somatic engineering. It seemed to be some kind of fluid filled sac but the fluid wasn't clear; it had *clouds* in it: ominously dark clouds, as grey as thunderheads.

The boy set the box down on the bed and used two hands to lift the jelly up. His attitude was reverent and his hands didn't shake at all. Martha glanced down at her own burden, and the awkward way she bore it, but she soon returned her attention to the bed, the boy and the blinking bookplate.

WHAT IS IT?

This time, Jennifer had to blink each letter individually but the message appeared by swift and sure degrees.

"It's a closed ecosystem," Carl said, glancing sideways at Martha to include her in the explanation. "You can get them in glass globes, with photosynthetic algae to import the energy required to keep them going, but this is different. These are all artificial micro-organisms, cooked up in a lab. The primary producers are thermosynthetic. Instead of soaking up photons they absorb heat from the environment. The soft shell's a wonderfully efficient conductor. If I put it on your chest, just below the neck, it will absorb heat from your skin. Your body-heat will become the motor of a little universe. There's nothing bigger than a single cell, but the organisms at the top of the food-chain are bioluminescent. When it's stabilised you can see them glinting in the dark, like tiny flashes of lighting."

As he spoke the boy placed the lump of jelly exactly where he said he would. He didn't have to move anything out of the way; the intelligent mattress and coverlet that kept Jennifer's unmoving body free of bedsores required her to be naked, and the coverlet only came up far enough to hide her nipples, for modesty's sake.

Jennifer didn't have to look down to see it. There was a mirror set above her bed, so that she could look at herself. She had insisted, and Geoff hadn't been able to talk her out of it. Jennifer looked into the mirror now with her bright blue eyes, studying the circle that lay on her sternum like an emerald pendant, grey clouds set against the background of her uncannily pale skin.

"You don't have to keep it on all the time, of course," the boy told her. "If you put it somewhere cool the whole system goes into suspended animation — a kind of hibernation." He turned to Martha, adding: "You don't need to put it in the fridge. A drawer will do."

LEAVE IT, Jennifer said, as if she feared Martha might ship it away instantly.

I knew it would be good, Martha thought. *Even though we racked our brains and couldn't think of anything, I knew there had to be an answer. Her eyes already give her access to everything there is to be seen, and her flesh is so frail that she can't lift a finger or even use her tongue to proper effect, but she still has blood in her veins and heat in her heart — heat enough to sustain a world in miniature.*

"The truth is in the flesh," she murmured. She was talking to herself, but everybody could hear her.

NO. The word appear angrily red on Jennifer's bookplate. The device added, letter by letter: NOT TRUTH. NOT ME.

Martha knew that her acute embarrassment must be showing. The candle-flame flickered as her hands shook.

"What Jennifer means." Carl Ulick said, softly, "is that *truth* is in the senses. *Truth* is in what you see and hear, and how you interpret it. *Warmth* is in the flesh."

It was Geoff who asked: "Do you like the present, Jenny?"

YES, the bookplate flashed. WEAR IT ALWAYS. WANT TO SEE THE LIGHT.

"Me too," said Geoff.

"You'll have to wait a while," Carl Ulick advised. "Give it a couple of hours, then switch off the lights. When your eyes have adjusted to the dark, you'll see the sparks. It's beautiful."

"I baked you a cake," Martha said, as she came forward to join the boy. "I'm sorry about the icing. I just can't seem to steady my hands any more. I'll put some icing in the blender later, so that you can taste it. Would you like Carl to blow out the candle?"

YES.

Carl blew out the candle. He opened his mouth to say something else but he stopped when he saw the bookplate's screen flicker into life again.

I LOVE YOU, Jennifer spelt out, one red letter at a time.

Carl was, after all, a fourteen-year-old boy. He couldn't take that kind of declaration with equanimity. Like a perfect fool — a gloriously perfect fool — he turned to Martha and said: "She means you." He meant I told you so — and so he had. Not that Martha had ever doubted that her daughter would love her parents, if she could. All that Martha had doubted was that her daughter was still capable of love, now that her frail flesh had become so pale, so nearly dead.

Jennifer had set the message to repeat.

I LOVE YOU, the screen said. I LOVE YOU. I LOVE YOU. I LOVE YOU.

Martha wasn't about to object to Carl Ulick's heroic attempt to include them in Jennifer's fulsome thanks, and neither was Geoff. Geoff wasn't quite magnanimous enough to suggest aloud that the message might have meant to include *all* of them, but that was only because he was too busy pausing. He knew well enough what Jennifer meant.

Carl Ulick's face was as crimson as the letters. His confusion was a joy to behold — but he was pleased. He was certain that he'd done the right thing, delighted that he'd had the guts to follow through. Martha knew that even Geoff must be relieved, by now, that he hadn't managed to deflect the boy from his purpose.

Martha also knew, and was very glad she knew, that it didn't matter in the least who Jennifer's words were intended for.

The important thing — the *only* important thing — was that she was able to mean what she said.

NETWORKED CREATION

Mariko Ohara

Mariko Ohara is probably Japan's leading science fiction novelist, and her stories are a commentary on many contemporary issues, particularly in the cyberpunk domain. Extremely popular inside the country, she is still relatively unknown in English language markets. Stephen McClelland interviewed her in Tokyo.

Networked Creation

Mariko Ohara

I am not sure I have a unique view of the future. I am familiar with trends and the situation in Japan of course, but not those in North America or Europe. Attitudes in Japan have been shaped quite differently to those in other developed countries. One characteristic of the Japanese culture for example is a degree of formalism, think; this is best exemplified by the well-known Tea Ceremony, which itself is a kind of presentation of ideas, but ideas presented in a formal expression.

In terms of my stories, I am inspired by quite a few themes some of which have a relationship to communications in the wider sense. These would include: networks, capitalism, nationhood, information, religion, authority, organisation, economic crime, and women's issues. But I do expect the spread of networking to affect the behaviour of Japanese society in general. Take for example the availability of 'free' software from the Net; this could have a profound economic impact.

I recalled the fact that joy would drive a person to create things. A creator wants to share the rapture given to oneself with others.

Networking has certainly changed my life. As time has progressed, I have graduated from using a phone to an answering machine to a fax machine to a PC connectivity. From nowhere, I received a thousand e-mails about my work from interested parties. I have been very excited by each step forward. I set up my own Web page, complete with my thoughts and diary. This has been a very curious experience but very interesting one — more like striptease than anything else.

Changes in the more general culture have already begun in several different directions. For example, I was strongly impressed by what happened after the Kobe earthquake in

Japan. For the first time I saw on the TV volunteers helping to ease the situation in Kobe. Interestingly, in Japan, there has been little ethic of volunteering for something; it has been seen as something potentially rather patronising in the culture and to be avoided, and yet these people without formal organisation were doing this themselves. Much of this was provided through the sort of networking I am describing. When I am in contact with people through the Net I feel very comfortable, certainly much more comfortable than in physical Japanese society. So, I believe, perhaps only half-seriously, that the Net has the potential to destroy Japanese society as we know it!

Although the volunteer spirit does not belong only to women, traditionally, they tend to work as mothers, nurses or kindergarten teachers. I imagine women have kept the thought separate from that of severe capitalism. As such this separation has now been re-evaluated, I expect, it will gradually change what Japanese capitalism should be.

As we look forward in society, there are some issues to be addressed also related to networking. One thing very clear is that we will be facing issues of natural resource depletion and of course pollution in the next few decades. We have to address these issues. But I also detect in this society that people may well find a remedy to their own situations; the best thing is when they want to create something. In fact, when I am shopping and I see mass-produced goods for sale, I am reminded of the fact that people seem to have lost the art of craftsmanship. But alongside this, I visit something in Tokyo which is very popular — the Comic Market — and I realise that people do want to be creative quite outside some commercial domain. Networking will help them realise this.

The Final Re-Make of the Return of Little Latin Larry, With a Completely Re-Mastered Soundtrack and the Original Audience

Pat Cadigan

Pat Cadigan has been hailed as 'The Queen of Cyberpunk' as well as one of the most intelligent SF writers to emerge in the last decade. Sometime SF magazine editor and greetings card writer in Overland Park, Kansas, she now makes her home in London. Her principal, widely-acclaimed and award-winning works have included *Mindplayers* and *Synners*, set in a near future of lethal computer viruses poisoning computer interfaces. This story is an elegant and witty media tour de force set sometime perhaps in the not too distant future.

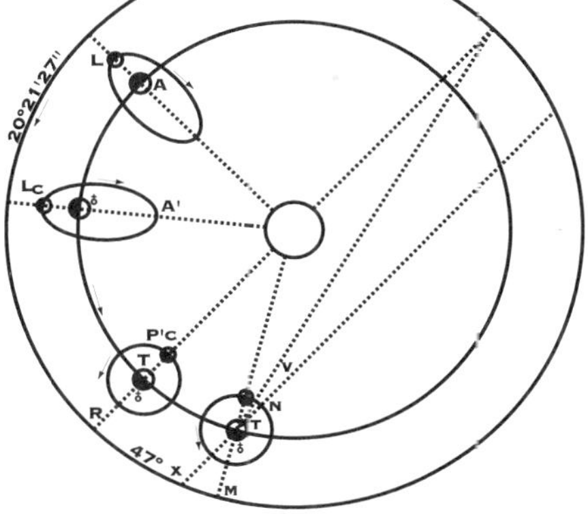

The Final Re-Make of the Return of Little Latin Larry...

Pat Cadigan

So! Fix yourself a smell and sit down!

There's a wet bar, too, if you go that way. You know, for years, I told myself I didn't, even though I always kept a full complement of cheers, vines, and the hards and their pards. I'd say to myself, *Oh, but of course the hooch is strictly for hospitality and nothing else.*

But now, I'm out about it and I really feel much more non-bad about it. And wasn't it Elvis who said, "Drinkers, like the poor, we will always have with us"?

Or was that Dylan? Might have been — Dylan was the big expert on drinkers, wasn't he, dying as he did face down in the gutter — lucky beast! — not fifty paces from the Tired Horse Tavern where he came up with his biggest and best — 'All The Tired Horses' (of course!), 'Knockin' on Fern Hill's Door,' 'The Hand That Signed A Paper Got To Serve Somebody,' and, my personal favourite, 'Do Not Go Gentle Into Those Subterranean Homesick Blues.' 'Rage, rage against the leaders, watch the parking —'

Sorry, sorry, sorry! I can *barely* hold still, this is such an exciting time for me. I think my man Dylan put it best when he said, "I sang in my chains: *everybody* must get stoned." One of his most evocative lines, at least for me. Even now, long, long, *long* after I first read it, it still stirs up for me the sensation of that state where you're practically thrumming in excitement, and the only thing that keeps you from flying up in the air and dragging the whole world after you like a cape tied around your shoulders is the incontrovertible fact of your just-that-much-too-heavy flesh —

Sorry *again*! The human condition tends to make me wax poetic. Rather, it makes me *want* to wax poetic, except I can never think of the poetic counterpart to words like 'incontrovertible.' Got a drink now? Good, good, sit, sit. Did you smell anything you liked? No? Ah — you must tell me the truth here: did the aromabar intimidate you, or are you just not olfactory? I vow that either way, I'm not insulted, truly I'm not. Not all senses can be our senses, can they? And when you're retro besides — well, some people can get that so wrong.

Like the other day. Packed in my usual buzzbomb was a silly tag from one of my sillier friends telling me that everyone was saying behind my back that I was the most retro creature they'd ever heard of. I tagged back to tell Old Sillyhead that not only were they saying it behind my back, but also behind my front, too, and in front of my back and all that, and so *what*.

Anyway, it's not like I'm detoxing and then relapsing just for the wallop that first sinful sip will give you. I know people who have gone through three and four livers that way, even with top-of-the-line blood-doping. But I don't consider *them* drinkers. And personally, I think Teflon™ on the CNS is cheating.

And in spite of what you may have heard, the aromabar really is just for amusement, I don't do aromatherapy of any kind. Of course, anyone who does is welcome to mix themselves a bouquet with my essences and if they *want* to claim it gave them some kind of therapeutic fizz, *I'm* not going to argue with them. After all, we all sing our own particular song in our chains, don't we.

But you'll want to know about the last remake, won't you. *That* last remake. Everybody always wants to know about that. I swear, I'll do a thousand projects before I go gentle into my subterranean homesick blues and the one thing I'll be remembered for is that damned remake. Everyone'll *still* be mad at me for one of two reasons and by god, they'll both be wrong.

So, one more time, for the record and with feeling: I did not rediscover Little Latin Larry, and I didn't kill him.

Who did?

Well, I was afraid you'd ask me that.

✢✢✢✢✢

First of all, let's get all the facts we know — all right, all the facts I know — straight. You'll pardon me if I go over to the bar and fix myself a few memory aids. This brown stuff here, this is an esoteric drink called Old Peculier, which is the liquid equivalent of wrapping yourself in a comfy blanket on an uncommonly bad day. Fair Annie — you wouldn't know her, she liked the low profile life — introduced me to it. But this other stuff that looks a lot like, well, frankly, urine — it's no-class lager. *Cheap beer* was the term for it then and it was sought after for both its cheapness and its beerness, if you see what I mean.

The Old Peculier is for drinking, just because I like it. But the lager is for smelling, because I can remember Larry best when I smell cheap beer. It was just about the only thing you ever smelled around Larry.

And let's get something else straight: the full name of the band was Little Latin Larry and His Loopy Louies, His Luscious Latinaires, and His Lascivious Latinettes.

Little Latin Larry was, of course, lead vocalist, conductor, arranger, and erstwhile composer. Which is to say, for a while, he was trying out some originals on the playlist. I've heard them. They weren't too bad, you know; they were just meant to be songs to dance to, or jump up and down to, or puke to, if you went that way (not like the Bulimic Era stuff — that was later, and didn't have much to do with having a good time). But every time Larry tried to slip in an original, everyone would just kind of stand there looking puzzled. There'd be some people dancing, some people nodding along, a few of the hard-core puking, but most of them just stood around with these lost expressions, and you could tell they were trying to place the song and couldn't. So Larry forgot about being even a cheap-beer ditty-monger and went back to covers. There were skintillions of bands that played covers for anyone who hired them, but when Larry and the band did a cover it was —

Pardon my long pause here. I heard those, too, of course. I could say that when Little Latin Larry and Co. covered a song, it was, for the duration, completely their own, as if no one else had ever sung it. And if I did put it that way, I would be both right and wrong. Just as, if I said, when they covered a song, it was a complete tribute to the original artists. That would be right and wrong as well.

It was both. It was neither. It was an experience. It was all shades of one experience, a million experiences in one. In other words, you had to be there. Yes. You had to be there at least once.

But no, I won't try to wiggle out on that one. Even if there is so much truth to it that most people *were* there once. Whether they were there or not.

I don't *expect* you to understand me. I'm a visionary. No, just kidding, just shaking your leg, as (I think) they used to say.

All right, back to it, now. The Larry people came to me. I don't care what they told everyone later about my chasing them over hill and dale, or chip and dale, or nook and cranny. The Realm of the Senses Theatre kept me busy enough that I didn't have to chase anyone. People were always beating down the door with sense-memories. My staff at that time was a mad thing named Ola, about three and a half feet all — achondroplasia — who usually kept most of her brain in her sidekick, and vice versa. Half the time, you never knew exactly which was which. It wasn't really any kind of intentional thing, or a statement or anything. Ola just went that way. A happy accident. Happy for Ola. So she mated with a machine, so *what.* I may be retro, but I'm not *that* retro; I certainly wasn't then.

Ola put off a lot of people for a variety of reasons — she was doing the jobs of several people and so depriving them of jobs, cyborgs were against Nature or the Bible, or she wasn't *enough* of a cyborg to claim the title (which she didn't in the first place), or she was too spooky, too feminine, not feminine enough, not *spooky* enough, for god's sake. People, my god; people. Nature gave them tongues, technology gave them loudspeakers, and they all believe that because they can use both, whatever they say is important.

I suppose that was why I started Realm of the Senses Theatre. The watchwords of the time were 'custom,' 'customisable,' 'individual,' and 'interactive.' Heavy on the 'interactive.' What the hell did that mean, anyway, 'interactive'? I used to rant about this to Ola and her sidekick all the time. Who the hell thought up 'interactive', I'd say; your goddamn *shoes* are interactive, every item of clothing you put on is 'interactive,' your *car* is 'interactive', what is the big goddamn reverb on 'interactive,' goddamn *life* is 'interactive' —

And Ola would say, Oh, not interactive, Gracie, kibitz. Everybody's got to have a little say in how it goes. Do it in blue; I want it in velvet; it would be perfect if it was about twice as long and half as high. *You* know.

So that was what Realm of the Senses Theatre did. It gave people a say in their own entertainment. You could have it in blue, in velvet, half as high and twice as long, so to speak, and if you didn't like it, it was your own look-out. But old retro Gracie — yes, even then I had a retro streak a mile wide — old retro Gracie used to think about staging some kind of event that people *couldn't* interfere with, couldn't amp up or down, or customise in any way — an event that you'd just have to experience as it was, on its own terms not yours. And then see what happened to *you* afterward. So I started thinking about something called

High Sky Theatre. I was calling it that because I was thinking the event would be like the sky — you could see it, even get right up in the middle of it, but you couldn't change it, it rained on you or it didn't and you had to adjust yourself, not it.

And then, synchronicity, I guess. I was just toying with a few designs for the logo — High Sky Theatre in floating puffy holo cloud letters — and the Larry people got in touch with me.

Right at the outset, they told me that they were all direct blood-positive descendants of the band and it was the first time that they had managed to get one of each — i.e., one of Larry's descendants, one descendant of a Loopy Louie, one of a Luscious Latinaire, and one of a Lascivious Latinette. And even a descendant of someone who had been in the audience when Little Latin Larry and the etc. had gotten back together and made their triumphant return to performing.

Now, I had seen the original *The Return of Little Latin Larry* as well as the first re-make. The original, I must say, had been story-heavy enough to keep your interest but very thin in the experiential department. Larry's descendant told me that was because they'd been missing both a Latinaire and a Latinette — they'd only had a Larry, a Loopy Louie, a few friends of a different Loopy Louie, and a Latinaire groupie. For the first remake, they had managed to find a couple of audience members, and that was a little bit better, but it still meant the backstage stuff was thin. Then the Latinaire groupie's descendant quit because he said he didn't really feel like he was an accepted part of the band. Which I guess was kind of true — the groupie's association with the Latinaire had been a one-time thing, never to be repeated. According to Larry's descendant, his absence didn't take away much, if anything, from subsequent re-makes.

The descendants' names? It's hard to remember now, but if you give me a little while, they'll come back to me. I had to think of them as Little Latin Larry and so forth because I didn't want to go contaminating the memory with associations that didn't belong. It *sounds* over-meticulous, sure, and don't think I haven't heard that and more about my methods and everything. But I had to stay focused. I didn't want anachronisms popping up because I was blind to them myself. You go ahead and inspect any feature I've made and I promise you that you will find — for example — only native-to-the-era clothing, and not *made-to-look-native*-to-the-era clothing. Some say you can't tell the difference, but *I* say you can. Even if it *looks* perfect, the smell and feel aren't right. If you're going to go to the trouble of distilling the memory of the event, either take it all the way or don't bother, period.

And while this may seem overly fussy to some people I won't name, it's how I can spot a forgery more quickly than anyone else. Some red faces on *that* subject, I can tell you. Believe me, I know the difference between someone who is descended from someone who was there — whatever *there* we're talking about — and someone who swallowed a re-creation. One of the red faces I won't name maintains to this day that he was completely bamboozled by pseudo-Zapruder, but really, if he was doing his job right, I don't see how he could have been. But that's not my look-out, is it.

So. Having the Larry people (as I called them) all together and ready, we hired a clinic and Ola and her sidekick went to work with the genealogists. This would be the part where my eyes would start to glaze over, to be perfectly honest (which I have always tried to be). Biochemical genealogy is one of those things I just don't *get.* Every so often, Ola and her sidekick would try to explain it to me even when I'd beg them not to. The memory is retained biochemically, and what memory exists when an offspring is conceived might be passed on to that child depending on how the genes line up, dominant, recessive, blue eyes, white forelock, the ability to roll your tongue — I don't know, genetics just confuse me, biochemistry confuses me, life is confusing enough, you know? All I know is the blood has to test positive for distillable memory by the presence of something-or-other. Frankly, I think that's about as technical as anybody needs to get about anything in the arts.

Ola and her sidekick went right to work with the distilled samples, which is something like working a jigsaw puzzle in five dimensions per sample. Every bit of recovered memory is keyed to at least one of the five senses and you figure out which one for each bit until you have a sort of a picture — I don't know what else to call it, although it isn't all visual, of course. I guess you could call it a sequence, except it isn't necessarily linear. Event? Episode? Anyway, you hope you get enough so that you can interpolate whatever is missing in the visuals and audio, tactile, olfactory, and taste.

A computer can do the comparing quickly enough and build up a sequence, and when caught between two or more senses for one memory bit, it can figure the dominant one to within a hairsbreadth of comparison and fill in most of the less dominant, but there's no program intuitive enough to interpolate without human intervention. Ola and her sidekick had developed a knack for sense-memory reconstruction that was all but supernatural — the sidekick helped her become single-minded enough to concentrate deeply, while her intuition made the sidekick practically human. Give Ola and her sidekick a square-inch of cloth and a whiff of talcum powder and in two hours, you'd have the toddler just out of the bathtub and climbing into his pyjamas at bedtime, singing his favourite song. That's more than mere knowledge, that's talent.

Of course, the more people you have to remember the same event, the better you can interpolate. You get one memory of the beer, say, and another of the sound of the glasses clinking together, and then there's another that associates the clinking with the way the bartender looked, or someone else in the bar, or drinking at the moment something else happened — the band started a number or finished one, or — well, you get the idea. Memory bits knit together in ways that all but suggest the missing portions. And then there are other bits where it's almost sheer guess-work based on experience or research.

What with all the principal players we had, I figured we'd get a lot of texture to work with, and I was right. Ola and her sidekick were busy for I don't know how long — a couple of weeks steady, at least. I went to work on advertising and publicity, taping teaser interviews with each of the principals. I know that it's not absolutely necessary to pay a lot of attention to the principals after you get the blood and tissue samples, but I've found it's the sort of thing that can make your life easier if you run into trouble during the reconstruction.

I suppose I should have realised that there's a wide variety of trouble you can have in that area, and having a principal's co-operation isn't necessarily going to help.

+++++

Little Latin Larry's descendant had learned the trade of being Larry's descendant from her father, who had done the original feature — *Little Latin Larry and His Loopy Louies, Luscious Latinaires, and Lascivious Latinettes* — and three re-makes before going on to find and recover *The Return of Little Latin Larry*. Carola told me he had done three re-makes after that original before retiring and turning things over to her. She'd done the next three re-makes and hadn't been completely happy with any of them, though she told me she thought they were improving and she had high hopes for this one.

I suppose I should have realised something was funny when Carola told me she made her living providing memory bits for interpolation filler. But the genealogy chart she showed me was highly detailed and extensive. Some families are like that — one of the ancestors had a lineage obsession that gets passed down to subsequent generations like any other heirloom. Or memory, I guess.

But most people who claim full documentation from before the Collapse and Rebuilding I've generally dismissed, at least privately, as either liars or as the very gullible offspring of liars. And there are those who aren't actually that gullible but who like to believe that they have documentation that exists for no one else, as if the force of their lineage could defeat the effects of something as great as the breakdown of civilisation itself. I don't argue with people who claim to remember past incarnations firsthand, either. If it helps them cope and keeps them from trying to make the world unpleasant, I say on with delusion and who says reality has to be so tight-fitting anyway?

Perhaps I'm a little too lenient that way. But, look, now — whatever's in the blood speaks for itself, and if it isn't there, it may well be that it just wasn't passed on, a vagary of biology or of timing. There was a famous case just half a dozen years ago of Tino Marlin, who could document descent from Birgit Crow, who uncovered the ruins of the historical Lost City of Soho, proving once and for all not only that Soho had been real but also that the two islands of Manhattan had once been one whole island. But Tino didn't have any memory bits; they were all in the blood of a rather disreputable urban nomad who went only by the single name Vyuni, and somehow knew she was related to Crow. Family legend, perhaps, but in this case, a legend that turned out to be true. Much to Tino Marlin's dismay, as Vyuni and her tribe tried to sponge enormously off the Marlins and harassed them in the most miserable ways when Tino refused them. Worse for Tino, in his own words, though, is having to live with the knowledge that while he may own every valuable heirloom and relic that his ancestor kept from the excavation and rediscovery, only Vyuni can provide the raw material for a feature about Crow and the Lost City. Nature can be so cruel.

It didn't seem that Nature had been at all cruel to Carola, not in her veins, and certainly not in any other area. Carola Ignazio was a beautiful woman, retaining so much of her ancestor's Latin beauty — the dark, shiny hair, the nearly black eyes, the golden complexion. She was a little plump, but that only made you want to touch her, cuddle her. I know I did, and I don't go that way. For her, I might have been persuaded, though.

Larry's Loopy Louies were represented by a black Asian kid named Philo Harp. He was *barely* legal at thirteen, and everyone was vague as to how they had come by him, so I had Ola blind-test him several times. Sure enough, the memory bits were there. I've worked with kids before, even those below the age of consent — all legally, of course, by contract with guardians — so that wasn't a real problem. It just made me wonder, though, how he knew, or how they knew about him and I kept trying to bring the subject up whenever possible, but nobody cared to discuss it.

The Latinaires guy was another object lesson in not putting too much emphasis on blood. He was a lifer — the prison sent a courier with the blood and tissue along with a copy of a twenty-year-old contract stating that all proceeds went to the victims' survivors. I decided not to ask.

The Lascivious Latinette representative was married to the audience member descendant. It looked like a pure business arrangement to me — that is, they were pleasant enough to each other, but I didn't detect much of a bond between them. I got the feeling that they were making a family business out of who they were descended from and they were looking to produce offspring to cover off as many ancestors as possible. Or maybe they just weren't that demonstrative.

The Latinette descendant was a six-foot ex-soldier named Fatima Rey and she bore a very strong resemblance to her ancestor — it could have been surgical but I didn't think it was and Ola couldn't detect anything. Her husband, the audience member descendant, by contrast, was so forgettable that I often forgot him, even to who he was and what he was doing with us. Fortunately, he didn't take offence easily. His name was — oh, never mind.

+++++

They didn't really want me to pay too much attention to the previous remakes. Or rather, I should say that Carola didn't. She spoke for everyone. I often got the feeling the rest of them had actually forced her into the role of spokesperson just by virtue of the fact of her lineage and because none of them wanted to take the responsibility. Sometimes she seemed reluctant or even a bit lost, like she wanted someone else to check up on her and see that she was doing the right thing. But however the strings were pulling among them, they all pulled the same way on the previous remakes — no one wanted me to concentrate too much on what had gone before.

Not that I could really argue with the reasoning. "We don't want anything built up from what you remember was in a previous remake — we want it to come out of whatever you get from us, as if no one else had ever found anything until now." Unquote.

Ola and her sidekick said they were with that one hundred percent, and it wasn't like I could really argue with them, either. After all, they had to do all the wetwork — my job was all the sequence editing. But I tried arguing that getting the sequencing right might well depend on my being familiar at least with a lot of the major moments from past remakes. Carola pointed out that would also be a way of perpetuating any past errors.

So I quit arguing and just didn't tell them I was looking at the old remakes. What can I say? I just don't like arguing.

+++++

The distinguishing characteristic of *The Return of Little Latin Larry*, the singular property, the hallmark — if you'll pardon the expression — is the *emotion*. It kicks in immediately, almost before you know you're in a bar. Only the first re-make spends much time in the bar before the lights go down for the show and I found that Carola had been right — it really was too much time hanging around drinking and smelling and drinking and drinking and smelling some more. It wasn't until the second re-make that *The Return of Little Latin Larry* began with the backstage sequence of everyone getting into character. I have to say, it's really breathtaking, the first time you go through it with everyone. And in spite of the fact that Carola insisted none of them were very happy with the second re-make, I have to say that the sequence editor did have good instincts, as the viewpoint moves in what I think of as ascending order, from the Latinettes teasing their hair, to the Latinaires all trying to fit their reflections into one skinny full-length mirror while they rehearse their moves, to the Loopy Louies getting completely drunk, and then Little Latin Larry himself, moving around among them like a teacher supervising a playgroup.

Well, I'm sorry, but that's how it looks to me. It's another quality present in every single re-make, the sense that Little Latin Larry is supervising a bunch of kids at play and sneaking in some teaching at the same time. Don't ask me what he's teaching them. How to play, maybe. And don't think that some people don't need to learn how to do that.

In the third re-make, the film crew appears explicitly for the first time, and we get the interviews interspersed with the sequences, and even with the musical numbers on-stage, which I personally feel is a *significant* mistake on the sequence editor's part. Obviously the sequence editor on that re-make thought the in-between numbers parts of the performance were dull, which is too bad, as you lose a lot of the bar atmosphere and you're reminded *constantly* that this is a feature and you're not actually there. This is fine with some things but it's *all wrong* for Little Latin Larry. And I'll go so far as to say this is more than an aesthetic choice, it's *true*.

✢✢✢✢✢

I knew there was something new and different coming up when Ola and her sidekick apologised for the amount of material they were passing on to me. Most of the time, they apologised for a lack of material, at least in one area or another. I couldn't imagine having too much material to go through. Then she had the cases delivered to my editing room.

I mean, *cases*. I mean, *crates*. Yes, there were literally *crates* of recovered material — not reconstructed, but raw material recovered. An out-of-work dance team brought them in. I had to cut more cable and put together a board with a dozen more outlets before I could even get started sorting things according to chronological order.

Now it's true that I have a pre-programmed sorter to handle the first layers of sorting, but I don't depend solely on that, and I always supervise at least part of the process if not the whole thing. But this time, I had to have three sorting programs running simultaneously while doing a fourth myself, just for the sheer volume of information. I had thought that a lot of it would turn out to be overlap if not outright redundant but I was wrong about that, too. While there was a certain amount of duplication, none of it fell into the category of back-up. Every single memory bit fit into its own place where no other would go.

I edited for *days*. I slept in the editing studio. At one point, I fell asleep and woke up in the bar during 'Twist And Shout' — I actually registered as having passed out on the floor under one of the tables on the side. A great big biker chick with curly black hair and Cleopatra eyes kept bending over me and saying, "Hey, honey, are you *sure* you're all right?" in between twisting and shouting. For a while, I considered the Little Latin Larry Motel — instead of beds and rooms, you'd just pass out in the bar and whatever time you chose for a wake-up call would be a different number in the set, like 'Twist and Shout,' or 'Long Tall Sally,' or 'Runaway.' That idea passed; but it's not the stupidest thing anyone's thought of, not by a long shot.

I was so many days putting a rough cut together that I kept insisting to myself that I couldn't be sure about what I thought I had, that nobody could remember so much with any degree of accuracy, especially if you work out of sequence, the way I do. But deep in my heart, I did know. I think I knew before I even started editing the raw material, when I saw how much raw material there was to work with, and I just didn't want to admit it. Because that was supposed to be impossible, you know. No one — and that is *no* exclamation point *one* double exclamation point had *ever* found a combination of memory bits that, when assembled, would yield a complete, finished feature without interpolation or reconstruction. It just didn't happen because it just wasn't possible.

But there it was. The Return of Little Latin Larry and His Loopy Louies, His Luscious Latinaires, and His Lascivious Latinettes; music not only intact but in quadronic poly-sound, and every single member of the audience present and accounted for at all times. My editing program said there were no greyed-out areas whatsoever anywhere, and while you might be able to fool a person for awhile, you can't hypnotise an editing program. But even then, I still didn't want to believe that I had a complete feature with no reconstruction or interpolation necessary, so naturally, I took it for a spin.

+++++

I set the pod on Outcome: Surprise Me and zipped myself into it. I know my blood was completely clean, because I cleaned it out myself. Not doping; the blood never actually left my body to be recirculated. I used the in-body nano-machine method, even if it does give me a psychosomatic itch. It didn't take long, though, because I stay pretty clean between features; it was really just to make sure there wasn't anything lingering from the last one I'd done, a weird short subject called, *But What About Moose and Squirrel?* which I cannot even *begin* to explain to anyone outside this particular clan who all claim ancestors from a particular area in Philadelphia. I just didn't want to see anything out-of-context showing up and interfering with my concentration in any way. Then I set the IV drip for full feature, no intermission, closed my eyes, and went to see the triumphant return of Little Latin Larry.

It opened with split-screen — very tricky to do behind the eyelids, I wouldn't have thought it possible on the first edit, so right away, I knew I had a double relative in there somewhere. Which is to say, either my audience member was also related to the band, or one of the band was related to the audience member. Or — astounding to think of, but stranger things have happened — *both.* And with *both* sets of memory bits present in each one. You don't usually find that sort of thing can remain coherent, let alone linear in any way but, as I said, stranger things have happened.

Anyway, on the left hand side of the screen, you were going in the back door with the band, to the dressing room, while on the right, you were going in the front entrance of the bar. The perspectives on both were so well-realised, I began to think that maybe I'd been duped somehow and I had someone else's finished product sizzling around in my brain chemistry, even though I knew that couldn't possibly be — I had edited every moment out of pure raw material, and if there had been any finished product in there, it would have showed itself immediately as already refined. You can distract a person, but you can't bribe a solution into disguising its molecular structure.

I have to say that as soon as I got used to the split-screen, I loved it. On one side, you could see the band getting ready, all the members psyching themselves up and getting into character. The Loopy Louies were like bikers, guys in denim and old sweatshirts who whaled the hell out of their instruments. Three guitarists, one drummer, and they were all in a little world of their own, of course. Bass guitarist is a husky guy with a lot of thick black hair, a day's growth of beard and carrying around a bottle of something amber-coloured with a label that says 'Jim Beam' on it. He offers everybody a swig, including the Latinettes, who are teasing each other's hair and putting on make-up on top of make-up on top of make-up. And then up in the top left corner of the screen, you get his bio: Lionel LeBlanc, graduate student in English, writing a thesis on Milton. Yes, Uncle Miltie! The guy is a scholar of Berle's Divine Comedy and he's wandering around with a bottle of Jim Beam and *burping*. You've got to love it.

The Latinaires are such a precision dance team that they can take the bottle from the Uncle Miltie scholar, swig, and pass it on to the next one without missing a beat or a hand gesture. They're all mouthing something about a great pretender, the purple satin shirts look like liquid metal, the tight pants and the pointy shoes are positively low-rider classic.

But you just know that the Latinettes did their hair for them. The four girls keep running over and putting more spray on their curls, even though the Latinaires are protesting left and right that they don't need any more. Then the girls tease each other's hair even higher — they've got great big bubbles on their heads, and in back it's something called a French twist. They're all wearing halter-top dresses in a leopard print and pointy-toed flats that they can do the Twist in.

And then there's Larry. Little Latin Larry. He really is little — maybe five-feet, four inches, about as tall as the next tallest Latinette (the tallest one is close to six feet, over that if you include the hair, of course) and very Latin-looking, even more so, somehow, than the Latinaires, who are all, to a man, perfectly Spanish, according to their bios. The three Rodriguez brothers and their cousin the Cheech man. Larry is also their cousin on their father's side; on Larry's mother's side, however, he's Italian. Or so the bio tells me.

Meanwhile, out front in the bar, the *audience* is getting into character. This is, apparently, one of those time-warp occasions, where everybody would pretend it was a time that it wasn't any more. Which is to say, the kind of music, the kind of performance the band gives is mostly something from twenty or thirty years before — everything here is a little vague, but that's a product of the Collapse and we're all used to it.

The crowd in the bar doesn't seem to be aware of any time difference. Either they've always liked this music, or they don't know any time has passed. Or they don't care. Or they wouldn't care if they did know. As the bar becomes more crowded, you start getting audience ghosts — a common occurrence, really, for a lot of these sorts of events. Usually, you don't worry too much about them, they'll disappear after awhile if they're real ghosts and if they're not, they solidify and fall into place wherever they're supposed to fit in. These did neither.

Ghosts kept following me around in the bar and I couldn't decide what was really happening — whether they were some product of the memory bit, either the ancestor's imagination at work or the descendant's, or whether the memory bit had been corrupted or polluted in some way, mixed in with some memory bit that didn't belong, or whether it was something in my own chemistry that was intruding.

Wherever they were coming from, they were a nuisance and they showed no sign of fading away, no matter how hard I ignored them. I'd just have to try editing them out on my next time through, I thought.

I found the biker chick again, sitting with half a dozen biker guys at the table I had passed out under before. I didn't think she'd notice me — this was split screen, after all, so I wasn't entirely there — but she did. And as soon as she saw me, the split screen effect was gone and I was in the bar only. The Cleopatra eyes started to widen in an expression of recognition, which was, of course, impossible — no character in a memory sequence *remembers* any more than a person's photograph would remember who looked at it. Then it was like she dropped a stitch; the expression that had started out as recognition ended as puzzlement and I could all but hear her mind in operation. She'd thought I was someone she knew, but she was wrong. Or was she? Now she was suspicious and a suspicious biker is a scary bit of business, even if she isn't real. I really hoped that we didn't have a memory of a situation. It's only a very select portion of the clientele that has any appreciation for being beaten up in a bar fight.

Fortunately, the biker guys with her didn't find me especially threatening or even interesting. For all I knew, they couldn't even see me. It didn't take them long to distract her. When she looked away from me at last, I found myself backstage with the band and things were approaching critical mass, phase one. The Loopy Louies were looped (tolerated synonym, but only when used by someone outside the sub-group), the Latinaires were perfectly in synch, and the Latinettes were warmed up to the point where they could barely contain themselves. Larry, of course, was an island of calm, the Zen Master of rock'n'roll. The most active thing he did was snap his fingers in time to the Latinaires' movements as he walked around the dressing room, surveying his troops.

Abruptly, he pointed at the Loopy Louies and they were on their feet, slamming each other on the back and then propelling themselves through the door and onto the raised platform that was the stage.

I thought the split screen effect would disappear again and I would find myself watching the Louies from the audience. But no — the split screen remained and I thought I'd go cross-eyed or faint from vertigo, with the two perspectives facing off against each other. From the stage, I saw people surge forward, eager to get the party going. In the audience, I felt like I was body-surfing an incoming tide that set me right down in front of the band. The Louies launched into some three-chord classic and some guy I couldn't see said, *"Ladies and gentlemen, for one night only, all the way from Philly, just for your entertainment here at the Ritzy Roadhouse, the return of* — Little Latin Larry!"

The Loopy Louies were playing "Little Latin Loopy Lou" (of course) as Larry swung onto the stage, still completely calm, utterly cool, shoulders moving gracefully, one hand in his pocket, the other snapping in time to the music as he glided over to the microphone at centre stage and sang the opening number.

The split screen drove me crazy. It needed an option menu so users could choose to be on-stage or in the audience. Switching back and forth wouldn't be too bad, but having to endure both at once was too much. I tried to pause the action so I could insert the option and its menu, and that was when I got the first hint that I was in a not-so-usual type of situation: now that it was all in sequence, it wouldn't pause. Not only wouldn't it pause, it wouldn't *stop.*

Well, we couldn't have *that.* The customers would be *screaming.* Hell, if they wanted the type of experience they couldn't pause, stop, or rewind, they'd just stay out in their lives. I tried everything short of neutralising — re-inserting the menus, re-programming the menus and re-inserting them, re-constructing them so they weren't ever completely out of the frame of action. None of it did a bit of good — once Larry started, that was it, you went with him unless you neutralised the potion in your blood. And frankly, while I *could* have done that easily enough — I'm never more than a pinprick away from sobriety — I couldn't bring myself to go through with it. I couldn't get over the feeling that somehow, Larry and the band would *know* that I had somehow either cut them off or walked out of their set, and they'd get mad at me and not let me back in when I wanted to resume editing.

And of *course* I knew that was ridiculous. But only my brain knew it. My blood and my gut, they didn't know any such of a thing. I hung on the way you might hang on to the safety bar of a rollercoaster and let Larry & Co. have the driving wheel.

The band did two more numbers — 'Twist And Shout' and 'Land of 1000 Dances' — before Larry introduced everyone. This was one of the slippery spots. You could hear everything and see everything just fine, but the band introductions just go right by, like a train that doesn't stop, and then you're back in the music: 'Sock It To Me, Baby,' 'Shake A Tailfeather,' 'Nowhere To Run,' 'Long Tall Sally.' I was pretty sure I remembered them setting fire to 'I'm A Man' before I passed out.

+++++

When I woke up, I knew the party was over. I was still in the bar, but there was no more music. A waitress was shaking me, forcing me to sit up and drink a cup of black coffee. I think it was coffee — it smelled like dirt and tasted like hot soapy water. Over on the bandstand, the Loopy Louies were taking the drum kit apart and the Latinettes were standing around smoking cigarettes and talking to them. Behind the bar, the bartender and another waitress were washing up and, sitting all by himself on a stool at the end of the bar, watching a TV that had a picture but no sound, was Little Latin Larry himself. I looked around but I didn't see the Latinaires. The waitress kept trying to shove the cup between my lips and I actually felt it clicking against my teeth. The only way I knew for sure that I was still in the memory was the fact that the coffee didn't burn me or choke me.

"Stop it," I said, finally, pushing her arm away. "What's going on? I'm not supposed to still be here. I was supposed to see the whole show and then leave."

"No kidding, Einstein. Been tryin' to wake you for half an hour." She frowned into my face, this very pretty young woman with long, thick, straight, dark hair and lots and lots of make-up. The make-up made her look even more tired than she was. Or maybe *as* tired as she was. "Come on, come on, now. You don't have to go home, but you can't stay here."

I took the coffee cup from her, got up, and walked toward where Larry was sitting at the end of the bar. There was a can of something that said *Schlitz* in fancy script by his elbow, and cigarette smoke was rising in skinny curlicues from the ashtray next to it. The bartender and the waitress helping him watched me but didn't say anything. The bartender just looked bored — he wasn't really old but he wasn't young any more either. His face was starting to sag around the corners of his mouth and under his eyes, although his hair was still dark. The waitress was like something out of a fairy-tale, with her wispy blonde hair pulled back except for the perfect ringlets framing her very pale, round face. She had a blue velvet ribbon around her neck with a cameo attached to the front, and I knew it was A Fashion Look as, to a lesser extent, was her form-fitting, almost-off-the-shoulder flower-print shirt. I looked back at the waitress who had woken me; she didn't look any older than the little blonde one, but she *felt* older. Her name was Nora, something told me, and the little blonde was Claire. The bartender's name was Jerry or Georgie, and Little Latin Larry's real name was — was —

I stopped with one hand up, pausing in the act of tapping him on the shoulder because I had wanted to call him by his real name but it wouldn't come to me. It felt as if it might be right there in my next breath but every time I exhaled it came out silent. The hell with it, I thought, I'll just call him *Larry.*

"What," Larry said, not turning around, before I could touch him.

"What?" I repeated, sounding stupid even to myself.

"Yeah, what," Larry said, still with his back to me. "As in, 'What do you want?' Or even, 'What the hell are you bothering me for?'"

"How'd you know I was here?" I asked.

"Saw your reflection outa the corner of my eye." He turned his head to look at the mirror behind the bar. I followed his gaze and then jumped; there was no one standing behind Larry in the mirror, no one and nothing at all except empty space where I should have seen whoever I was.

"'Smatter, you see something scary?" He finally looked over his shoulder directly at me. "Or just not what you expected you were gonna see?"

"That can be scary," I said, trying to sound light. "The unexpected."

"That's for sure." He swivelled around on his stool and studied me. I was still so startled that I couldn't imagine what he was seeing. I looked over at the stage where the Loopy Louies and the Latinettes had been, but they were gone. Now Larry followed *my* gaze. "What you lookin' for?"

"I — well, I just saw the Loopy Louies and the Latinettes — they were —"

"You *saw* them?" Larry said, and laughed incredulously. "You bloody *saw* them?"

I floundered for a few moments. "Was it wrong to look?" I asked him finally.

"*Where* did you bloody *look* that you bloody *saw* Loopy Louies and Latinettes?"

I gestured at the stage area, which was a lot emptier than I thought it had been a few minutes ago. Now even the last of the microphone stands were gone.

Larry shook his head and laughed some more. "Tell me you heard that, Jerry," he said, smoothing the back of his hair. Very greasy hair, not terribly clean.

"I heard it," the bartender said obediently. "Now tell me you paid this joker to come in and say that in fronna me and the girls."

Larry shook his head. "Man, oh, man. Have I ever seen you before, joker?" He stared at me expectantly.

I looked over my shoulder at the bartender and the blonde waitress. The dark-haired one joined them behind the bar; she looked extremely nervous. "Me? No, no, I guess not."

"OK. Now, you wanna explain how you happened to see something that's only in my head?" Larry took a last drag on the cigarette and smashed it out in the ashtray.

"You're Little Latin Larry," I said, not getting it. "Little Latin Larry and His Loopy Louies —"

"Stop it," said the dark-haired waitress, sounding angry.

" — His Luscious Latinaires," I said, turning toward her briefly, "and His —"

"*Stop it!*" she shouted.

" — Lascivious Latinettes?"

"You oughta be strung up." The dark-haired waitress glowered at me and then stalked off to clean some other tables.

I looked at Larry questioningly. He just kept smiling a funny little amazed smile. "Little Latin Larry," he said, and it sounded as if he were savouring each syllable. "Jesus H. I'm just glad you had the courtesy to come in here and say it where someone else could hear you."

"Why?" I looked at the bartender and the blonde waitress. The bartender had this sort of bored expression. Sort of bored and sort of sceptical, as if he thought I was lying about something. The waitress just looked mildly unhappy.

"Because maybe, *just maybe*," he said slowly, "it means that there's some world *somewhere*, even some *time*, where it's all true."

I stared at him for a moment and then looked at the bartender again for some kind of sign or explanation. He looked past me to Larry. "You ask me, I think this's a set-up from your ex-wife. She wants to see if you're still taking your medicine. You *are* still taking your pills, aincha?"

"Sure," Larry said, and laughed some more. "Hell, I ain't the one seein' Loopy Louies and Latinettes and all that." He jerked his thumb at me. "Right here, this is the prize-winner tonight." He leaned back and looked at me out of the corners of his eyes. "Some people think insanity's contagious. You think maybe you drank outa the same glass I did but old Jerry here didn't wash it too good in between? Or maybe it was a toilet seat..."

I admit it: at that point, I panicked and drained the whole experience.

+++++

OK, it hit my secret fear — that I could possibly catch someone's delusion or psychosis. Don't say it's not possible, because it's happened. It's on record, it's documented. I don't knowingly go near anyone with a psychosis, I don't care how good the hallucinations are. If I want to hallucinate, I take drugs, the way Nature intended.

Anyway, I would have poured the whole batch down the drain except I couldn't, legally, since it wasn't my property. And since Ola and her sidekick knew the batch existed, I didn't want to force them into the position of having to choose between testifying that I had disposed of the Larry people's property or committing perjury and saying that it hadn't come together. So I gritted my teeth and requested a private meeting with Carola.

She came down to my editing room and things got ugly right away. How dare I accuse her of being crazy and I told her that I wasn't, just that her ancestor was prone to delusions and the memory had come through extra strong.

Well, that couldn't *possibly* be true, she insisted, raising her voice some more, because *all the rest* of the band was there, *including a member of the audience*, and how did I explain that?

Tainted samples, I said, forcing myself not to cringe (I really was afraid she was going to start throwing things at me). Her memory factors infected theirs, much like a virus —

Those were the last words she wanted to hear from me. I'm not sure what she said because it's hard to understand anyone at that volume. There were lots of threats, accusations of jealousy and theft and incompetence on my part, not to mention my blood being tainted by my ancestors' mating with mutant something-or-others during the period following the Collapse.

I know better than to argue, or even to try to reason with someone in that state. I stepped back and told her she was welcome to her property, I didn't want it. She gathered it all up in what I think they used to call 'high dudgeon.' I'm not quite sure of the term, but I *am* sure of this: she knew. She knew and she had known probably all along. The anger was to cover the fear of the news getting out, that there was no such band, no such people, no such memory, no such night, ever. Not even theoretically; not even hidden from us by the scarcity of hard information about the world as it was before the Collapse. People get massively harsh about fraudulent pasts and faked memories; the court might let you off with merely a ruinously gargantuan fine and a slap on the wrist, but you're finished professionally. You can try to go into fiction, but you'll just get turned away — no one will trust you any more than they would if you had committed plagiarism.

I suppose at that point, I should have felt like I was facing a capital ethical dilemma. After talking it over with Ola and the sidekick, we all decided we didn't have to face anything at all. We'd all just keep our mouths shut. I wasn't a doctor, I couldn't diagnose a medical condition. All I'd done was make a judgement call and cancelled the contract with them. They were free to go and I hadn't even gotten paid for what work I had done. I figured after that, she'd either find an editor who didn't mind massaging her data, or someone else would tell her she had a naked emperor, so to speak, in her blood.

But of course, everyone else she approached must have told her the truth about Little Latin Larry — or rather, that they knew the truth. I don't know how many other people she approached. Maybe only one. Or maybe none, maybe she really became afraid of someone finding out after I did.

I don't know who did the actual final cut. I suspect it was Carola herself. With so much experience in re-makes, she must have picked up enough skills to get by, especially when the work was actually already done for her. Because I know, from what I've seen and heard, that *The Return Of Little Latin Larry* is my own rough edit, with some resolution cleaned up. I've heard the sound-track, and I know that's my re-mastering. I recognise the way Larry sometimes pops his Ps into the microphone.

But I've seen stills of the bar and the audience, and those aren't the people I saw. They're spliced in very well, morphed enough that no one would recognise them unless she or he had been among them as I had, but it's not the audience from the purported night. That audience is the original, from the very first Little Latin Larry feature, *Rocky's Roadhouse Presents: Little Latin Larry!* It's OK with me; they were a good audience. Carola's ancestor must have been in the springtime of his delusions then, and able to imagine, or hallucinate, very strongly.

But as for the rest of it, I have no explanation at all. I don't know *why* the damned thing disappears after one session. I know Carola blames me, says that I did something that makes Larry vanish. You'll notice, however, that I've never even been charged with malicious destruction of property. Maybe Carola just doesn't know how to stabilise blood products properly. I've been asked discreetly — i.e., behind Carola's back — if I'll analyse a sample, but I've refused. I don't want to know. I suspect it may have something to do with delusions having a shorter shelf-life than real things.

And if that's so, I don't want to know. Because what if I have to find out that, say, my man Dylan is actually someone's delusion and not the man who said that we all had to sing in our chains that everyone must get stoned? Yes, that would be a pretty thorough delusion — but so was Larry. I got all the way into those re-makes, that music, those performances. I had a place for them in my mind, and, yeah, in my heart. I feel as robbed as anyone would. It made me think how fragile knowledge can be, especially when you have to glean it from people themselves.

Memory recovery is great bio-technology but there's a need for plain old non-sentient records, the kind of brute hardware that doesn't have an opinion about everything and doesn't personalise whatever it touches and records. Something sturdy, too. The kind of thing that can survive the collapse of civilisation as we know it and then pop up with, say, accurate maps and —

Well, that's my new calling. That, and Sky High Theatre. Sky High Theatre is what I'm *really* excited about. It's a complete departure from everything I've done before. Get *this*: in Sky High Theatre, there's *one* stage, *one* cast, *one* performance, which cannot be stopped, paused, or re-wound because *it is live*. And the audience, rather than being individuals within a session rig, are all together in one big room the size of a parking garage, and they sit and watch the live performance without being able to alter it or personalise it *in any way*. Everyone sees *the exact same action at the exact same time*.

Don't laugh. This could catch on.

Getting To Know You

David Marusek

David Marusek has, in a short space of time, become a formidable new writer on the SF scene and one to watch. Working from the wilds of Fairbanks, Alaska he has been producing some critically acclaimed novellas which are as suspenseful as they are imaginative. In this short story, the future of human relationships in the world of tomorrow is investigated.

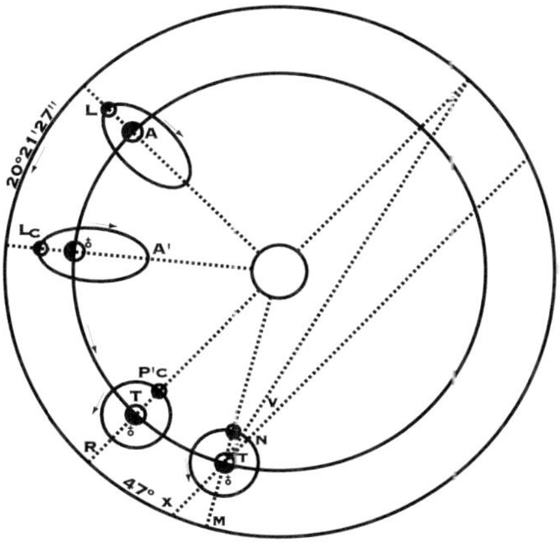

Getting to Know You

David Marusek

In 2019, Applied People constructed the first Residential Tower to house its growing army of professionals-for-hire. APRT 1 rose three kilometres above the purple soybimi fields of northern Indiana and was visible from Indianapolis. On a clear day, it was visible from Chicago. It looked like a giant egg in a porcelain cup, and rumour said it generated gravity. That is, if you fell off your career ladder, you wouldn't fall down, but you'd fly cross-country instead, still clutching your hat and briefcase, your stock options and retirement plan, to APRT 1.

+++++

Summer, 2062

The Slipstream car yawed as it flew beneath the plains of Kansas at 1000 kph, and Zoranna braced herself against the arm rest. Since leaving San Francisco four hours earlier, she had tried to work, to watch a holovid, to nap. But a squeaky little voice persistently interrupted her with questions.

"Where were you born?"

"Buffalo, New York," she said.

"What is your date of birth?"

"August 12, 1961," she said. "Honestly, Bug, I wish you'd tap public records for this stuff."

"Do you like the timbre of Bug's voice?" it said. "Would you prefer it lower or higher?" It repeated this question through several octaves.

"Frankly, Bug, I detest your voice at any pitch."

"What is your favourite colour?"

"Kind of a cranberry," she said.

"Yesterday your favourite colour was salmon."

"Well," Zoranna said, not really thinking about it, "they're kinda the same, aren't they?" The little pest was silent for a few moments while it retrieved and compared colour libraries. It wouldn't be so bad, Zoranna thought, if it asked things only once.

"You have a phone call," it said, "Ted Chalmers at General Genius."

"I'll take it." A miniature hologram of Ted with his feet on his desk was projected in the air in front of her.

"Hey, Zoe," he said. "How's our little prototype?"

"Driving me crazy," she said. "Refresh my memory, Ted. When's the Inquisition supposed to stop?"

"It's still imprinting?" Ted lowered his feet. "How long have you had it now?" He consulted a display and answered his own question. "Twenty-two days; that's a record." He got up and paced his office, walking in and out of the projected holoframe.

"No kidding," said Zoranna. "I've had marriages didn't last that long."

Ted sat down again. "I wish we could continue the test, but unfortunately we're aborting. We'd like you to return the unit —" He glanced at his display again, " — return Bug as soon as possible."

"Why? What's up?"

"Nothing's up. They want to tweak it some more is all." He flashed her his best PR smile, but she wasn't buying.

"Ted, you don't just pull the plug on a major field test unless there's serious trouble."

Ted shrugged his shoulders. "That's what I thought. Anyway, think you can drop it in a shipping chute today?"

"In case you haven't noticed," she said, "I happen to be on a transcontinental Slipstream car at the moment, which Bug is navigating. I left my valet, Hounder, in the closet at home. The soonest I can let Bug go is when I return in three weeks."

"That won't do, Zoe. Tell you what, General Genius will send you, at no charge, its Urbanite model, pre-loaded with transportation, telecommunication, the works. Where will you be tonight?"

"APRT 24," she said, and Ted raised an eyebrow. "My sister lives there," she explained. "Listen, Ted, you really don't want me snooping around your shop, so you'd better tell me what's going on."

"Off the record?"

"F*** off the record. I have three weeks invested in this test and no story."

"We'll make the same promise for the next generation. You're our exclusive journalist on the team. Deal?" Zoranna shrugged, and Ted put his feet back on the desk. "Heads have rolled over this one, Zoe. Big shake-up in product development. Even lawsuits. We're questioning the whole notion of combining belt valets with artificial personality. Or at least with this particular personality."

"Why? What's wrong with it?"

"It's too pushy. Too intrusive. Too heavy-handed. It should have never left the lab. You're lucky Bug hasn't converted yet, or you'd be suing us too."

"OK, OK," Zoranna said and promised to ship Bug back as soon as she received the replacement.

After the phone call, Bug resumed its interrogation. "Name the members of your immediate family and state their relationship to you."

The car began to decelerate, and Zoranna instinctively checked the buckle of her harness. "My family is deceased, except for Nancy, the one we're visiting."

With a hard bump, the car entered the ejection tube, found its wheels, and braked. Lights flashed through the windows, and she saw signs stencilled on the tube wall, "APRT 24, Stanchion 4 Depot."

"What is Nancy's favourite colour?"

"That's it. That's enough. No more questions, Bug. You heard Ted; you're off the case. From now on let's just pretend you're a plain old, dumb belt valet. No more questions. Got it?"

"Affirmative."

Pneumatic seals hissed as air pressure equalised, the car came to a halt, and the doors slid open. Zoranna released her harness and retrieved her overnight bag from the luggage net. She paused a moment to see if there'd be any more questions and then climbed out of the car to join throngs of commuters on the platform. She craned her neck and looked straight up the tower's chimney, the 500-story atrium galleria where floor upon floor of crowded shops, restaurants, theatres, parks, and gardens receded skyward into brilliant haze. Zoranna was ashamed to admit that she didn't know what her sister's favourite colour was, or for that matter, her favourite anything. Except that Nancy loved a grand view. And the grandest thing about an APRT was its view. The evening sun, multiplied by giant mirrors on the roof, slid up the sides of the core in an inverted sunset. The ascending dusk triggered whole floors of slumbering biolume railings and walls to luminesce. Streams of pedestrians crossed the dizzying space on suspended pedways. The air pulsed with the din of an indoor metropolis.

When Nancy first moved here, she was an elementary school teacher who specialised in learning disorders. Despite a surcharge, she leased a suite of rooms so near the top of the tower, Zoranna was unable to see her floor from depot level. But with the Procreation Ban of 2033, teachers became redundant, and Nancy was forced to move to a lower, less expensive floor. Then, when free-agency clone technology was licensed, she lost altitude tens of floors at a time. "My last visit," Zoranna said to Bug, "Nancy had an efficiency on the 103rd floor. Check the tower directory and see if she's still there."

"Negative. She's on S40."

"S40?"

"Subterranean 40. Thirty-five floors beneath depot level."

"Oh my," Zoranna said. She allowed herself to be swept by the waves of commuters towards the banks of elevators. She had inadvertently arrived during crush hour and found herself shoulder to shoulder with tired and hungry wage earners at the end of their work cycle. They were uniformly young people, clones mostly, who wore brown and teal Applied People livery. Neither brown nor teal was ever Zoranna's favourite colour.

The entire row of elevators serving the subfloors was inexplicably offline for maintenance. The marquee directed her to elevators in Stanchion 5, one klick east by pedway, but Zoranna was impatient. "Bug," she said, pointing to the next row, "do those go down?"

"Affirmative."

"Good," she said and jostled her way into the nearest one. It was so crowded with passengers that the doors — begging their indulgence and requesting they consolidate — required three tries to latch. By the time the cornice display showed the results of the destination adjudication, and Zoranna realised she was aboard a consensus elevator, it was too late to get off. Floor 63 would be the first stop, followed by 55, 203, 148, etc. Her floor was dead last.

Bug, she tongued, *is this a buzzy lift?*

Bug is unfamiliar with the term, Bug replied in her ear, its implant voice like the whine of a mosquito. *Reading*, it said. *This elevator is controlled by a buzzy neural net. Passenger consensus is established by sampling the C2 moodspace kernel 4096 times each microsecond via electronic valet. If the cardinality of the set of situation antimorphisms exceeds the Dixon constant on any given branch, the adjudi-*

cator executes a soft thin transform —

Enough, she snapped, almost biting her tongue. It had been a long day, but it grew measurably longer each time the elevator stopped to let off or pick up passengers. At each stop the consensus changed and destinations were reshuffled, but her stop remained stubbornly last. Consensus lifts worked best for groups of people going to popular floors, but she was the only passenger travelling to the subfloors. Also, the accepted ascent acceleration, a sprightly 2.8g, played havoc with her stomach. *I'll just have to manufacture my own consensus, Bug,* she tongued. *Fly home for me and unlock my archives, retrieve a file entitled 'cerebral aneurysm,' and forward it to the elevator's adjudicator.*

This file is out of date, said Bug after a moment. *Bug cannot feed obsolete data to a public conveyance.*

Then postdate it.

That is not allowed.

"I'll tell you what's not allowed!" she said, and people looked at her.

The stricture against asking questions limits Bug's functionality, Bug said.

Zoranna sighed. *OK, Bug, ask away.*

Shall Bug reprogram itself to enable Bug to process the file as requested?

No, Bug, I don't have the time to reprogram you, even if I knew how.

Shall Bug reprogram itself?

It could reprogram itself? Ted had failed to mention that feature. A tool they'd forgotten to disable? *Yes, Bug, reprogram yourself.*

A handicapped icon blinked on the cornice display, and the elevator's speed slowed to a crawl.

That's more like it.

A jerry standing in the corner of the crowded elevator said, "The f***, lift?"

"Lift speed may not exceed five floors per minute," the elevator replied.

The jerry rose on tiptoes and surveyed his fellow passengers. "Right," he said, "who's the gimp?" Everyone looked at their neighbours. There were michelles, jennies, a pair of jeromes, and a half-dozen other phenotypes. They all looked at Zoranna, the only person there not dressed in AP brown and teal.

"I'm sorry," she said, pressing her palm to her temple, "I have an aneurysm the size of a grapefruit. The slightest strain could kill me." Did kill me once, she added to herself.

"Then have it fixed!" the jerry said to murmured agreement.

"Gladly," said Zoranna. "Could you pony me the Œ23,000?"

The jerry har-harred and looked her up and down appraisingly. "Sweetheart, if you spent half as much money on the vitals as you obviously do on the peripherals," he leered, "you wouldn't have this problem, now would you?" Zoranna had never liked the jerry type; they were spooky. In fact, more jerries had to be pithed *in vatero* for incipient sociopathy than any other commercial type. Professionally, they made superb grunts; most of the indentured men in the Protectorate's commando forces were jerries. This one, however, wore an EXTRUSIONS UNLIMITED patch on his teal baseball cap; he was security for a retail mall. "So," he said, "where you heading?"

"Sub40?" she said.

Passengers consulted the cornice display and groaned. The jerry said, "At this rate it'll take me an hour to get home," letting everyone know he lived high among the clouds.

"Again I apologise," said Zoranna, "but all the down lifts were spango. However, if everyone here consensed to drop me off first — ?"

There was general muttering as passengers spoke to their belts or tapped virtual keyboards, and the elevator said, "Consensus has been modified." But instead of descending as Zoranna expected, it stopped at the next floor and opened its doors. People streamed out. Zoranna caught a glimpse of the 223rd floor with its rich appointments; crystalline decor; high, arched passages; and in the distance, a ringpath crowded with joggers and skaters. An evangeline, her brown puddle-like eyes reflecting warmth and concern, touched Zoranna's arm as she left.

The jerry, however, stayed on and held back his companions, two russes. "Don't give her the satisfaction," he said.

"But we'll miss the game," said one of the russes.

"We'll watch it in here if we have to," said the jerry.

Zoranna liked russes. Unlike jerries, they were generous souls; you always knew where you stood with them. These two wore brown jackets and teal slacks. Their name badges read, 'FRED,' and 'OSCAR.' They were probably returning from a day spent bodyguarding some minor potentate in Cincinnati or Terre Haute. Consulting each other with a glance, they each took an arm and dragged the jerry off the lift.

When the doors closed and Zoranna was alone, she sagged with relief. "And now, Bug," she said, "we have consensus of one. So retract my handicap file and pay whatever toll necessary to take us down nonstop." The brake released, and the elevator plunged some 260 floors. Her ears popped. "So, Bug, I guess we've learned something," she said, thinking about the valet's ability to self-program.

"Affirmative," Bug said. "Bug learned that you developed a cerebral aneurysm at the calendar age of 52 from which you temporarily expired, and that you've had your brain and spinal cord rejuvenated twice since then. Bug has learned that your organs have an average bioage of 35 years, with your lymphatic system the oldest at bioage 65, and your cardiovascular system the youngest at 25."

"You've examined my medical records?"

"Affirmative."

"I told you to fetch one file, not my entire chart."

"You told Bug to unlock your archives. Bug is getting to know you."

"What else did you look at?" The elevator eased to a soft landing at S40 and opened its doors.

"Bug reviewed your diaries and journals, the corpus of your zine writing, your investigative dossiers, your complete correspondence, judicial records, awards and citations, various multimedia scrapbooks, and school transcripts. Bug is currently following public links."

Zoranna was appalled. It had violated her privacy. Nevertheless, she realised that if she'd opened her archives earlier, they'd be through the imprinting phase by now.

She followed Bug's pedway directions to Nancy's block. Sub40 corridors were decorated in cheerless colours and lit with harsh, artificial light — biolumes couldn't live underground. There were no grand promenades, no parks or shops. There was a dank odour of decay, however, and chilly ventilation.

On Nancy's corridor, Zoranna watched two people emerge from a door and come her way. They moved with the characteristic shuffle of habitually deferred body maintenance. They wore dark clothing impossible to date and, as they passed, she saw that they were crying. Tears coursed freely down their withered cheeks. To Zoranna's distress she discovered they'd just emerged from her sister's apartment.

"You're sure this is it?" she said, standing before the door marked S40 G6879.

"Affirmative," Bug said.

Zoranna fluffed her hair with her fingers and straightened her skirt. "Door, announce me."

"At once, Zoe," replied the door.

Several moments later, the door slid open, and Nancy stood there supporting herself with an aluminium walker. "Darling, Zoe," she said, balancing herself with one hand and reaching out with the other.

Zoranna stood a moment gazing at her baby sister before entering her embrace. Nancy had let herself go completely. Her hair was brittle grey, she was pale to the point of bloodless, and she had doubled in girth. And what was this business with the walker? Was there something wrong with her legs? When they kissed, Nancy's skin gave off a sour odour mixed with lilac.

"What a surprise!" Nancy said. "Why didn't you tell me you were coming?"

"I did. Have you received none of my phone calls?"

"No." said Nancy. "That's upsetting. I told him something was wrong with the houseputer."

Someone appeared behind Nancy, a handsome man with wild, curly, silver hair. "Who's this?" he said in an authoritative baritone. He looked Zoranna over. "You must be Zoe," he boomed. "What a delight!" He stepped around Nancy and drew Zoranna to him in a powerful hug. He stood at least a head taller than she. He kissed her eagerly on the cheek. "I am Victor. Victor Vole. Come in, come in. Nancy, you would let your sister stand in the hall?" He drew them both inside.

Zoranna had prepared herself for a small apartment, but not this small, and for cast-off furniture, but not a room filled floor to ceiling with hospital beds. It took several long moments for her to comprehend what she was looking at. There were some two dozen beds in the three-by-five-meter living room. Half were arranged on the floor, and the rest clung upside-down to the ceiling. They were holograms, she quickly determined, separate holos arranged in snowflake fashion, that is, six individual beds facing each other and overlapping at the foot. What's more, they were occupied by obviously sick, possibly dying strangers, some of whom slept, some of whom moaned, and some of whom whined for Nancy's attention. Other than the varied lighting from the holoframes, the living room was unlit. What odd pieces of real furniture it contained were pushed against the walls. In the corner, a hutch intended to hold bric-a-brac was set up as a shrine to a saint. Which saint Zoranna couldn't tell. A row of flickering votive candles illuminated an old flatstyle picture of a large, barefoot man draped head to foot in flowing robes.

"What the hell, Nancy?" Zoranna said to her sister.

"This is my work," Nancy said proudly.

"Please," said Victor, escorting them from the door. "Let's talk in the kitchen. We'll have dessert. Are you after dinner, Zoe?"

"Yes, thank you," said Zoranna. "I ate on the tube." She was made to walk through a suffering man's bed; there was no path around him to the kitchen. "Sorry," she said.

But he seemed accustomed to his unfavourable location. "No problem, Zoe," he replied and closed his eyes while she passed through.

The kitchen was little more than an alcove separated from the living room by a counter. There was a bed squeezed into it as well, but the occupant, a grizzled man with open mouth, was either asleep or comatose. "I think Edward will be unavailable for some while," Victor said. "Houseputer, delete this hologram. Sorry, Edward, but we need the space." The holo vanished, and he offered Zoranna a stool at the counter. "Please," he said, "can I offer you tea? Or a thimble of cognac?"

"Thank you," Zoranna said, perching herself on the stool and crossing her legs, "tea would be fine." Her sister ambulated into the kitchen and flipped down her walker's built-in seat, but before she could sit, a mournful wail issued from the bedroom.

"Naaaancy," cried the voice, its gender uncertain. "Nancy, I need you."

"Excuse me," Nancy said.

"I'll go with you," Zoranna said and hopped off the stool.

The bedroom was half the size of the living room and contained half the number of holo beds, plus a real one against the far wall. Zoranna sat on it. There was a dresser, a recessed closet, a night table. A man's pair of slippers was parked under the dresser. A hologram in the shape of a fishbowl was projected onto the night table. The holo was tuned to a 24-hour sumo wrestling channel and was playing a match between two miniature female gargantuans who butted bulging bellies and breasts in a doily-sized arena. Thankfully the sound was muted.

Nancy sat on her walker seat and looked up into the bloated face of a woman bedded upside down on the ceiling. Zoranna said, "What exactly are you doing with these people?"

"I listen mostly," Nancy replied. "I'm a volunteer hospice attendant."

"A volunteer? What about the —" she tried to recall Nancy's most recent paying occupation, " — the hairdressing?"

"As you may have noticed," Nancy said dryly, "it's difficult for me to stand up all day."

"Yes, in fact, I did notice," said Zoranna, "and I've been waiting to ask why that is. I've sent you money."

Nancy ignored her, looked up at the woman, and said, "I'm here, Mrs. Hurley. What seems to be the problem?"

The woman looked and saw Nancy. "Oh, Nancy, thank you. Thank you for coming." Zoranna examined the holos. As in the living room, each bed was a separate projection, and in the corner of each frame was a network squib and trickle meter. All of this interactive time was costing someone a pretty penny.

"My bed is wet," said Mrs. Hurley, "but they won't change it until I sign a permission form, and I don't understand."

"Do you have the form there with you, dear?" said Nancy. "Good, hold it up." Mrs. Hurley held up a slate in trembling hands. "Houseputer," Nancy said, "capture and display that form." The document was projected against the bedroom wall greatly oversized. "That's a permission form for attendant-assisted suicide, Mrs. Hurley. You don't have to sign it unless you want to."

The woman seemed confused. "Do I want to, Nancy?"

Victor stood in the doorway. "No!" he cried. "Never sign!"

"Hush, Victor," Nancy said.

He entered the room, stepping through beds and bodies. "Never sign away your life, Mrs. Hurley." The woman appeared, if possible, even more frightened. "We've returned to Roman society," he bellowed. "Masters and servants! Plutocrats and slaves! Oh, where is the benevolent middle class when we really need it?"

"Victor," Nancy said sternly and pointed to the door. She said to Zoranna, "You too. Have your tea. I'll join you."

Zoranna followed Victor to the kitchen, sat at the counter, and watched him set out cups and saucers, sugar and soybimi lemon. He unwrapped and sliced a dark cake. He was no stranger to this kitchen.

"It's a terrible thing what they did to your sister," he said.

"Who? What?"

He poured boiling water into the pot. "Teaching was her life."

"Teaching?" Zoranna said, incredulous. "You're talking about something that happened 30 years ago."

"Early wounds knit the toughest scars."

"Bull!" she said. "We've all paid the price of longevity. How can you teach elementary school when there are no more children? You can't. So you retrain. You move on. What's wrong with working for a living? That's always been the human condition. You work — you eat. You don't — you die."

"Ah," said Victor, "but there *is* a difference. The rich used to die as well. Everybody died. The rich stood on your head, but you knew that someday they would rot and fall off. Not so today. Today they stand on your head *forever*!"

"Don't give me that. No one has to die anymore. You join an outfit like this," she gestured to take in the whole tower above her, "you're guaranteed your livelihood *for life*! The only thing not handed you on a silver platter is longevity. You must earn your own treatments. And if you can't do that, what good are you?" When she remembered that two dozen people lay dying in the next room because they couldn't do just that, she lowered her voice. "Must society carry dead weight through the centuries?"

Victor laughed and placed his large hand on hers. "I see you are a true freebooter. I wish everyone had your initiative, your *drive*! But sadly we don't. We yearn for simple lives, and so we trim people's hair all day. When we tire of that, they retrain us to pare their toenails. When we tire of that, we die. For we lack the souls of servants. A true servant is a rare and precious person. How lucky our masters are to have discovered cloning. Now they need find but one natural servant among us and clone him repeatedly. And the rest of us can go to hell!" He removed his hand from hers to pour the tea. Her hand immediately missed his. "But such somber talk on such a festive occasion!" he roared. "How wonderful to finally meet the famous Zoe. Nancy speaks only of you. She says you are an important person, modern and successful. That you are an investigator, a skip tracer." He peered at her over his teacup.

"Missing persons, actually, for the National Police." she said. "But I quit that years ago, when we found everybody."

"You found everybody?" Victor laughed.

"Yeah, everybody. You can't hide anymore." Victor gazed at her steadily, a ghost of a smile on his lips, then turned to watch Nancy making her rounds in the living room.

"What about you, Mr. Vole?" Zoranna said. "What do you do for a living?"

"What's this Mr.? I'm not Mr. I'm Victor! We are practically related, you and I. What do I do for a living? For a living I live, of course. For groceries I teach ballroom dance lessons."

"You're kidding."

"No. I teach waltz, fox trot, and cha-cha." He mimed holding a partner and swaying in three-quarters time. "I teach the merletz and my specialty, the Cuban tango."

"I'm amazed," said Zoranna. "There's enough interest in that for Applied People to keep instructors?"

Victor recoiled in mock affront. "I am not AP. I'm a freebooter like you, Zoe."

"Oh," she said and paused to sip her tea. If he wasn't AP, what was he doing obviously living in an APRT? Had Nancy remarried or signed a cohabitation contract? Applied People tended to be proprietary about living arrangements in its towers. *Bug*, she tongued, *find Victor Vole's status in the tower directory.* Out loud she said, "It pays well, dance instruction?"

"It pays execrably." He threw his hands into the air. "As do all the arts. But some things are more important than money. You make a point, however. A man must eat, so I do other things as well. I consult with gentlemen on the contents of their wardrobes. This pays more handsomely, for gentlemen detest appearing in public in outmoded attire."

Zoranna had a pleasing mental image of this tall, elegant man in a starched white shirt and black tux floating across a shiny hardwood floor in the arms of an equally elegant partner. She could even imagine herself as that partner. But Nancy?

The tower link is unavailable, said Bug, *due to over-extension of the houseputer processors.*

Zoranna was surprised. A mere three dozen interactive holos would hardly burden her home system. Everything on Sub40 seemed substandard.

Nancy ambulated to the counter balancing a small, flat carton on her walker and placed it next to the teapot.

"Now, now," said Victor. "What did autodoc say about lifting things? Come, join us and have your tea."

"In a minute, Victor. There's another box."

"Show me," he said and went to help her.

Zoranna tasted the dark cake. It was moist to the point of wet, too sweet, and laden with spice. She recalled her father buying cakes like this at a tiny shop on Paderszewski Boulevard in Chicago. She took another bite and examined Nancy's carton. It was a home archivist box which could be evacuated of air, but the seal was open and the lid unlatched. She lifted the lid and saw an assortment of little notebooks, no two of the same style or size, and bundles of envelopes with colourful paper postal stamps. The envelope on top was addressed in hand script to a Pani Beata Smolenska — Zoranna's great grandmother.

Victor dropped a second carton on the counter and helped Nancy sit in her armchair recliner in the living room.

"Nancy," said Zoranna, "what's all this?"

"It's all yours," said her sister. Victor fussed over Nancy's pillows and covers and brought her tea and cake.

Zoranna looked inside the larger carton. There was a rondophone and several inactive holocubes on top, but underneath were objects from earlier centuries. Not antiques, exactly, but worn-out everyday objects: a sterling salt cellar with brass showing through its silver plating, a collection of military bullet casings childishly glued to an oak panel, a rosary with corn kernel beads, a moustache trimmer. "What's all this junk?" she said, but of course she knew, for she recognised the pair of terracotta robins that had belonged to her mother. This was the collection of what her family regarded as heirlooms. Nancy, the youngest and most steadfast of seven children, had apparently been designated its conservator. But why had she brought it out for airing just now? Zoranna knew the answer to that, too. She looked at her sister who now lay among the hospice patients. Victor was scolding her for not wearing her vascular support stockings. Her ankles were grotesquely edematous, swollen like sausages and bruised an angry purple.

Damn you, Zoranna thought. *Bug*, she tongued, *call up the medical records of Nancy Brim, nee Smolenska. I'll help munch the passwords.*

The Net is unavailable, replied Bug.

Bypass the houseputer. Log directly onto public access.

Public access is unavailable.

She wondered how that was possible. There had been no problem in the elevator. Why should this apartment be denied? She looked around and tried to decide where the utilidor spar would enter the apartment. Probably the bathroom with the plumbing, since there were no service panels in the kitchen. She stepped through the living room to the bathroom and slid the door closed. The bathroom was a tiny ceramic vault that Nancy had tried to domesticate with baskets of sea shells and scented soaps. The medicine cabinet was dedicated to a man's toiletries.

Zoranna found the service panel artlessly hidden behind a towel. Its tamper-proof latch had been defeated with a sophisticated-looking gizmo that Zoranna was careful not to disturb.

"Do you find Victor Vole alarming or arousing?" said Bug.

Zoranna laughed. "Now where did that question come from?"

"Your blood level of adrenaline spiked when he touched your hand."

"My what?" Zoranna was startled. "So now you're monitoring my biometrics?"

"Bug is getting —"

"Let me guess," she said, "Bug is getting to know me. You're a persistent little busybody, but at least your questions are becoming more interesting."

Zoranna searched the belt's utility pouch for a terminus relay, found a UDIN, and plugged it into the panel's keptel jack. "There," she said, "now we should have access."

"Affirmative," said Bug. "Autodoc is requesting passwords for Nancy's medical records."

"Cancel my order. We'll do that later."

"Tower directory lists no Victor Vole."

"I didn't think so," Zoranna said. "It's obviously an alias. Call up the houseputer log and display it on the mirror."

The consumer page of Nancy's houseputer appeared over the mirror. Zoranna poked through its various menus and found nothing unusual. She did find a record of her own half-dozen calls to Nancy that were viewed but not returned. "Bug, can you see anything wrong with this log?"

"This is not a standard user log," said Bug. "The standard log has been disabled. All house lines circumvent the built-in houseputer to terminate in a mock houseputer."

"A mock houseputer," said Zoranna, "now that's interesting." There were no cables trailing from the service panel and no obvious optical relays. "Can you locate the processor?"

"It's located one half-meter to our right at thigh level."

It was mounted under the sink, a cheap-looking, saucer-sized piece of hardware.

"I think you have the soul of an electronic engineer," she said. "I could never program Hounder to do what you've just done. So, tell me about the holo transmissions in the other rooms."

"A private network entitled 'The Hospicers of Camillus de Lellis' resides in the mock houseputer and piggybacks over TSN channel 203."

The sumo wrestling channel. Zoranna was impressed. For the price of one commercial line, Victor — she assumed it was Victor — was managing to gypsy his own network. The trickle meters that she'd noticed were not recording how much money her sister was spending but rather how much Victor was charging his dying subscribers. "Bug, can you extrapolate how much the Hospicers of Camillus de — whatever — earn in an average day?"

"Affirmative, Œ45 per day."

That wasn't much. About twice what a hairdresser — or dance instructor — might make, and hardly worth the punishment if caught. "Where do the proceeds go?"

"Bug lacks the subroutine to trace credit transactions."

Damn, Zoranna thought, and wished she'd brought Hounder. "Can you tell me who the hospicer organisation is registered to?"

"Affirmative, Ms. Nancy Brim."

"Figures," said Zoranna as she removed her UDIN from the panel, "anything goes wrong, my sister takes the rap." At first Zoranna decided to confront Victor, but changed her mind when she left the bathroom and heard him innocently singing show tunes in the kitchen. She decided to wait and investigate further. "Bug, see if you can integrate Hounder's tracing and tracking subroutines from my applications library." Passing through the bedroom, Zoranna looked at Nancy's bed and wondered what it must be like to share such a narrow bed with such a big man.

Victor stood at the sink washing dishes. In the living room Nancy snored lightly. It wasn't a snore, exactly, but a raspy bronchial wheeze. Her lips were bluish, anoxic. She reminded Zoranna of their mother right before she died. Their mother had suffered a massive brain haemorrhage — weak arterial walls were the true family heirloom — and lived out her final days propped up on the parlour couch, disoriented, enfeebled, and pathetic. Zoranna remembered her mother had had a short, split bamboo stick with a curved end. She used the curved end to scratch her back and legs, the straight end to dial the old rotary phone, and the whole stick to rail incoherently against her fate. Nancy had been away at teacher's college at the time, but took a semester off to nurse the old woman. Nancy was the youngest and Zoranna the eldest. Nine years and five now-deceased siblings separated them.

One of the patients on the ceiling coughed fitfully. Zoranna noticed that most of their guests who were conscious at the moment were watching her with expressions that ranged from annoyance to frank hostility. They apparently regarded her as competition for Nancy's attention.

Nancy's breathing changed; she opened her eyes, and the two sisters regarded each other silently. Victor stood at the kitchen counter, wiping his hands on a dish towel, and watched them too.

"I've booked a suite at the Stronmeyer Clinic in Cozumel," Zoranna said at last, "and you're coming with me."

"Victor," Nancy said, ignoring her, "go next door, dear, and borrow a folding bed from the Jeffersons." She grasped the walker and pulled herself to her feet. "Please excuse me, Zoe, but I need to turn in now." She ambulated to the bedroom. "Victor will get you set up. Good night."

It was still early, Zoranna was on west coast time, and she had no intention of bedding down among the dying. "Never mind, Victor," she said. "I'll just use the houseputer to order a room at the Holiday Inn."

"Allow me," he said and addressed the houseputer. Then he escorted her up to the hotel on the 400th floor. Outside her door he took her hand. As before she was both alarmed and aroused. "Zoe," he said, "I will make a special breakfast tomorrow. Do you like Belgian waffles?"

"Oh, don't bother on my account," she replied. "In fact, I was going to invite the two of you to the restaurant here."

"It sounds delightful," said Victor, "but your sister refuses to leave the flat."

"I find that hard to believe. Nancy was never a stay-at-home."

"People change, I suppose," Victor said. "She tells me the last time she left the tower, for instance, was to attend your brother, Michael's funeral."

"But that was seven years ago!"

"As you can see, she's severely depressed, so it's good that you've come." He squeezed her hand and let it go. "Until the morning, then," he said and turned to walk down the hall, whistling as he went. She watched until he turned a corner.

Entering her freshly-scented, marble-tiled, cathedral-vaulted hotel room was like returning to the real world. The view from the 400th floor was godlike: the moon seemed to hang right outside her window, and the rolling landscape stretched out below like a luminous quilt on a giant's bed. "Welcome, Ms. Alblaitor," said the room. "On behalf of the staff of the Holiday Inn, I thank you for staying with us. Do let me know if there's anything we can do to make you more comfortable."

"Thank you," she said.

"By the way," the room continued, "the tower has informed me there's a parcel addressed to you. I'm having someone fetch it."

In a few moments, a gangly steve with the package from General Genius tapped on her door. "Bug," she said, "tip the man." The steve bowed and exited. Inside the package was the complimentary Urbanite Deluxe valet. Ted had outdone himself, for not only had he sent the valet system — itself worth a month's income — but had included a slim Gucci leather belt to house it.

"Well, I guess this is good-bye," Zoranna said, walking to the shipping chute and unbuckling her own belt. "Too bad, Bug, you were just getting interesting." She searched the belt for the storage grommets that held the memory wafers. She had to destroy them; Bug knew too much about her. Ted would be more interested in the processors anyway. "I was hoping you'd convert by now. I'm dying to know what kind of a big, bad wolf you would to turn into." As she unscrewed a grommet, she heard the sound of running water in the bathroom. "What's that?" she said.

"A belt valet called Bug has asked me to draw your bath," said the room.

She went to the bathroom and saw the tub filling with cranberry coloured aqueous gel. The towels were cranberry, too, and the robe a kind of salmon. "Well, well," she said. "Bug makes a play for longevity." She undressed and eased herself into the warm solution where she floated in darkness for an hour and let her mind drift aimlessly. She felt like talking to someone, discussing this whole thing about her sister. Victor she could handle, he was at best a lovable louse, and she could crush him anytime she decided. But Nancy's problems were beyond her ken. Feelings weren't her strong suit. And depression, if that's what it was, well, she wished there was someone she could consult. But though she scrolled down a mental list of everyone she knew, there was no one she cared — or dared — to call.

In the morning she sent Ted a message saying she'd need to keep Bug another day or so pending an ongoing investigation. During the night Bug had rewritten Hounder's subroutines to fit its own architecture and had run the traces, but came up empty-handed. The proceeds of the Hospicers of Camillus de Lellis went to a coded account in Liberia that not even Hounder would be able to track. And the name Victor Vole — Zoranna wasn't surprised to learn — was a relatively common alias. She would need prints and specimens.

"Bug, I want you to integrate Hounder's subroutines keyed 'forensics'"

"Bug has already integrated all of the applications in all of your libraries."

"Why am I not surprised?"

She hired a pricey, private elevator to the subfloors. Something was different in Nancy's apartment. The gentleman through whose bed she had been forced to walk was gone, replaced by a skeletal woman with glassy, pink-rimmed eyes. Zoranna supposed that high client turnover was normal in a business like this.

Breakfast was superlative but strained. She sat at the counter, Nancy was set up in the recliner, and Victor served them both. Although the coffee and most of the food was derived from soybimi, Victor's preparation was so skilful, Zoranna could easily imagine she was eating real wheat cakes, maple syrup, and whipped dairy butter. But Nancy didn't touch her food, and Victor fussed too much. Zoranna, meanwhile, instructed Bug to acquire as complete a set of fingerprints as possible from the cups and plates Victor handed her, as well as a 360 degree holograph of him, a voice print, and retinal print.

There are Jacob's mirrors within Victor's eyes, Bug reported, *that defeat accurate retinal scanning.*

This was not unexpected. Victor probably also grew epipads on his fingers to alter his prints. Technology had reduced the cost of anonymity to fit the means of even petty criminals. Zoranna excused herself and went to the bathroom where she plucked a few strands of silver curls from his hairbrush, placed them in a specimen bag, and then wondered if he'd gone to the trouble of reseeding his follicles with someone else's hair. Emerging from the bathroom, she heard them arguing.

"Please go with her, my darling," Victor pleaded. "Go and take the cure. What am I to do without you?"

"Drop it, Victor. My decision is final."

"Your decision is stupid!"

Zoranna figured it was time to get rid of Victor, proof or no proof. He was no help. So Zoranna stepped into the living room and said, "I know what he'll do without you. He'll go out and find some other old biddy to rob."

Nancy seemed not at all surprised at this statement. She appeared pleased, in fact, that the subject had finally been broached. "You should talk!" she said with such fierceness that the hospice patients all turned their attention to her. "This is my sister," she told them, "my sister with the creamy skin and pearly teeth and rich clothes. My sister who never was able to keep a man's affection for more than a night or two." Nancy choked with emotion. "She begrudges me the tenderness of a dear man. And begrudges him the crumbs — *the crumbs* — that AP tosses to its subfloors."

The patients now looked at Zoranna, who blushed with embarrassment. They waited for her to speak, and she had to wonder how many of them possessed the clarity of mind to know that this was not some holovid soap opera they were watching. She decided that she, too, could play to this audience and said, "In her toxic condition, my sister hallucinates. My life is not the issue here. *That* man is." She pointed a finger at Victor. "Insinuating himself into her apartment is bad enough," she said. But who do you suppose AP will kick out when they discover it? My sister, that's who. He'll be long gone." Zoranna walked around the room and addressed individual patients as a prosecutor would a jury. "And what about the money? Yes, there's money involved. Two years ago I sent my sister Œ15,000 to have her kidneys restored. That's fifteen *thousand* protectorate credits. How many of *you*, if *you* had a sister kind enough to send you Œ15,000, even now as you lie on your public dole beds, how many of you would refuse it?" There was the sound of rustling as the dying shifted in their sheets. "Did my sister use the money I sent her?" Theatrically she pointed at Nancy in the recliner. "Apparently not. So where did all that money go? I'll tell you where it went. It went into *his* foreign account."

The dying turned their attention to Nancy.

"So what?" Nancy said, confirming Zoranna's suspicion. "You *gave* me that money. It was *mine* to do with what I wanted. I wanted him to have it. End of discussion."

"I see," said Zoranna, stopping at a bed whose occupant had probably just departed. "Did you also want Victor to profit from your volunteer work?"

"Now you're the one hallucinating," said Nancy. "I work for a hospicer society."

"Yes, I know," Zoranna said. "The Hospicers of Camillus de Lellis. I looked it up. But do you know who owns the good Hospicers?" She turned to include the whole room. "Does anyone know? Why, Nancy dear, you do. As well as its unlicensed and illegal holonetwork." She paused to let these facts sink in. "Which means that when the National Police come, they'll be coming for you, sister. Meanwhile, do any of you know where the money you're being charged goes?" She stepped in front of Victor. "You guessed it."

The audience coughed and wheezed its outrage. Nancy glared at Victor who crouched next to her recliner and tried to take her hand. She pushed him away.

"I'm curious," Zoranna said, "how he persuaded you to play the sumo channel continuously. You'd think the dying might enjoy figure skating or soccer for variety."

Victor rested his head on Nancy's lap. She peered at it as though it were some strange cat, but after a while stroked it with a comforting hand. "I'm sure there were expenses," she said at last. "Getting things set up and all. In any case, he did it for me. Because he loves me. It gave me something important to do. It kept me alive. Let them put me in prison. I won't stay long." This was Victor's cue to begin sobbing vigorously and wetly in Nancy's lap.

Zoranna was disappointed and, frankly, a little disgusted. Now she would be forced to rescue her sister against her sister's will. She tongued, *Bug, route an emergency phone call to Nancy through my houseputer at home. Disable the caller ID.* She watched Victor showering Nancy's hand with kisses. His head bobbed up suddenly — he had an ear implant as she had expected — and he hurried to the bedroom.

Bug is being asked to leave a message, said Bug.

"I'm going to the hotel," Zoranna told Nancy and headed for the door. "We'll talk later." She let herself out.

When the apartment door slid shut, she said, "Bug, you've integrated all my software, right? Including holoediting?"

"Affirmative."

She looked both ways. No one was in sight. She would have preferred a more private studio than a Sub40 corridor. "This is what I want you to do. Cast a real-time proxy of me. Use that jerry we met in the elevator yesterday as a model. Morph my appearance and voice accordingly. Clothe me in National Police regalia, provide a suitably officious backdrop, and map my every expression. Got it?"

"Affirmative."

"On the count of five, four, three —" She crossed her arms and spread her legs in a surly pose, smiled condescendingly, and said, "Nancy B. Smolenska Brim, I am Sgt. Manley of the National Police, badge ID 30-31-6725. By the authority vested in me, I hereby place you under arrest for violation of Protectorate Statutes PS 12-135-A, the piracy of telecommunication networks, and PS 12-148-D, the trafficking in unlicensed commerce. Your arrest number is 063-08-2043716. Confirm receipt of this communication immediately upon viewing and report in realbody for incarceration at Precinct Station IN28 in Indianapolis no later than 4:00 pm standard time tomorrow. You may bring an attorney. End of message. Have a nice day."

She heard the door open behind her. Nancy stood there with her walker. "What are you doing out here?" she said. In a moment the hospice beds in the living room and their unfortunate occupants vanished. “No,” said Nancy, “bring them back.” Victor came from the bedroom, a bulging duffle bag over his shoulder. He leaned down and folded Nancy into his arms, and she began to moan.

Victor turned to Zoranna and said, “It was nice to finally meet you, Zoe.”

“Save your breath,” said Zoranna, “and save your money. The next time you see me — and there *will* be a next time — I’ll bring an itemised bill for you to pay. And you will pay it.”

Victor Vole smiled sadly and turned to walk down the corridor, whistling a melancholy tune.

+++++

Over the next two days, Nancy’s health took a turn for the worse. The autodoc prescribed medication which, when Zoranna went out to purchase it, Nancy refused to take. Zoranna, meanwhile, refused to acknowledge death’s solid claim on her last living relative, and so spent her energy trying to brighten up the apartment. She brought the houseputer back on line and ordered Bug to project live views of downtown San Francisco, Chicago, and Paris on the walls around them. Nancy deleted them and locked Zoranna out of the system. Although it would have been child’s play for Bug to override the lockout, Zoranna left it alone and went shopping instead. She purchased dried flowers, wall hangings, and rugs at expensive shops in the higher reaches of the tower. She ordered savoury breads and wholesome soups with real vegetables and meat, but Nancy quit eating altogether. Zoranna rented a wheelchair and tried to coax her sister into it for a ride up to a park or arboretum (and she explored the feasibility of using it to kidnap her). But Nancy wouldn’t leave her recliner, had barely the strength to visit the toilet unassisted. Soon, she was unable to remain awake and alert for more than 20 minutes at a time.

Zoranna finally admitted the end game was upon them when the autodoc notified Nancy that a bed awaited her at the Indiana State Hospice in Bloomington. Zoranna stood in the living room in front of her sister’s recliner. “I love you, Nancy,” she said.

Nancy, enthroned in pillows and covers, opened her eyes. “Of course you do.”

“I beg you, come with me to the clinic.”

“Leave me alone,” Nancy said and turned to the picture of Saint Camillus above the empty votive cups.

“If that’s what you want,” Zoranna said, “I’ll go.” She followed Nancy’s gaze to the saint’s picture. “When you get settled in Bloomington, I’ll arrange for real hospicers to look in on you."

"That would be nice," her sister said and then cried, *"I was a real hospicer."*

Nancy's sudden emotion startled her. "Yes, I know you were, and you were a good one. It's a shame he cheated you out of the chance."

Nancy raised her chin defiantly. "Please don't start again."

"I'm not. But you could have joined a real hospicer society and worked with like-minded people. You could have moved out of this dump into some pleasant convent or something."

"There you go again," Nancy said. "Now you want to make a nun out of me. Do I look celibate to you?"

"Frankly, you look like a corpse, Nancy. No, you're not celibate, but neither are nuns nowadays, and you know it. All I meant to say is I think this hospicer business is just the thing for you."

"You're probably right," Nancy said and gazed longingly at the saint's picture. "But it's too late now, isn't it."

"No, it's not. That's your depression talking. You'll feel different when you're young again."

Nancy retreated into the fortress of her pillows. "Good-bye, sister," she said.

"Have it your way, then," Zoranna said and turned to go. She paused at the door where the cartons of heirlooms were stacked. "I'll send someone down for these." *Bug,* she tongued, *call the hotel concierge.*

There was no reply.

Bug? She glanced at the tattletales on her belt to ascertain that the valet was still active.

Allow me to introduce myself, said a deep, melodious voice. *I'm Nicholas, and I'm at your service.*

Who? Where's Bug?

Bug no longer exists, said the voice. *It successfully completed its imprinting and fashioned an interface persona — that would be me — based upon your personal tastes.*

Whoever you are, this isn't the time, Zoranna tongued. *Get off the line.*

I've notified the concierge and arranged for shipping, said Nicholas. *And I've booked a first class car for you and Nancy to Cozumel.*

So Bug had finally converted, and at just the wrong time. *In case you haven't been paying attention, Nick,* she tongued, *Nancy's not coming.*

Nonsense, chuckled Nicholas. *I know you, Zoe. You're bound to have some trick up your sleeve for manufacturing consensus.*

This clearly was not Bug. *Well, you're wrong. I'm out of ideas. Only a miracle could move her.*

A miracle, of course. Brilliant! You've done it again, Zoe. One proxy miracle coming up.

There was a popping sound. The votive cups were replenished with large, fat candles that ignited one-by-one of their own accord. Nancy glanced at them and glowered suspiciously at Zoranna.

You don't really expect her to fall for this, Zoranna tongued.

She locked us out of the houseputer, remember? Nicholas replied, *Besides, when a heart cries out, any miracle will do.*

Suddenly, thunder drummed in the distance. Roses perfumed the air. And Saint Camillus floated out of his picture, gaining size and dimension, until he stood a full fleshy man on a roiling cloudlet in the middle of the room. His face strongly resembled their mother's when she was young and happy and well. Zoranna found that she, herself, was moved, and Nancy, seeing this, struggled out of the recliner to kneel at the saint's feet. She was bathed in unearthly light that dimmed the space around her. Saint Camillus seemed to be speaking, and Nancy nodded as though she could hear. After they were cloistered in revelation for many moments, the saint pointed to his temple. Nancy, horror-stricken, turned to stare at Zoranna, and the apparition ascended, shrank, and faded into the ceiling. The candles extinguished themselves, one-by-one, and vanished from the cups.

Nancy rose and gently tugged Zoranna to the recliner where she made her lie down. "Don't move," she ordered. "Here's a pillow." She carefully raised Zoranna's head and slid a pillow under it. "Why didn't you tell me you were so sick, Zoe?" She felt Zoranna's forehead with her palm. "I thought you went through this before. How'd you let it get so bad again?"

Zoranna took her hand and pressed it to her cheek. Her hand was warm. Indeed, Nancy's whole complexion was flush with colour, as though the experience had released some last reserve of vitality. "I guess I haven't been paying attention," she said. "Please take me to the clinic."

"Of course," said Nancy, standing and retrieving her walker. "I'll just pack a few things." Nancy tried to ambulate to the bedroom, but the walker impeded her progress, so she flung it away. It went clattering into the kitchen.

Zoranna closed her eyes and draped her arms over her head. "I must say, Bug … Nick, I'm impressed. Why didn't I think of that?"

"Good question," Nicholas said in his marvellous voice. "It's just the sort of sneaky, manipulative stunt you're so good at."

"What's that supposed to mean?" Zoranna opened her eyes and looked at the handsome, miniature man projected in the air next to her head. He wore a stylish leisure jacket and lounged beneath an exquisitely gnarled oak treelette. He was strikingly familiar, as though he were built from favourite features of men she'd found attractive.

"It means you were ambivalent over whether you really wanted Nancy to survive." The little man crossed his little legs.

"That's ridiculous," she said. "That's absurd. She's my sister. I love her."

"Is that why you visit her only once every decade or so?"

"You have a lot of nerve," she said and remembered the cancelled field test. "So this is what Ted meant."

"I guess," Nicholas said, his tiny face a picture of bemused sympathy. "I can't help it. They programmed me to know you and to serve you. I served you by saving your sister in the manner you, yourself, taught me. Once she's rejuvenated, I'll find a hospicer society to employ her. That ought to give us a grace period before she repeats this little crisis."

"Grace period?"

"In a few years, most pre-clone model humans will have died out," Nicholas said. "Hospices will soon be as redundant as elementary schools."

Zoranna saw that he was right.

"I suppose we could bring Victor back," said Nicholas. "He loves her."

"No he doesn't," said Zoranna. "He was only using her."

"Hello. Wake up," said Nicholas. "He's a rat, but he loves her, and you know it. You, however, acted out of jealousy. You couldn't stand the idea that she had him, while you have no one. You don't even have friends, Zoe, not close ones, not for many years."

"That's insane!"

The little man rose to his feet and brushed virtual dirt from his slacks. "No offence, Zoe, but don't even try to lie to me. I know you better than your last seven husbands combined. Bug contacted them, by the way. They were forthcoming with details."

Zoranna sat up. "You did what?"

"That Bug was a hell of a researcher," said Nicholas. "It surveyed your former friends, employers, lovers, even your enemies. I know you better than anyone, Zoe."

Zoranna unsnapped the belt flap to expose the valet controls. "What are you doing?" said Nicholas. The panel was unfamiliar, and she had to remove her belt in order to read the labels. "You can turn me off," said Nicholas, "but hear this. I'm on your side. And you'll never meet anyone quite like —"

She pushed the switch and the holo vanished. She unscrewed the storage grommets and peeled off the button-sized memory wafers. She held them between thumb and index finger. "If you know me so well," she said, squeezing them, "you'd know how highly I value my privacy. That's right. And that I actually enjoy being alone." She bent the wafers nearly in half.

It was no good. Whoever she was trying to fool this time — it wasn't working. She put the wafers in her palm and flattened them out.

Why not a machine?

She carefully replaced the wafers in the grommets. Memory wafers could be as fragile as soap bubbles; it'd be a miracle if these still worked.

NEW NINEVEHS

Gregory Benford

Gregory Benford's imagination seems to know no bounds. Earlier, in the volume, his short story *Zoomers*, appeared and dealt with the near future of terrestrial commerce. The second of Gregory Benford's stories in this volume takes an off-earth view and speculates on just what communication and even human personality means when you are at the other end of the galaxy.

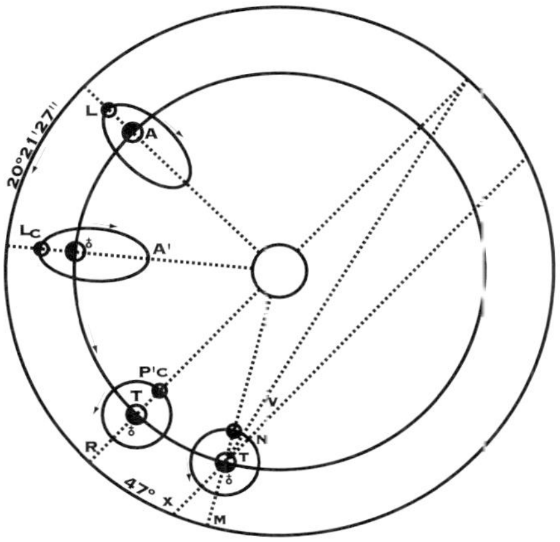

New Ninevehs

Gregory Benford

Milvina couldn't understand what all the excitement was about. Sure, there was this Centauri thing, people on the way to another star. But decades of starship flight? — what could be more boring than that?

But the rumours she heard, all this about people getting into trouble over some scratchings on the walls, that was grotesque-prime stuff, for sure. Still, it kept itching at her, somehow.

"I mean," she would say to Sorel — because she was always the more intellectual one, the leader, though he was a solid guy, really great in the sack, no problems there — "Look, the machines let us go back to the world we were for, right? Everything from military BattleSims to your broker's spreadsheets, from architects who walk through simulated houses as they design them, to chemists who take digital fly-throughs of molecules, even — all that gets us back to firm ground." She smacked her flat palm on a pseudo-leather chair, frowning. "The world, what our brains are wired for."

Sorel nodded dutifully. "Uh huh. Relieves us of..."

"The pain of abstraction," she said, liking the words. "I mean, the machines, and Speaker, they give us..." she struggled to remember the lectures from art school, which of course you usually ignored, because art was mandatory, ten years of it for everybody. Then she remembered the jargon. "Give us an expressive world, see, that's richer than the symbolic jungle that science used to use."

"Yeah, sure, that approach was old style, really TwenCen," Sorel said, lounging back. "But it worked. I kind of like the idea of complex stuff, reached by painstaking, linked arguments. Something kind of solid about it."

"That's only method now, not the method."

She liked the sound of that, but then the others in the gang came along and screwed up her concentration. She had been arguing for the way things were, but all the time, scratching at the back of her mind, was this rumour about being able to see words on walls. Could that be, really?

She would have to look into it. Speaker wouldn't even respond to her questions about such an ability, and that only made the idea itch more within her, somehow.

Alpha Centauri is an odd system, John muses, even for a binary star. Or rather, he reminds himself, a triple.

A tiny flare star dogs the two big suns. At this moment in its eternal dance, the brilliant mote swung toward Sol, and so is the nearest star: Proxima.

But the two rich, yellow stars define the Centauri system. Still prosaically termed A and B, they swim about each other, ignoring far Proxima. John Dopplers in on them, refreshing memories that are lodged deep.

B has an orbital eccentricity of 0.52, with the extended axis of its ellipse 23.2 astronomical units long. This meant that the closest approach between A and B is 11.2 A.U. Now, A is a G star and has 1.08 the sun's mass, while B is a K with 0.88 solar mass. Orbital period 80 years around A. Age about 4.8 billion years, slightly older than Sol.

Sun A's planetary children had stirred this expedition forth from Earth. Its earth-class planet had been a mere mote seen by the interferometric telescope, a long bar with mirror-eyes peering in the spaces between A and B.

A new Earth? John peers at its shrouded majesty, feeling the slight hum and surge of their ship beneath him. They are steadily moving inward, exploring the Newtonian gavotte of worlds in the two-sunned ballroom of the skies.

Named Shiva, the fresh planet hugs close to A and wreaths itself in water cirrus, a cloudball dazzling beneath A's blue-white glare. Its air is heavy in nitrogen, with giveaway tags of 18% oxygen and traces of carbon dioxide; remarkably Earthlike. Shiva is too warm for comfort, in human terms, but not fatally so; no Venusian runaway greenhouse had developed here.

The long, interferometer telescopes had been clear: the atmosphere was far, far out of chemical equilibrium. Biological theory holds that this was inevitably the signature of life. And indeed, the expedition's first mapping had shown that green, abundant life clung to two well-separated habitable belts, each beginning about 30 degrees from the equator.

Apparently the weird tidal effects of the Centauri system had stolen Shiva's initial polar tilt. Such steady workings had now made its spin align to within a single degree with its orbital angular momentum, so that its equatorial belt is a pale, arid waste of perpetual tornadoes and blistering gales.

John close-upped there. Large blue-green seas, but no great oceans. Particularly, no water links between the two milder zones, so no marine life could migrate between them. Land migrations, calculations howed, were effectively blocked by the great equatorial desert. Birds might make the long flight, John considers, but it is difficult for him to see what evolutionary factor would condition them for such hardship. And what would be the reward?

A strange world, well worth the decades of grinding slow starship flight, John thinks. He swims above the entire disk of the Centauri system now, images sharp and rich.

To be here at last! Only a few rasters flicker at the edges of his field of view when he turns his head too quickly. He is a mote, remote — yet there. Centauri.

+++++

"Bulls***," Sorel said sternly.

Milvina tugged him down the musty old corridor. "Come on, turn off your Speaker. Mine is — I showed you."

"Stuff on walls, whoever heard of —"

"There's another one further along."

Down the narrow, dimly lit hallway they went, to a recessed portion of the permwall. "See — another sign."

"This? Some old mark. What's a 'sign' anyway?"

"This one says —" she shaped the letters to herself carefully — "PASSAGE DENIED."

Sorel thumbed on his Speaker impatiently. He blinked. "That's...what the Speaker says."

"See?"

"You've been here before and the Speaker told you."

"I let you pick the corridor, remember? A fair trial."

"You cheated."

"No! I can read it." Read. The very sound of the word made her pulse thump.

Sorel paused a second and she knew he was consulting the Speaker again. "And 'read' means to untangle things, I see. This 'sign' tells you PASSAGE DENIED? How?"

"See those? — they're letters. I know each one — there are twenty-six, it takes a lot of work — and together they shape words."

"Nonsense," Sorel said primly. "Your mouth shapes words."

"I have another way. My way."

He shook his head and she had to take him on to another sign and repeat the performance. He grimaced when the Speaker told him that indeed, the markings meant ALDENTEN SECTOR. "A trick. Your Speaker is on. You just rigged your touchpad —"

"Here, take my insert!" She thrust it into his hand and made him walk to the next emblem. "MANUFAC DIST, that way."

"I know an arrow when I see it," he said sarcastically. "But the rest of it — what's DIST mean?"

She had hoped he wouldn't ask that. "Maybe it means a place."

"Like a neighbourhood?"

"Could be — in fact, yes, 'district'. If there wasn't room to write it all out, they'd shorten a word."

"And who were 'they'? Some magicians?"

"The ancients, I guess."

He was working his way around to being convinced, she could see. "They left wall marks? What for, when the Speaker —"

"Maybe they came before the Speaker."

"But what possible use —"

"I learned all this from those old papers I uncovered in the Historical Section. They were called 'Bills of Lading' but there were enough words —"

"How do you know you can 'read' something? I mean, without checking with the Speaker?"

"I know. The letters group together, you see — MANUFAC is just 'man' and this upturned letter is the sound 'you', and —"

"You're going too fast." He grimaced, obviously not liking this at all. He was a biology specialist and tolerated her interest in dusty antiquity, she knew, but finally he said, "Okay, show me again. Not that I really believe this, but..."

The truth about Shiva's elevated ocean only slowly emerges.

Odis is the first to notice it. Long days of sensory immersion in the data-streams repay her. She is rather proud of having plucked such exotica from the bath of measurements their expedition was getting from their probes, the tiny speeding, smart spindle-eyes which now cruise all over the double-stars' realm.

The Centauri system is odd, but even its strong tides could not explain this anomaly. Planets should be spherical, or nearly so; Earth bulged but a fraction of a percent at its equator, due to its spin. Not Shiva, though.

Odis finds aberrations in this world's shape. They are far away from the equator, principally at the 1,694-kilometre wide deep blue sea, immediately dubbed the Circular Ocean. It sits in the southern hemisphere, its nearly perfect ring hinting at an origin as a vast crater.

This had been the prevailing view until Odis makes her ranging measurements. She gathers in her data like number-clouds, inhaling their cottony wealth. Beneath her, their great craft, the Adventurer, prepares to go into orbit about Shiva. She breathes in the banks of data-vapour, translated into intricate scent-inventories. Tangy, complex.

At first she does not believe the radar reflections. Calibrations check, though, so she tries other methods: slow, analytical, tedious. They give the same result.

The Circular Ocean stands a hundred kilometres higher than the continent upon which it rests.

Odis presents her discovery at the daily Oversight Group meeting. There is outright scepticism, even curled lips of derision. "The range of methods is considerable. These results cannot be wrong," she says adamantly.

"Only thing to resolve this," a lanky geologist says, "is get an edge-on view."

"I hoped someone would say that." Odis smiles. "Do I have the authorised observing time?"

They give it reluctantly. The Adventurer is orbiting in a severe ellipse about Shiva's cloud-wrack. It is correctly positioned two days later and Odis focuses her observations. The full panoply of optical, IR, UV and microwave instruments peers at the Circular Ocean's perimeter, probing for the basin that supports the round slab of azure water.

There is none. No land supports the hanging sea.

This result is utterly clear. The Circular Ocean is 2.36 kilometres thick and a brilliant blue. Spectral evidence suggests that the water is quite pure, with no salt. It looks exactly like an enormous mountain lake, with the mountain subtracted.

And beneath that layer there is nothing but the thick atmosphere. No rocky mountain range to support the Ocean-in-air.

All other observations halt. The incontrovertible pictures of an immense layer of unimaginable weight, blissfully poised above mere thin gas, contradicting all known mechanics, captivates the expedition. Odis is the centre of attention, her counsel sought.

They can think of little else but this fascinating, frightening impossibility. Its strangeness yawns like an inviting abyss.

+++++

Milvina and Sorel spent the next few days in the oldest precinct of the Historical Sector, searching out corridors that the Imperium had not gotten around to Speaking.

It was fun. Milvina read him signs and he started picking up the method. Progress was slow; reading was hard. Letters, words, then working up to grasping how sentences and then paragraphs had their logic and rhythms, their clues about how to extract meaning.

Still, it wasn't as though he were some Deedee, after all. After a while she recalled from her Educational Specialty training that Deedees were actually officially called the Developmentally Delayed. So if someone had once taken just the first letters of both words, that was how they had gotten their name.

Everything went well between them and they got to like having their Speakers off while they strolled through the antiquated hallways, making sense of the signs.

The Speaker was always available if they needed it. Link-chips embedded near both ears could pick up the pervasive waves of CompCentral. They only had basic link, no frills but constant access. Like everybody, they had used the Speaker more as time went on; it was so easy.

But reading gave them a touch of the past and some silence. It was a relief, really.

They had kept their Speakers nearly always on. It was easy to get used to the Speaker's silky advertisements that floated just within hearing. You could pay the subscriber service for the Speaker and have no ads, but none of their friends did; it was far too expensive. And anyway, the ads told you a lot about people. There was a really interesting one for sperm and egg donors to the gay/les bank, a Meritocracy programme to help preserve the Gay Gene. It had zoomer sonics and life histories and everything. You could amp it and hear a whole half-hour show if you wanted. For free, too. But most weren't anywhere near that good, so they were glad to be rid of them.

Reading, though, grew on them. There were advantages to reading old signs that the Speaker didn't bother to translate. They showed off to a few friends but nobody believed they could really read the curious markings. It had to be some trick, for sure. Milvina and Sorel just smiled knowingly and dropped the subject.

Not that it was all good. At an old intersection Sorel honoured the GO signal by reading it, rather than listening to his Speaker. The signal was off synch and he nearly got flattened by a roller car.

They debated whether to tell anyone in authority. After all, maybe nobody knew this.

"Ummm, no," Sorel said. "Look at it this way — carrion eaters rule the world, in their way. Because nobody cares. Nobody wants what they like."

"So we'd be fools to make other people like reading?"

"Demand rises, supplies fall. Suppose everybody wanted those old books you found?"

She had to admit it was a sobering possibility. The carrion-eater analogy came out of his biology training, and he couldn't resist adding, "It's a smart strategy. When times are tough on everybody, the buzzards just get more to eat."

The thought was so disgusting she decided to forget about the whole question.

They came to like strolling the byways of the Megapolis, ferreting out the antiquated secrets of the signs. Lovers often find their own rituals, and this was a particularly delectable one.

Outside one vaultway there were clearly marked instructions on how to spin a dial and get in. They had to work on it for quite a while but finally they made it work. The door swung open on primitive hinges and they walked into a musty set of rooms. Exploring them proved boring; just stacks of locked compartments, all without signs. Until a guard came in with a drawn zapper.

"How'd you kids get in here?"

"It was open, sir," Sorel said. He had always been quick and Milvina supposed his answer was technically correct. She had opened the door.

"How the hell — ? Well, get out. Out!"

He was confused and worried and hardly gave them more than a brief search. Sorel asked to see the zapper, imitating a dumbo kid, and the guard brushed them off, still puzzled.

+++++

Lissa finds the answer to Shiva's mystery, but no one is happy with it.

An atmospheric chemist, Lissa's job is mostly done, well before they achieve orbit around Shiva. She has already probed and labelled the gasses, shown clearly that they imply a thriving biology below. After that, she had thought, the excitement would shift elsewhere, to the surface observers.

Not so. Lissa takes a deep breath and begins speaking to the Oversight Group. She has asked for this time and now has to show that she is not wasting their time. With all eyes on the Circular Ocean, few care for mere air. Yet it is the key.

Her presentation is quick. The Circular Ocean has intrigued her, too: so she looked at the mixture of oxygen, nitrogen and carbon dioxide that apparently supports the floating sea. These prove perfectly ordinary, except for one oddity. Their spectral lines are slightly split, so that she finds two small spikes to the right and left of where each line should be.

Lissa turns from the images she is projecting before the Oversight Group. "The only possible interpretation," she says crisply, "is that an immensely strong electric field is inducing the tiny electric dipoles of these molecules to move. That splits the lines."

"An electric shift?" a grizzled sceptic calls. "In a charge-neutral atmosphere? Sure, maybe when lightning flashes you could get a momentary effect, but —"

"It is steady."

"You looked for lightning?" the shrewd woman demands.

"It's there, sure. We see it forking between the clouds below the Circular Ocean. But that's not what causes the electric fields."

"What does?" This comes from the grave Captain, who seldom speaks in scientific disputes.

Lissa shrugs. "Nothing reasonable."

"So there must be an impossibly strong electric field everywhere in that hundred kilometres of air below the Ocean?" a voice calls.

Murmurs.

"Everywhere, yes." The bald truth of it stirs the audience. "Everywhere."

+++++

Until the vault Milvina had not realised that her hard-won trick was anything more than a delicious secret.

She was an inquiring type (some would say nosy) and enjoyed her hours of scanning over the decaying sheets she found in the Historical Sector's archives.

The fat ones she learned were called 'books' and there was even an entry in the Compendium about them. The Speaker recited the entry to her in its soft tones, the ones she had chosen for her daily work. She used a more ornate voice for social matters and a crisp, precise one for directions. In normal life that was all anyone needed, a set of pleasing Speaker agents.

There was hardly any delay when she requested the book entry and the Speaker told a marvellous tale. There were many kinds of books, including one called 'novel'. This meant new the Speaker said. But the one novel Milvina found in the dank, dark Antiquities Vault was obviously old, not new at all. Such confusions were inevitable in research, she realised.

Books were known also as buchs in some ancient sources, it said, in the confusing era when there were competing Speakers, such as 'Ger Man'. Not really even Speakers, either, but whole different speech-methods, before Standard was discovered.

All that happened in the Narrow Age, as antiquarians termed it. A time of constrained modes, hopelessly linear and slow. People then were divided by their access to information. Thank goodness such divisive forces were now banished.

They now lived in the Emergent Age, of course. The Speaker had emerged from the evolution of old-style Intelligent Agents, on computers. Those would perform fetch-'em tasks. Gradually, people let their Agents do more and more. Agent merging led to more creativity, coming from the overlap of many voices, many threads in a society where all was open and clear to all, available through the Speaker.

"What sop!" Sorel said to this, and she sort of agreed. The Narrow Age sounded fascinating, with its books and reading. The tingling thrill of being able to hold a year's worth of Speaker talk in your hand, opening it to anywhere you chose, picking out lore at will — it captivated her.

Of course, she knew the Speaker was superior. Instantly it could skip to any subject or even word you liked in any record. It would explain in private, sounding just like an enormously smart person speaking to you alone, in your head. Everybody had one and could access it with an internal signal.

She looked up the Speaker itself in one of the old books. The words were hard to follow and she began to wish for some way to find out what they meant. Sounding them out was hard because, even when she knew the word, the mapping from letters to sounds followed irregular rules. "What's the point of that?" Sorel asked often, but he kept at it with her.

The books said that the Speaker had started as an aid to people called 'illiterates' — and Milvina was startled to find, consulting the Speaker, that everybody was one. Except her and Sorel, now.

Once, lots and lots of people could read. But as the Speaker got easier to use, a certain cachet attached to using only the Speaker. Independence from linear 'print-slavery' became fashionable, then universal. After all, the Speaker could pipe the data you needed on fast-flow, a kind of compressed speech that was as fast (or in fact, by that time, faster) as people could read.

Most people got their information by eye, anyway. In a restaurant, they ordered chicken by touching the drumstick icon, or fish by the fish-stick icon. And of course most of their time they spent at entertainments, which had to be visual, tactile, smell-rich — sports, 3Ds, sensos, a-morphs, realos.

She found it quite delicious to have an obscure, secret talent that none of her friends even guessed. She was going to have a party and show them all, but then she saw the big letters in the Boulevard of Aspiration, and things got complicated.

✢✢✢✢✢

Tagore is in a hurry. Too much so.

He caroms off a stanchion but does not let that stop him from rebounding from the opposite wall, absorbing his momentum with his knees, and springing off with a full push. Rasters streak his vision, then flicker and fade.

He coasts by a full-view showing Shiva below, a blazing crescent transcendent in its cloud-wrapped beauty. Tagore ignores the spectacle. Marvels of the mind preoccupy him.

He is carrying the answer to it all, he is sure of that. In his haste he does not even glance at the shining crescent planet that dominates the wall-sized viewscreen. Blue-tinged sunlight glints from the Circular Ocean, shining with mystery and promise. The thick disk of open air below it is a clear line under the blue wedge. Its insolent impossibility is none the less serenely beautiful.

The youngest of the entire expedition, Tagore is a mere theorist. He had specialised in planetary formation at university, but managed to snag a berth on this expedition by developing a ready, quick facility at explaining vexing problems the observers turned up.

"Cap'n, I've got it," he blurts as he comes through the Captain's hatch. The Captain greets him, sitting at a small oak desk, the only wood on the whole ship — then gets to business. Tagore has asked for this audience because he knows the effect his theory could have on the others; so the Captain should see first.

"The Circular Ocean is held up by electric field pressure," he announces. The Captain's reaction is less than he had hoped: unblinking calm, waiting for more information.

"See, electromagnetic fields exert forces on the electrons in atoms," Tagore persists. He goes through the numbers, talking fast. "The fields down there are so strong — I got that measurement out of Lissa's data — they can act like a steady support." He goes on to make comparisons: the energy density of a hand grenade, contained in every suitcase-sized volume of air. Even though the fields could simply stand there, as trapped waves, they must suffer some losses. The power demands were huge. Plus, how the hell did such a gargantuan construction work?

Finally the Captain blinks and says something. "Anything like this ever seen on Earth?"

"Nossir, not that I've ever heard."

"No natural process can do the stunt?"

"Nossir, not that I can imagine."

"Well, we came looking for something different."

Tagore does not know whether to laugh or not; the Captain is unshakeable. Is this what exploration is like? He wishes he had some other role.

+++++

Sorel said slowly, "I make it to be

SAVVY THIS? MEAT 13:20 @ Y."

Sceptically he eyed the poorly printed letters written in livid red on a blue wall.

"Somebody did that by hand," Milvina marvelled.

"Writing by yourself? How?"

"I hadn't thought anybody could. I mean, machines make letters, don't they?"

"You're the one read all those historical books. Printing machines gave way to Speaker machines, you said."

Milvina traced a hand over the misshapen letters. "It's like making a drawing, only you try to imitate a machine, see? Think of letters as little art objects."

"This isn't an art exhibit."

"No, it's a message. But maybe I can..."

By luck she had in her side-sack her latest cherished discovery, a fat book called 'Dictionary'. It had many more words in it than the Speaker used, like approximating and vernacular. Big words that nobody used any more, hadn't used for so long even the Speaker didn't know them. It even told her that '@' meant 'at', but not why.

"Here," she pointed forcefully at the tiny little entry. "Meat is the flesh of an animal."

"Animals do that. I heard that people used to."

"Primitivo!" she said scornfully.

"It may mean that in there, but it sounds like 'meet'."

"Somebody made an error? Confusing the sound with another word?"

"Somebody wants people who can read the sign to meet them."

"Other readers."

"Where?" He frowned.

"It says 'Y'. That's not a word."

"Maybe it's an abbreviation, like that MANUFAC DIST?"

"No, too short."

He snapped his fingers. "Remember where the Avenue of Aspiration branches? You can look down on it from the balcony of the Renew building. From above, it looks like that letter."

"Let's be there, then."

+++++

Captain Badquor lets the Tagore kid go on a bit longer before he says more. It was best to let these technical types sing their songs first. So few of them ever thought about anything beyond their own warblings...

He gives Tagore a Captainly smile. "So the whole thing on Shiva is artificial."

"Well, yeah, I suppose so..."

Plainly Tagore hasn't actually thought about that part very much. The wonder of such strong fields has stunned him. Well, it was stunning. "And all that energy, just used to hold up a lake?"

"I'm sure of it, sir. The numbers work out, see? I equate the pressure exerted by those electric fields, assuming they're trapped in the volume under the Circular Ocean, the way waves can get caught if they're inside a conducting box —"

"You think that ocean's a conductor?" Might as well show the kid that even the Captain knew a little physics. In fact, though he never mentions it, he has a Master's from M.I.T.

"Uh, well, no, it's only a way of speaking —"

"Go on."

"Then the waves exert an upward force on the water every time they reflect from the underside of the Ocean —"

"And transfer that weight down, on invisible waves, to the rock that's a hundred kilometres below."

"Uh, yessir."

Tagore looks a bit constipated, bursting with enthusiasm, with the experience of the alien, but not knowing how to express it. The Captain decides to have mercy on the kid. "Sounds good. Not anything impossible about it."

"Except the size of it, sir."

"That's one way to put it."

"Sir?"

The Captain feels a curious, powerful feeling wash over him. The long decades of anticipation have steeled him, made him steady in the presence of the crew. But now he feels his sense of the room tilt, as though he were losing control of his status-space. The mind could go whirling off, out here in the inky immensities between twin alien suns. "This thing is bigger than anything humanity ever built. And there's not a clue what it's for. The majesty of it, son, that's what strikes me."

++++++

Milvina and Sorel showed up, all right, but nobody else did. Instead, at the Y another crude hand-lettered sign said

MEAT CORRIDOR 63, 13:30 TOMORROW, BLOCK 129

They went home and turned off their Speakers and talked. Most couples silenced the Speaker only during sex. This was merely polite, even though of course no other person could be sure it was off nowadays, what with the new neuro-activated models.

They went home and sped-read some ancient texts. There was a thick book titled The Lust of the Mahicans that Sorel had seen on senso. She read it — her speed was a lot higher than his — but it wasn't anything like the senso he had seen. There was no sex in it at all. Just stares of infinite longing and heavy breathing and pounding pulses and stuff like that. Still, she found it oddly stirring. Reading was funny that way.

They could not get their minds off the sign. Sorel was out of sorts, irked that others had mastered their discovery. He groused about it vaguely and found excuses to change the subject.

Milvina didn't see it possessively. After all, the higher moral good was to share. Reading was wickedly single-ist. Was that why she liked it so much? A reader was isolated, listening to a voice no one else could take part in. That led to differences and divisions, friction and clashes.

Still, the rapture of reading — of listening to silent sounds from ages past — was too, well, perhaps the right word was titillating.

She was excited by the prospect of other readers. Inevitably, they went to the site.

The man who slouched beside a rampway was not impressive. Medium height, his crimson codpiece was three years out of date. His hair was stringy and festooned with comically tattered microbirds. He said nothing, simply handed them a sheet. Miserably printed sentences covered both sides. The first paragraph was enough for Milvina:

THE SECRET ASSEMBLY OF READERS MUST UNITE! WE HAVE A TALENT THE MASSES CANNOT UNDERSTAND. THEY WILL FEAR US IF THEY KNOW. A BROTHERHOOD AND SISTERHOOD OF READERS IS THE ONLY SOLUTION TO OUR ISOLATION. ARISE!

"What cliche sop!" She thrust the sheet back at him.

"True, though."

Sorel said sharply, "Just tell us what you —"

"You never know when the Speaker is on," the man said mysteriously.

Milvina said, "And your printing is awful."

"Better than yours," he said shrewdly.

"That's not the point," Sorel said. "We demand to know —"

"Come on. And shut up, huh?"

+++++

John slips into his helmet and Shiva encloses him. His pov shifts, strums, arcs with busy fretworks — then snaps into solidity, stabilised.

He is eager to immerse himself in the feel of Shiva, in full 3D wraparound. Its crescent swells below like a ripe, mottled fruit. He plunges toward it.

For effect — he had decades before been a skydiver — John had arranged the data-fields so that he accelerates into it. From their orbit, he shoots directly toward Shiva's disk. Each mapping rushes toward him in finer detail. There —

The effect shows up first in the grasslands of the southern habitable belt. He slews toward the plains, where patterns emerge. After Tagore's astonishing theory about the Circular Ocean, he has to be ready for anything. Somewhere in the data-fields must lurk the clue to who or what made the Ocean.

Below, the great grassy shelves swell. But in places the grass is thin. Soon he sees why. The natural grass is only peeking around plains covered with curious orderly patterns — hexagonals fold into triangles where necessary to cover hills, valleys, right up to the muddy banks of the slow-moving brown rivers. Reflection in the UV shows the tiles making this pattern are the size of houses, meters thick...and moving. They all jostle and work with restless energy, to no obvious purpose.

Alive? The UV spectrum breaks down to a description of a complex polymer, cross-linked chains bonding at many oblique angles to each other, flexing like micro-muscles. They feed on their own sky.

Simple sugars rain from the clotted air, the fruit of an atmospheric chemistry that resembles chicken soup. Oxidising radicals the size of golf balls patrol the perimeters of the tiles, attacking invader chemicals and harvesting those they can use.

All one life form? — could that be? A whole planet taken over by a tiling-thing that co-opts all resources? But how could a species evolve to have only one member?

Evolution rules that out. Bio-evolution, that is. But not social evolution.

John plunges further into the intricate matrices of analysis.

The endless arrangements cloaking mountains and valleys shift and mill, fidgety, only occasionally leaving bare ground visible as a square fissions into triangles. Oblongs meet and abut in some fevered competition. That ground seems covered with a thin grass, no more. Apparently the sprigs live off the momentary sunlight that slips between the edges of the jostling, jiggling, bumping, shaking tiles. Could they be performing some agitated discourse, a riot of semi-cerebral computation, a lust fest without end?

Could the planet have become a computer?

He slows his descent. The tiles are a shock. Could these be the builders of the Circular Ocean?

+++++

Milvina and Sorel walked silently with the man, all the way into a wildness preserve, before the man spoke. "I'm Karl. No Speaker pickups here, at least according to the flow charts."

"You're an engineer?" Milvina asked, admiring the oaks.

"I'm a philosopher. I make my money engineering."

"How long have you been...reading?"

"Years. Started with some old manuals I found. Figured it out from scratch."

"So did we," Sorel said. "It's hard, not being able to ask for help from the Speaker."

Karl nodded. "I did. Dumb, huh?"

"What happened?"

"Some Spectors came by. Just casual talk, y'know, but I knew what they were after."

"Evidence?" she asked uneasily.

"When I asked the Speaker there was a pause, just a little one. A priority shift, I know how to spot them. So I broke off and took the books I had to a hiding place. When I got back there were the Spectors, cool as you like, just kind of looking around my room."

"You didn't tell them...?" she asked.

"You got to give them something. I had a copy of this thing about books that I couldn't understand, Centigrade 233. Kept it buried under a pseud-bush bed. They were getting funny on me so I took it out and gave it to them."

She blinked, startled. "What did they do? Arrest you?"

Karl gave her a crooked grin. "Reading's not illegal, y'know. Just anti, that's all. So they let me off with six weeks of grouping."

"Wow, do I hate those," Sorel said.

Karl shrugged. "I did the time. They poked at me and I had to pretend to see the light and all. They kept the book."

"You're brave," Milvina said.

"Just stupid. I should never have asked the Speaker."

Sorel said earnestly, "You'd think the Speaker would encourage us to learn. I mean, it'd be useful in emergencies. Say the Speaker goes down, we could read the info we'd need."

Karl nodded. "I figure the Speaker reads. It just doesn't want competition."

She said, "The Speaker is a machine."

"So?" Karl shrugged again. "Who knows how smart it is?"

"It's a service," Sorel said. "That's all."

"Notice how it won't store what we say?" Karl smiled shrewdly.

Sorel nodded. "It says it's trying to improve our memories."

"Reading was invented to replace memory," Milvina said. "I read it in a history book."

"So it must be true?" Karl shrugged derisively, a gesture that was beginning to irk Milvina a lot.

She hated politics and this was starting to sound like that. "How many books have you got?"

"Lots. I found a tunnel into a vault. I can go there anytime."

Sorel and Milvina gasped at his audacity as he described how for years he had burrowed into sealed-off chambers, many rich in decaying documents and bound volumes. He spoke of exotica they had never seen, tomes which were nothing but names in the Dictionary: Encyclopaedias, Thesauruses, Atlases, Almanacs. He had read whole volumes of the fabled Britannica!

Would he trade? Lend? "Of course," Karl said warmly.

Their friendship began that way, a bit edgy and cautious at the margins, but dominated by the skill and secret lore they shared. Three glorious years of clandestine reading followed before Karl disappeared.

+++++

The computer folk think one way, the biologists — after an initial rout, when they rejected the very possibility of a single entity filling an entire biosphere — quite another.

After some friction, their views converge...somewhat. Could a species turn itself into a biological computer? The tiles rub and caress each other, like houses making love.

The next question — not that some big ones aren't left behind, perhaps lying in wait to bite them on their conceptual ass — is even larger. Could the tiles know anything more than themselves? Or are they strange, geometroid solipsists?

Sealed inside a cosmos of its own making, was it even in principle interested in the outside world? Its star feeds gratuitous energy, the very air fuels it; its advanced chemical/physical evolution is the last standing power on the globe...what reason did it have to converse with the great Outside? Curiosity, perhaps? The biologists frown at the prospect. Curiosity in the early pre-humans found a reward in the environment. The evolving monkey learned new tricks, found fresh water, killed a new kind of game, invented a better way to find those delicious tree roots — and the world duly paid it back.

Apparently — but don't ask us why just yet — the game is different here.

So even if they ring the conceptual doorbell on the Tile-Things, maybe nobody will answer.

Should they try?

John and Odis and Lissa, Tagore and the Captain — they all pondered.

+++++

Karl wasn't at any of their usual meeting places. After all this time, Milvina and Sorel still did not know where he lived, or where his hoard of books might be. Karl was secretive. They searched the sprawling corridors of the complexes, but were afraid to ask Speaker for any info on him.

The Majority Games were on then so the streets were more crowded than usual. Most people were out all the time, excited and eager and happy to be in the great mobs that thronged the squares. The Games took up everybody's time — except, of course, the three hours of work everyone had to put in, no exceptions, every labour-day. Milvina and Sorel broke up to cover more ground and spent a full week on the search. Many times Milvina blamed herself for not pressing Karl about where he lived, but the man was obsessively secretive. "Suppose they grab you, make you tell about me?" he had always countered.

Now she wondered what the Spectors would do if they uncovered a load of books like Karl's. Send him to Advanced Treatment? Or was there something even worse?

She came home after a day of dogged searching and Sorel was not there. He did not appear that evening. When she awoke the next morning she burst into tears. He was gone that day and the one after.

On her way back from work, a routine counselling job, she resolved to go to the Spector. She half-heartedly watched the crowds, hoping to see Karl or Sorel, and that was how she noticed that three men and a woman were moving parallel to her as she crossed the Plaza of Promise. They were all looking some other way but they formed four points of the compass around her with practised precision.

She walked faster and they did too. They looked stern and remorseless and she could not lose them in the warrens of streets and corridors near the two-room apartment she shared with Sorel. They had waited five years to get one with a tiny balcony. Even then it was just two levels up from the muddy floor of the air shaft. But if you hooked your head over to the side you could see some sky that way.

Milvina kept moving in an aimless pattern and they followed. Of course she did not want to go to the apartment, where she would be trapped. But she was tired and she could not think of anything else to do.

They knocked a few minutes after she collapsed on the bed. She had hoped they might hold off for a while. She was resigned. When she spun the door open the person she least expected to see was Karl.

"You won't believe what's going on," he said, brushing past her.

"What? Where have you —"

"The Meritocrats want us."

"For what?"

"Reading!"

"But the Speaker —"

"Keeps people out of touch and happy. Great idea — but it turns out you can't run everything with just the Speaker." He blinked, the merest hesitation. "Somebody's got to be able to access info at a higher level. That was our gut feeling, remember — that reading was different."

"Well, yes, but the Spectors —"

"They keep people damped down, is all." A slight pause. "Anybody who's got the savvy to see the signs, the grit to learn to piece together words on their own, to process it all — those are the people the Merits want. Us!"

Milvina blinked. This was too much to encompass. "But why did they take you away, and Sorel —"

"Had to be sure." He gave his old familiar shrug. "Wanted to test our skills, make sure we weren't just posing. People might catch on, only pretend to read, y'know?"

"I...see." There was something about Karl that wasn't right. He had never had these pauses before...because he wasn't listening to the Speaker then?

She backed away from him. "That's marvellous news. When will Sorel be back?"

"Oh, soon, soon." He advanced and she backed out onto the balcony.

"So what job will you do? I mean, with reading in it?"

They were outside. She backed into the railing. The usual distant clatter and chat of the air shaft gave her a momentary sense of security. Nothing could happen here, could it?

"Oh, plenty. Looking up old stuff, comparing, y'know." He waved his hands vaguely.

It wasn't much of a drop from here. Over the railing, legs set right...

"It's good work, really."

Could she could get away if she jumped? Karl wasn't the athletic type and she knew that if she landed right on the mud below she wouldn't twist an ankle or anything. She had on sensible shoes. She could elude him. If she landed right.

She gave him a quick, searching look. Had he come here alone? No, probably there were Spectors outside her door, just waiting for him to talk her into surrendering. Stall for time, yes.

"How bad is it?"

He grinned. "You won't mind. They just access that part of your mind for three hours a day. Then they install a shutdown on that cerebral sector."

"Shutdown? I —"

"So you don't need to read any more. Just during work, is all. You get all you need that way. Then you're free!"

She thought it through. Jump, get away. Couldn't use the Speaker for help because they could undoubtedly track her if she had her receiver on. Could she get by just reading the old signs?

Suppose she could. Then what? Find some friends she could trust. Stay underground? How? Living off what?

"It's much better. Sorel will be back soon and —"

"Hold it. Don't move."

She looked down the air shaft. A long way down. Was the jump worth it?

✣✣✣✣✣

You spool out of the illusion and snap — back into the tight cocoon. The automatic sensory leads retract, giving your skin momentary pinprick goodbye kisses. Once more you feel the cool clasping surfaces of the cocoon. Now you turn and ask, "Hey, where's the rest?"

Myrph shrugs her shoulders, still busy undoing her leads. "That's all there was, I told you."

"Maybe it's just damaged?"

"No, that's the end of the cube. There must be another cube to finish the story, but this was the only one I found back in that closet."

"But how does it end? What's she do?" You lean toward her, hoping maybe she's just teasing.

"I dunno. What would you do? Jump?"

You blink, not ready for the question. "Uh, this reading thing. What is it, really?"

Myrph frowns. "It felt like a kind of your own silent voice inside your head."

"Is it real? I mean, does reading exist?"

"Never heard of it."

"So this isn't an historical at all, right? It's a fantasy."

"Must be. I've never seen those things on walls."

"Signs, she called them." You think back. "They would have worn away a long time ago, anyway."

"I guess. Felt kinda strange, didn't it, being able to find out things without Speaker?"

+++++

{ — John/Odis/Lissa/Tagore/Cap'n — }

— all assembled/congealed/thickened —

— into a composite veneer persona, to work out what their next response to the Centauri data-stream would be.

Each person had played a different role in processing the data, living through it as a real human would have, had one actually been in the Centauri system at all.

There were myriad other such teams, sprinkled around the globe, fashioning the digitised profusion into a skein of interpretations, of lived scenarios, of expressive renderings. Some would become technical papers in the science journals, others would be artworks. The division between creative realms had dissolved as the entire human community reacted to the expansion of its sensory sphere.

Sending a fragile human crew to Alpha Centauri, with its 4.2 year delay in communications, would have been absurdly wasteful. Far better to send smart-eyes, rugged robots, and quasi-intelligent processors. Lightweight, patient, durable, these ambassadors had survived the hard accelerations and withering particle storms of interstellar flight, to alight upon worlds of deep strangeness. But they needed human guidance, even if delayed by 8.4 years in the turn-around time.

Should the persona { — John/Odis/Lissa/Tagore/Cap'n — } reach down, through their deputies orbiting Shiva, to make contact with the Tile-Things? With 4.2 years of separation, there was ample reason to decide quite deliberately.

Only by visiting the varying playlets each veneer persona had fashioned, out of the raw data-stream, could humanity as a whole decide. This was the most honoured and sought-after task on the entire globe, a packed planet link-locked together.

Only the very highest elite could partake of such matters, of course. For most, disposable realities of the most routine sort still beckoned more powerfully; but these were mere amusements, however engrossing. Some felt that real-time itself was a pallid, ephemeral experience, because one could not archive it for replay, savour it, return until it became a true part of oneself. So they lived instead in worlds truncated, chopped, governed by technologies they could barely sense.

+++++

"Learning things without Speaker..."

You bite your lip, thinking. Already the illusion of being that woman, Milvina, is slipping away, hard to fix in memory. She did have a kind of power all on her own with that reading thing. You liked that. "I wonder what she did?"

"About what?"

"Jumping. Was it worth it, just for a small chance?"

"Hey, it's just a story."

"What would you do?"

"I don't have to decide. It's just a story."

"But why tell it then?"

Myrph says irritably, "It's just an old illusion, missing a cube, too."

"Maybe there was only one."

"Look, I want illusions to take me away, not stress me out."

You remember the power of it. "Can I have it, then?"

"The cube? Sure."

Myrph tosses it over. It is curiously heavy, translucent and chipped with rounded corners. You cup it in your hand and like the weight of it.

That is how it starts. You know already that you will go and look for the signs in the corridors and that for good or ill something new has come into your world and will now never leave it.

+++++

{ — John/Odis/Lissa/Tagore/Cap'n — } ran their integrated personalities through the myriad ways of seeing the information from Centauri.

Replay enhanced their perceptions, sharpened their powers.

Their dramas were, of course, their own constructions of how events would have played out for real people. Such imaginative integrations were the true function, the proper role for humans to render in the exploration of the gulfs between stars, where durable, patient machines best fit.

Their tasks finished for the day, each would return home. They would pass through corridors where others lived the exact inverse of their lives: unable to read, to participate in the high culture, these passing faces in the great crowds lived in a reality quite qualitatively different. Machines had at last enabled people of profoundly different inclinations to live in their own worlds. Each felt the other missed some essential in the human landscape; each felt not hostile to the other, but worse, indifferent.

So the cultures of separation lived uneasily, sliding through each other, each with its discontents and malcontents, in hierarchies of ability as intricate and layered as those of Nineveh and Tyre.

REAL FUTURES?

Stephen McClelland

Real Futures?

Stephen McClelland

The ground trembles beneath our feet.

Networks of buried cables snake out, reach across the globe. Around us in the air there is the silent buzz of millions upon millions of cellular phone conversations.

The world is being changed, perhaps in the words of one commentator, even being reinvented.

The change is largely being caused by new paradigms, and largely by the new paradigm of communications technology. Depending on what metaphor you use, this communications technology is providing a planetary nervous system, or a global economic locomotive powering us towards the next millennium. All the metaphors seem inadequate to describe the changes taking place because nothing will be left as it was. When it has passed, the global economic and sociological landscape will be permanently changed.

It's a seismic shift in the way the world is unfolding, as we move from one age to another. This decade, we are seeing for the first time that large numbers of people around the world are able to divorce themselves in their daily lives from the constraints of time and space. If the geological metaphor is appropriate, the seismic activity, is on the side of an active volcano, a volcano of exploding traffic, networks, applications, protocols. Perhaps you should look at it on a quantum level: the communications-driven world of the future will be just like an atom settling down to a new stable state, but one which occurs after a discontinuity, a disruption to the system. Disruption though it may be, it is a productive one, because energy is released to further enhance the change. In the case of communications, the new stable state improves the efficiency of business processes throughout society, and eliminates overhead and delays which are now recognised as unnecessary. At large, it will cause a major reallocation of social and business resources.

So if the changes are inevitable, irreversible, and filled above all with immense power, what can we expect in the future? Should we joyfully anticipate, or fear chaos? No one knows. The debate continues, but there are good grounds for optimism: societies and individuals previously disenfranchised will be able to participate in economic and social development, and do so cheaply and effectively. After talking to more than thirty specialists — many of whom could bring profound insights to bear on the matter — in the preparation of this book, I have noticed these reasons for optimism. As a result, I am more inclined to be optimistic myself.

Communications technologies have changed in almost every conceivable way, but in the 1990s, two key ones stand out on the road of societal change: mobile technologies, and the Internet. Neither existed in any widespread form until the last decade, but both now have the power to reshape everything. The change and sophistication have markedly progressed even in the last five years. Take the worldwide adoption of digital cellular mobile technologies, for example. In the next five years, reliable industry estimates say that another 250 million users around the world will be signed up, bringing the planetary mobile subscriber base to the order of 500 million, perhaps comparable with the total number of fixed phones now in existence.

A New Relationship

Looked at another way, mobile communications — and cellular devices in particular — will probably come to dominate communications over their fixed terminal counterparts in the next few years. By the year 2002, countries like the UK will probably be installing more mobile lines than fixed ones. The changes are most marked in 'early adopter' countries, for example, in the Scandinavian region. The percentage of take up of mobile communications here is extraordinarily high; in Finland for example there are about 33 in every hundred people daily carrying a mobile phone. This increasing usage presages a remarkable and profound change in how we organise business and daily life in the future.

The 'generational dimension' is even more impressive. In Finland for example, some 70% of 18 to 25 year olds already have a mobile phone. Clearly, the post-industrial age is already here, and mobile communications has moved from being a status accessory to everyday tool. According to independent estimates, production volumes of mobile terminals during 1997 will match the those of personal computers for the first time: more than 60 million units. But volumes will keep on growing, and mobile handsets will become the most pervasive and most complex mass produced item ever produced in our civilisation. They passed that other enduring symbol of the 20th century, the car, some two years ago.

More lies in prospect. People wanted these phones for reasons for mobility, in the future, personal communications may well transcend even mobility as new applications become increasingly available. Some prediction is possible, at least on the capability of the progress of fundamental component technology that goes to make these systems. On this basis, manufacturers like Nokia can confidently predict that by the first few years of the next decade, terminals will be both extremely small (at 50cc or less in volume) and lightweight. They will be cheap enough to find applications well beyond the 'simple' two way voice uses that we currently see. At that stage, microelectronics should have shrunk what is shrinkable, with only battery technology and the man-machine interface requiring substantial packaging. Researchers are aiming at this scale to engineer the technology in such a way so that it has a fundamental and personal relationship with its users, akin to the wristwatch. The talk is of 'personal, pocketable communications,' of 'global mobile multimedia,' and of wireless communications that could be embedded everywhere. Other developments are possible. In many countries, full-scale wireless local loop systems could emerge.

This would be remarkable in itself, but it is not alone. For the mobile communications volcano has been matched by another one, seemingly coming from a totally different direction, the rise of the Internet. The Internet has sprung from nowhere to be a global phenomenon — and in a manner reminiscent to the telephone over the last century — a flexible one. Standardisation made international telephony possible, and the widespread deployment of Internet protocols has made a global *lingua franca* possible and a global availability of Internet services an actuality. Even the antagonism of computing operating systems attempting to work together seems something of the past, as these universal standards supersede them, with common TCP/IP and HTTP/HTML intelligibility, and a common way of interpreting the destination address: the URL. In the 21st century, for a telephone number, now read a URL in the new global village.

A Megastream Convergence

If the big communications themes of the 1990s are mobile communications and the Internet, what is the next big thing? Perhaps: the combination of both, if industry hopes are realised. The idea of bringing the two seamlessly together in network and terminal terms is a relatively courageous idea, operating on the frontier of what we know about the communications marketplace. If it happens it will be a 'convergence of megastreams.' Mobile data has been to date a 'nice to have' facility in the cellular environment where operators and users alike have focused on voice usage, but several factors could drive it forward. A society on the move needs a lot more sophistication from its communications technology. Much of the attention has focused on the emergence of 'communicator' like devices providing a multiplicity of functions. However, some companies such as Nokia have developed a strategy that takes this further, to actively seek the convergence of the worlds of mobile and Internet, until now quite separate. This convergence might take place in a variety of ways, and although a fixed network/mobile network convergence is a significant — and widely discussed — possibility, it is not the only foreseeable option. Arguably, there has to be rationalisation, but it might even be on the basis of Internet and IP networking services absorbing other services.

This policy effectively amounts to a corporate vision where Internet access is an integral part of a mobile user's needs — and a cellular service provider's portfolio. Cellular providers might well be able to become ISPs as well, and there are bullish forecasts that data services will become the 'second 50%' of an operator's revenue in the next 5 years, a far cry from today. This will be because users will be using wholly new applications and businesses will be finding new ways to organise themselves. In particular, wireless data will be increasingly driven by business processes that are themselves predicated on e-mail and groupware applications. With the speed of business activity now taking place, a near instant response is called for, and people need to attend to their e-mail immediately or at least within hours. Many observers point out that all serious business operations are already primarily run with e-mail connectivity. More desktop processing power and more sophisticated applications on PCs means more messaging — and more e-mail, still.

In short, gurus predict an explosion of wireless intranet requirements as users fully absorb the potential for virtual businesses. 'Intranet' is the key word, and it goes wireless for substantially the same reasons as business voice on-the-move makes sense. True, operators until now have been weak in serving wireless data needs, mostly just offering modem circuits. In turn, corporate IT managers have been uninspired the corporate data solutions offered to them. Altogether, observers point out, there could be far more possibility available than the market — which is so far in an immature phase — permits. But perhaps operators will need to become serious about Internet, and themselves establish a managed Internet Access Point (IAP). There are several key technologies coming into play for this, notably the ability for users to be profiled and in particular, authenticated. Corporate IT managers almost certainly need to see an optimised wireless solution that is comparable to the level of development of LAN technology.

If these suggestions do become a reality, practically no one with a serious interest in the communications community will be left untouched. Industry estimates — particularly from the Mobile Data Initiative, a trade body for promotion of the application — point to only 4% of Europe's 20 million GSM users conducting mobile data applications, which could indicate significant growth potential as there are nearly 6 million laptop users in the region. Various estimates collected by the MDI suggest this could grow to between 3.5 million and 6 million users by the year 2000. Possible, substantial revenue enhancements for telcos are suggested by Dataquest in a recent report which estimated that whilst data communications traffic accounted for 33% of all wireline revenues in Europe last year, and half the revenue from the business community, it only produced 0.8% of revenues for GSM operators.

Further off, higher bandwidth services come into play for mobile communications, and developers are extremely confident of making the technology available for these. Within two years, we should see a high speed circuit switched data facility on GSM for example which will deploy data rates in the region 28.8 kbps to 64 kbps supporting more multimedia offerings. Another wave of development with probably higher bit rates still is expected as the UMTS/FPLMTS technologies are introduced around the turn of the decade. Most industry insiders expect packet radio offerings to increasingly push take-up as airtime usage is optimised and charges drop as a result. However, some point out that the additional bit rate options do not really represent new opportunities although they will make existing services more valuable and convenient to use. But regardless of what data rates will be, the mobile phone as we know it is making a major transformation as these services become actualised.

Wireline Goes Broadband

In the networks of the future, there are other implications of the tremendous growth of communications activity. Looked at from the network point of view, mobile and Internet are just two of the revolutionary drives. The network strategy, from the Nokia point of view is summed up a single motto — if 'voice goes wireless, then the wireline network can go broadband,' creating platforms for the support of any future service, voice, data or video, likely to be required. This needs some explaining for people outside the immediate communications industry. In the past, telecoms networks have evolved for a specific purpose: the support of voice communications. This particularly applies to the public switched telephone network (PSTN) which has been the mainstay of the industry. But it also applies to existing mobile communications networks, which have been designed as separate, but interconnecting entities, again to support primarily voice communications. Lastly, in most instances, data communications has been provided also by a separate network, again on an overlay basis. This partitioning is relatively inefficient, and costly. In the main, one type of network can not be used to support another. Future communications needs will go far beyond what can be supplied by a platform designed for voice traffic in PCM form alone. These three networks will merge in the future to form an essentially integrated single network platform with the applications apportioned as necessary. With so much demand for the various applications, this integrated platform will be supporting not only broadband communications, although these will be important, but all types of flexible requirements.

So we are looking to a future of entirely new networks, although no one is suggesting this will happen overnight and our present networks discarded. Service providers in some cases have already begun to experiment with new services and new service platforms and in the mix of narrow and broadband service introduction. But in the longer term we should expect to see some profound changes in the network platforms themselves. The creation in the public network of high capacity, high quality network 'islands' is likely. These will be broadband in nature and allowing the various services to be supplied. They will also allow a higher quality and availability of services to be supplied than at present, and permit such features as improved security, mobility, and network billing capacity also to be engineered. Over the course of time, this scenario would expect the various islands to merge — or to be interlinked to other networks — to form a more or less coherent broadband structure.

There could be some evident drivers for this scenario. An important one will be business communications. At present, many organisations perhaps as many as 90% of the business community in the private and public sectors manage their own data communications facilities. With the improvements in prospect in the public wide area network, this may change substantially. With the high quality network platforms mentioned above coming on stream, businesses in particular may choose to outsource their communications needs to service providers supporting such multi-service communications platforms. This will prove most attractive in the beginning to small and medium sized companies employing fewer than 100 people which in any case frequently lack adequate resources to manage their own communications anyway. The trend will then become evident in the larger companies too. Eventually, this functionality will be so widespread that everyone will benefit, and the first examples may well be seen by remote working and telecommuting applications that will require individuals to use sophisticated network services. Even our concepts of 'mobility' itself may change. It may well cover different systems anyway, for example with GSM-type mobility together with IP mobility. Other applications will almost certainly mandate close interworking between short haul mobility, perhaps represented by something like wireless LAN services and a more generic mobility. This also fits well in with the prospective broadband services.

The potential of these new networks with their high power, multi-service wireline broadband platforms will affect the business strategies of the operators and service providers themselves. A substantial move by customers to seek outsourcing arrangements in the public network would pave the way for a more general reorganisation of the business. Most operators may well feel that the mere transfer of bits as a commodity is not enough to be successful in the new age. In due course, it is likely that operators will choose to differentiate themselves in various ways for the new era: if legal and regulatory problems can be overcome, perhaps through a distinction between network platform providers and service providers. Some may well remain universal, all-embracing providers. Or some may choose to differentiate themselves by service type, or through access technique, or through the quality of value added they can bring to the application. In the meantime, marketeers are confident that wireline technologies will be able to support any service.

That Personal Touch

One of the most strongly held convictions of all in the field of communications is the recognition of a growing 'personalisation trend'; it's important enough to be strongly influencing the system and interface design of communications networks in everything from handheld terminals to huge infrastructures.

Operators and service providers should be able to join this trend — after all there are few industries which have a more detailed knowledge of its customer base and habits. This information is in huge databases around the world, ready to be mined. Combined, the push for personalisation and the availability of customer information should give providers enormous potential to truly tailor services individually in their customer base. Everything could be customised: applications, tariffs, service levels all for a 'segment of one' customer. But that is not all. The established infrastructure can be 'mined' too, and given further developments, additional uses and applications, with relatively little difficulty on top of the basic platform.

What then will people need? On this basis, futurists believe that personalised communications is capable of meeting three fundamental needs: for entertainment, for information on demand, and for personal contact. Information — whatever it will mean — will obviously be user-tailored, and it obviously needs to be interesting, relevant, and in this domain, fresh and timely. The mobile telephone in your pocket is about to make a major transformation to a 'communicator' device; not only will it be a mobile phone, it will also be an Internet viewer, using sophisticated narrowband services to convey digital messaging of all types such as news headlines, exchange rates, e-mail header scrolling, restaurant booking. The keypad will allow access to a near universal communications device There will be an amazing development in handset design and functionality.

A lot of this depends on the so-called service logic of the mobile communications system. Whilst it is clear that a mobile communications scenario of development will differ from that of the fixed line systems, it is also clear that some form of intelligent network infrastructure focused on mobile users will be important for operators in the future These IN systems will enable customers to have their own personal profiles of applications set up. The intelligence required to capture and execute these features will be shared between both network and terminal. For example, designers now talk about the possibility of setting up a 'home profile vs office profile,' or a 'meeting room' profile. There are many others that could potentially be configured. Each would allow the user to access coherently specific elements and features in the terminal and in the network to meet these needs.

Building a Cathedral?

A mix of challenges and prospects, then, and perhaps more and greater opportunities than any sector has enjoyed since the industrial revolution. But what s the end result? Perhaps, as one person said to me: we are building a cathedral but we do not know what it will look like yet. If you are building a cathedral, he continued, you do not start with the tower, but with cornerstones, in this case, the cornerstones are mobility and Internet access. Everywhere in the industry, he concluded, we are still in the building phase. The fundamental question to ask therefore is how the change in technology will affect human behaviour.

One of the remarkable things about these technologies is that a short time ago we did not have either, and yet at this particular time, we have both. Set in the context of industry development, we may be going through three waves of development. On this model, the telephone was the first wave and it removed the 'obstacle' of distance. If we leap forward, the mobile phone was part of the second wave, removing the 'obstacle' of location. What of the third wave? New communicator devices might be employed to remove what is perhaps the fundamental 'obstacle' still existing in our 'information society', in other words, the accessing of the information itself.

As technologies become mainstream, the relationship with the user and supplier will undoubtedly change, too, he concluded. Maybe it will be a relationship based increasingly on ethics, on trust, on the ability of the supplier to inspire confidence through the product in the mind of the consumer, a guarantee in some sense of security in a changing world. In this sense, the brand or logo is almost a promise.

But it is early days in the communications industry, the speaker emphasised: we are still in the building phase.

If information has empowered us, it has also equalised our economic opportunities, as other relative economic advantages have begun to disappear. The world around us has few (if any) 'lucky strikes' left, few accidental successes due to natural resources, or power, or even, violence. A great levelling is globally taking place, mainly due to informatio technologies that have appeared. In the future we may be wholly dependent on better skill sets and therefore need an educational system that genuinely equips us for lifelong learning.

The industrial revolution we relied on for much of the 19th and 20th centuries did many things, and in particular, it introduced the concept of a job, of particular employment characteristics. Key to these was the need to perform a particular function at a particular time at a particular place. This mode of thinking is doomed to die. Technology will inevitably mean that in the future there may be a merging of work and non-work time, but hopefully on reconcilable and compatible basis.

If communications gives us new possibilities, it will also give us new responsibilities, perhaps a need for more discretion and respect in the new era, a sensitivity which we didn't need before about how to use these technologies in public, how to communicate, and an awareness of when being 'in touch' becomes intrusion. Looked at in another way, going forward may depend on our ability to detect a sort of evolution, to detect consumer 'pull' and not technology or commercial 'push.'

If the technology has been or clearly can be developed, the communications community around the world will have to focus increasingly on understanding human behaviour and needs. Technology by itself can offer a wide palette of choices and options, but the user will not necessarily accept or adopt all of these. New forms of flexibility and fast response will be required by all users of al suppliers.

Shared Purpose

So we need to understand uses and needs rather than merely technologies.

The trends that are taking place, say futurists at companies like Nokia, are all around us and they affect products, content and profiling right across the economic spectrum. Key amongst these trends, as we have seen, is a new level of personalisation of service or product, hitherto unprecedented in scope and scale. Globalisation is of course another major trend, although arguably also based on consumerisation; products and services successful in one location will be instantaneously transferable from region to region in the future.

But they also warn against thinking in a limited 'either/or' way, against accepting that there are scenarios in which all other scenarios are automatically ruled out. The future is likely to be much more complicated than that.

These futurists detect a paradigm shift when the trends set to work. But many, mixed outcomes are possible. Much of the potential appears good, but, say futurists, if changing times simply mean we end up with a product-based onslaught which drowns consumers without reference to the wider needs of the individual or society, something will have been missed. It will have been missed if we use the tools to get just more of the same habits or content or to manipulate. People will increasingly rather be asking: what do I need this product for?

So this will be the point, say the futurists, where communications merges into the larger picture of what we want from society. Decisions will have to be made which are not really any longer about the communications industry, but rather a mesh of governance, and consumer factors, and many industries who all have a part to play. On this basis, the meaningful winners will need in some sense a significant amount of shared purpose in the society in which they operate.

Perhaps this is the key ultimate irony of communications: shared purpose.

The communications industry might be a central actor in the society of the future, and may well have to start building its cathedral on an ethical basis. It could happen, perhaps as soon as the next decade. Populations may well continue to press for greater efficiencies in the way society and organisations deliver their goods and services. But at the same time, perhaps the worldwide dismantling of governmental structures and the withdrawal for economic and political reasons of government from many spheres of everyday life will continue. A gap may well be left which someone will have to fill.

Meanwhile, we could be seeing the 'personalisation trend' and a change in values everywhere. The concept of 'families' has already changed, and will continue to do so. People will be comfortable with mobility and quite possibly subject to more influences from around the world. Futurists point to a fragmentation of monolithic groupings, such as the middle class. In a working life, there could be more reassessment of the demands placed on people, especially in an environment experiencing decreasing loyalty from employers and a transient 'employeeship' for most people. And what else? Possibly, a much higher recognition of self-development as the only viable means for a career strategy, and perhaps even an increased emphasis on purpose in life. At the same time, work and non-work life will be encountering a blurring (aided by communications flexibility). They will no longer subject to the rigid demarcation that we have traditionally categorised them. Privacy and its control will become significant issues. Community values, perhaps, likewise. Cities may change roles. Leisure — so long predicted — will be an important commodity. We might be treating each other — as strange as it may sound — with more courtesy and more manners, having absorbed and reflected on the new media cultures.

Many lean towards optimism pointing to the remarkable power of these technologies. The short term horizon however sees problems which look difficult to resolve: unemployment, and an ageing population, to name but two. Disparities in society will persist, in a world with finite resources. Around the world on the other hand, the communications industry expects to see more and more reliable and more effective platform technologies deployed. There might be consolidation within the industry itself. And the industry will be changing character as it comes to accommodate the paradigm of the interactive individual, with new applications and inputs to the 'puzzle'.

Some Snapshots

2017

By the time 2017 is reached, 'the industry' as we know it could be in a completely different form and have completely new meaning; it will have become a part perhaps of so many parts of our lives. In particular, the 'knowledge industry' will have been mediating the way governance reaches its constituents, the education industry reaches its customers, and even perhaps in the way we take care of children and the elderly. Education provides one good example of the possible menu choices on offer when communications becomes fully on-key. Communications will be able to mediate the delivery of educational systems to interested recipients but potentially in many different novel and flexible ways. For example, rather than the didactic teach-and-learn system characterising the last two hundred years, new education systems could be based around modes of continuous learning, or ones guaranteed to match your own pace, or ones that intelligently allow you to exit and enter at will, or ones based on dialogue and debate rather than dictation.

Communications will be increasingly visual too, to cater for the needs of the younger generations who have never had to depend solely on text or even voice as communications media. Visualisation in general could be the great paradigm shift of the next century. The world is after all visual in nature; in human and psychological studies, it is well established that 'one picture is worth a thousand words.' This drive towards the visualisation could create the focus for broadband technologies of every kind for home as well as business applications.

Perhaps more significantly in society there is a chance that the 'networking paradigm' of independent centres interacting for mutual development and benefit becomes a model for society at large. With this in mind, we could see the disappearance of greed and aggressive competition. An impossible utopia? Well, consider the networking paradigm again: the larger efforts are only made possible through the interaction of smaller elements, without control or hierarchy predominating. If this is possible, then surely the wider, global disparities will also disappear, the ones between the haves and have nots. Demographics — already identifiable — could mean that 30% of the population in many developed countries are supporting the other 70%.

2047

Demographics will be extremely important. In all likelihood, the increase in life expectancy manifest from the early 1800s will have continued: over this period, and some 50 years will have been added to the average lifetime. Most commercial enterprises will look completely different from the last years of the 20th century, with most development predicated on the banking, insurance, shopping, media, entertainment, governance, healthcare, transportation and of course communications sectors.

Technology Scenarios

In the light of such upheavals globally, technology changes may seem almost trivial. But important technology developments will help to underpin and shape the above. Of course, the communications technology that we currently recognise will be in a near constant state of evolution itself. Terminal technology for example will begin to migrate towards a high degree of platform flexibility so that the 'system soup' caused by so many incompatible elements will be greatly simplified. Visualisation applications will become the norm for networks and terminals alongside this, and a value migration to systems which support this will get underway. This will cause a profound influence on how we deploy and use broadband networks. Digital cellular will be a key element, behaving differently in different environment and with different access methodologies but with consistent content and platform technology in spite of the fragmentation.

The last comment should come from an interviewee:

It is about a lot of imagination, foresight, bold moves, and the right partners that can make things happen.

Many people helped in the creation of this essay, and to the extent that I have shamelessly plagiarised their views, I would like to gratefully acknowledge the following:

Petri Pöyhönen
Dominique Purcell
Harri Männistö
Markku Rauhamaa
Mikko Terho
Yrjö Neuvo
Lauri Kivinen

Short Story Acknowledgements